TWICE NEOKOROS

RELIGIONS IN
THE GRAECO-ROMAN WORLD

FORMERLY

ÉTUDES PRÉLIMINAIRES
AUX RELIGIONS ORIENTALES
DANS L'EMPIRE ROMAIN

EDITORS

R. VAN DEN BROEK   H.J.W. DRIJVERS
H.S. VERSNEL

VOLUME 116

TWICE NEOKOROS

EPHESUS, ASIA AND THE CULT OF
THE FLAVIAN IMPERIAL FAMILY

BY

STEVEN J. FRIESEN

E.J. BRILL
LEIDEN • NEW YORK • KÖLN
1993

The series Religions in the Graeco-Roman World presents a forum for studies in the social and cultural function of religions in the Greek and the Roman world, dealing with pagan religions both in their own right and in their interaction with and influence on Christianity and Judaism during a lengthy period of fundamental change. Special attention will be given to the religious history of regions and cities which illustrate the practical workings of these processes.
Enquiries regarding the submission of works for publication in the series may be directed to Professor H.J.W. Drijvers, Faculty of Letters, University of Groningen, 9712 EK Groningen, The Netherlands.

The paper in this book meets the guidelines for permanence and durability of the Committee on Production Guidelines for Book Longevity of the Council on Library Resources.

BL
813
.E64
F75
1993

Library of Congress Cataloging-in-Publication Data

Friesen, Steven J.
    Twice Neokoros : Ephesus, Asia, and the cult of the Flavian imperial family / by Steven J. Friesen.
    p.   cm. — (Religions in the Graeco-Roman world, ISSN 0927-7633 ; v. 116)
    Includes bibliographical references and index.
    ISBN 9004096892 (alk. paper)
    1. Ephesus (Extinct city)—Religion. 2. Emperor worship, Roman.
3. Flavian family. 4. Asia (Roman province) I. Title.
II. Series.
BL813.E64F75   1993
292.9—dc20

                         92-31027
                         CIP

ISSN   0927-7633
ISBN   90 04 09689 2

PRINTED IN THE NETHERLANDS

To Janie,

For reasons she and I know

CONTENTS

Acknowledgements IX
List of Figures XI
Abbreviations XIII
Maps XV

Introduction 1

I. Early Provincial Cults in Asia 7
   Pergamum 7
   Smyrna 15
   Miletus 21
   Imperial Cults of Other Provinces 26
   Summary 27

II. The Temple Inscriptions from Ephesus 29
   Discovery of the Inscriptions 29
   The Texts of the Inscriptions 32
   The Date of the Cult of the Sebastoi 41
   Summary 49

III. Developments in Cultic Traditions 50
   Ephesus, Neokoros of the Emperors 50
   Architecture, Sculpture, and the Emperors 59

IV. Provincial Highpriesthoods 76
   Provincial Highpriests 77
   Provincial Highpriestesses 81
   Responsibilities of the Highpriesthood 89
   Asiarchs 92
   Summary 112

V. Games and Festivals of the Cult 114
   Provincial Games 114
   The Ephesian Olympics 117
   The Harbor Bath-Gymnasium 121
   The Date of the Ephesian Olympics 137
   Summary 140

VI. Cult, City, Province, Empire 142
   Imperial Cult 142
   Human or Divine? 146

Neokoros 152

Grace 158

Reverence 160

Domitian, the Emperors, and the Cult of the Sebastoi 165

Appendixes 169

    I. Provincial Highpriests, Provincial Highpriestesses,
      and Asiarchs 169

    II. Dates of the Asiarchs from a Family of Cibyra 215

Bibliography 218

Indices 226

  Inscriptions and Coins 226

  General 233

ACKNOWLEDGMENTS

The development of this study from its inception as a proposal for a doctoral dissertation to its appearance in the form of a book was assisted by many people. I am indebted to those who read chapters of the manuscript and offered valuable advice. These include Bernadette Brooten, Sterling Dow, Rosalinde Kearsley, John Lanci, Greg Riley, Christine M. Thomas, and Roy Ward. My advisors Helmut Koester and David Mitten saw all the chapters through many drafts, and their guidance is evident throughout. Finally, David Orton and Thea Tilanus skillfully took the results of these labors through the editorial process at Brill. I would also like to thank Ann Brock for her help in locating secondary materials and Barry Barnes for initiation into the realm of graphics software. And, of course, I must recognize the contribution of my family—Janice, David and Daniel—who endured and aided these efforts with love and understanding.

LIST OF FIGURES

MAPS

Map 1	Western Asia Minor	xv
Map 2	The City of Ephesus	xvi

CHART

Chronological Chart of the Inscriptions from the Temple of the Sebastoi.	46–47

TEXT FIGURES

Fig. 1	Plan of Double Cella Temple at Ephesus.	12
Fig. 2	Plan of Upper Agora and Temple of the Sebastoi	59
Fig. 3	Temple of the Sebastoi Excavations	64
Fig. 4	Reconstructed Plan of the Altar and Temple of the Sebastoi	64
Fig. 5	The Ephesian Harbor Bath-Gymnasium and Environs	120
Fig. 6	Plan of Miletus Highlighting Bath Buildings	125
Fig. 7	Reconstructed Plan of the Bath-Gymnasium at Aizanoi	126
Fig. 8	The Baths of Agrippa at Rome	127
Fig. 9	The Baths of Nero at Rome	128
Fig. 10	The Stabian Baths at Pompeii	129
Fig. 11	The Baths of Titus at Rome	130
Fig. 12	The Baths of Trajan at Rome	131
Fig. 13	Plan of Priene, with Gymnasia Highlighted	132
Fig. 14	The Palaestra, Gymnasium, and Western End of Precincts at Olympia	133
Fig. 15	Bath Designs at Ephesus	136

PLATES

Plate I	One of the Augustan cistophoroi showing the Temple of Augustus and Rome, Pergamum. *BMCRE* 1.114 #705. Courtesy of the Trustees of the British Museum.	12
Plate II	Tetradrachma of Asia showing temple with the statue of Rome crowning the statue of Augustus (Claudian). *BMCRE* 1.196 #228. Courtesy of the Trustees of the British Museum.	14
Plate III	Bronze coin of Smyrna (29-35 CE). Obverse: Livia and Senate; reverse: Tiberius sacrificing in temple. *BM Ionia* 268 #267. Courtesy of the Trustees of the British Museum.	20
Plate IV	Statue base with inscription commissioned by the city of Keretapa for the dedication of the Temple of the Sebastoi. *IvE* 2.234.	30
Plate V	Text of the Keretapa inscription. Note erasure of Domitian's personal names. This inscription was not reinscribed with a dedication to Vespasian.	31

Plate VI   Statue fragment: Head of Titus. Archaeological Museum,
              Izmir. Courtesy of Helmut Koester.   60

Plate VII   Statue fragment: Arm of Titus. Archaeological Museum,
              Izmir. Courtesy of Helmut Koester.   61

Plate VIII   Ephesian coin showing Temple of the Sebastoi (right?), Tem-
              ple of Hadrian, and Temple of Artemis (center). *BM Ionia* 83
              #261. Courtesy of the Trustees of the British Museum.   65

Plate IX   Ephesian coin showing Temple of the Sebastoi (lower right?),
              Temple of Hadrian, Temple of Caracalla, Temple of Artemis
              (uppper left). *BM Ionia* 91 #305. Courtesy of the Trustees of
              the British Museum.   66

Plate X   Overview of temple terrace from Mt. Pion, facing south.   66

Plate XI   Remains of stairway and stoa on north side of temple terrace
              opening onto plaza. Facing southwest.   71

Plate XII   Engaged figures of Attis and Isis on facade of temple terrace
              stoa.   72

ABBREVIATIONS

AA	*Archäologisher Anzeiger. Beiblatt zum Jahrbuch des Deutschen Archäologischen Instituts.*
AD	Ἀρχαιολόγικον Δελτίον.
ABSA	*Annual of the British School at Athens.*
ANRW	*Aufstieg und Niedergang der Römischen Welt.*
AnSt	*Anatolian Studies.*
AntCl	*L'Antiquité Classique.*
AnzWien	*Anzeiger der Österreichischen Akademie der Wissenschaften in Wien, philos.-hist. Klasse.*
ABAW	*Abhandlung der Bayerischen Akademie der Wissenschaften, philos.-hist. Klasse.*
APAW	*Abhandlung der Königlichen Preussischen Akademie der Wissenschaften, philos.-hist. Klasse.*
ARNTS	*Archaeological Resources for New Testament Studies.*
AthMitt	*Mitteilungen des Deutschen Archäologischen Instituts, Athenische Abteilung.*
AvP	*Die Altertümer von Pergamon.*
BASOR	*Bulletin of the American School of Oriental Research.*
BCH	*Bulletin de Correspondance Hellénique.*
BM	*A Catalogue of the Greek Coins in the British Museum.* London: 1873-1922.
BMCRE	H. Mattingly, et al., eds. *Coins of the Roman Empire in the British Museum.* 6 vols. London: Trustees of the British Museum, 1923-62.
CIG	*Corpus Inscriptionum Graecarum.* 4 vols. Berlin: G. Reimer, 1828-77.
CIL	*Corpus Inscriptionum Latinarum.* Berlin: G. Reimer, 1893- .
ClRev	Classical Review.
CollWadd	Babelon, E., ed. *Inventaire sommaire de la collection Waddington.* Paris: Chez C. Rollin et Feuardent, 1898.
EpAn	*Epigraphica Anatolica*
FiE	*Forschungen in Ephesos* (1906-)
GRBS	*Greek, Roman, and Byzantine Studies.*
HuntColl	MacDonald, G., ed. *The Hunterian Coin Cabinet.* Glasgow, 1933.
IBM	*Ancient Greek Inscriptions in the British Museum.* 4 vols. 1874-1916.
IG	*Inscriptiones Graecae.* Berlin: G. Reimer, 1878- .
IGR	*Inscriptiones Graecae ad Res Romanas Pertinentes.* 4 vols. Paris: Ernest Leroux, 1906-27
IGS	*Inschriften griechischer Städte aus Kleinasien.* Bonn: Rudolf Habaelt, 1972- .
Insc. Louvre	Alphonse Dain, ed. *Inscriptions grecques du musée du Louvre, textes inédits.* Paris: Les Belles lettres, 1933.
IvDid	R. Harder, ed. *Didyma 2: Die Inschriften.* Vol. 2 of *Didyma.* Berlin: Mann, 1958.
IvE	*Die Inschriften von Ephesos* = *IGS* 11.1-17.4.
IvI	*Die Inschriften von Iasos* = *IGS* 28.1-2.
IvMag	Otto Kern, ed. *Die Inschriften von Magnesia am Maeander.* Berlin: W. Spemann, 1900.
IvMyl	*Die Inschriften von Mylasa* = *IGS* 34-35

IvPr	F. Frhr. von Gaertringen, et al. *Die Inschriften von Priene*. Berlin: Georg Reimer, 1906.
IvSar	W. H. Buckler and David M. Robinson. *Greek and Latin Inscriptions*. Vol. 7,1 of *Publication of the American Society for the Excavation of Sardis*. Leiden: Brill, 1932.
IvSm	*Die Inschriften von Smyrna* = *IGS* 23-24.
IvStr	*Die Inschriften von Stratonikeia* = *IGS* 21-22.
JBL	*Journal of Biblical Literature*.
JHS	*Journal of Hellenic Studies*.
Kl.P.	*Der Kleine Pauly*. 5 vols. Munich: Alfred Druckenmüller, 1975.
MAMA	W. M. Calder, et al. *Monumenta Asiae Minoris Antiqua*. 8 vols. Manchester: Manchester University Press, 1928-62.
Milet 1,7	Hubert Knackfuss. *Der Südmarkt und die benachbarten Bauanlagen*. Berlin: Verlag von Schoetz und Parrhysius, 1924.
Milet 1,9	Armin von Gerkan, et al. *Thermen und Palaestren*. Berlin: Verlag von Hans Schoetz, 1928.
Mionnet	T. E. Mionnet, *Description de médailles antiques, grecques et romaines*. 7 vols. Paris: 1806-8.
Mionnet Sup	T. E. Mionnet, *Description de médailles antiques, grecques et romaines*. *Supplément*. 10 vols. Paris: 1819-37.
OCD	N. G. L. Hammond, and H. H. Scullard. *Oxford Classical Dictionary*. 2d ed. Oxford: Clarendon, 1970.
OGIS	*Orientis Graeci Inscriptiones Selectae*. 2 vols. Hildesheim: Georg Olms, 1960.
ÖJh	*Jahresheft des Österreichischen Archäologischen Instituts*.
PASCSA	*Papers of the American School of Classical Studies at Athens*.
PIR	*Prosopographia Imperii Romani*.
PW	*Paulys Realencyclopädie der classischen Altertumswissenschaft*. Stuttgart: J. B. Metzlerscher Verlag/Alfred Druckenmüller, 1894- .
PWSup	*Paulys Realencyclopädie der classischen Altertumswissenschaft*. *Supplement*. Stuttgart: J. B. Metzlerscher Verlag/Alfred Druckenmüller, 1903- .
RBN	*Revue Belge de Numismatique*.
REA	*Revue des Études Anciennes*.
REG	*Revue des Études Grecques*.
RevNum	*Revue Numismatique*.
RevPhil	*Revue de Philologie*.
Sardis	*Archaeological Exploration of Sardis*.
SEG	*Supplementum Epigraphicum Graecum*. Leiden: A. W. Sijthoff, 1923- .
SIG	W. Dittenberger, et al. *Sylloge Inscriptionum Graecarum*. 4 vols. 3d ed. Leipzig: S. Hirzel, 1915-24.
SNG Cop	Niels Breitenstein and Willy Schlabacher. *Sylloge Nummorum Graecorum. The Royal Collection of Coins and Medals, Danish National Museum*. Copenhagen: Munksgaard, 1942- .
SNGvA	*Sammlung von Aulock. Sylloge Nummorum Graecorum; Deutschland*.
ZfN	*Zeitschrift für die Numismatik*.
ZPE	*Zeitschrift für die Papyrologie und Epigraphik*.

Map 1. Western Asia Minor.
(after Jones)

BLACK SEA

Herakleia
Perinthos
Byzantium
Chalkedon

PROPONTIS

Nikomedia

Nikaia
BITHYNIA

Kyzikos

TROAS
Skepsis

Rhyndacus

Mytilene

MYSIA

Pergamum
Kaikos
Stratonikeia
Aizanoi

Thyateira
Synaos

Kyme

Hermus
CHIOS
Smyrna
Sardis
LYDIA

Klazomenai
Tmolos?
Philadelphia
Eumeneia

Teos
Hyaipa

Kaystros
Makedones
Hyrkanioi?
Hierapolis
PHRYGIA

Ephesus
Meander

Samos
Magnesia
Laodikeia
Lycus

Priene
Aphrodisias
Keretapa?

Miletus
KARIA
Stratonikeia

AEGEAN
SEA
Jasos
Mylasa

Halykarnassos
Indus
Cibyra

Kos

RHODOS
LYCIA

Map 2. The City of Ephesus.
(after Akurgal, 144)

1. Temple of the Sebastoi
2. Upper Agora
3. Magnesian Gate
4. East Baths
5. Prytaneion
6. Fountain of Trajan
7. Slope Houses
8. Varius Baths
9. Byzantine City Wall
10. Mt. Pion
11. Theater
12. Celsus Library and Tetragonos Agora
13. Temple of the Egyptian Deities
14. Arcadian Street
15. Harbor Bath-Gymnasium Complex
16. Theater Baths
17. Basilica
18. Unidentified Temple (Olympieion?)
19. Heroon
20. Stadium
21. Vedius Baths
22. Temple of Artemis
23. Isa Bey Mosque
24. Church of St. John
25. Ancient Processional Way
26. Hellenistic City Wall
27. Mt. Koressos

INTRODUCTION

This study is an examination of one particular cult: Asia's provincial cult of the emperors, established during the late first century of the Common Era in the city of Ephesus. This cult has been mentioned often in a wide variety of scholarly and popular works, but the cult itself is not well understood. There has been no consensus about the date when the cult was established nor about the emperors to whom it was dedicated. After an examination of earlier provincial cults in Asia, an argument will be presented for a specific date and dedication of the cult.

The goal of this study, however, is to move beyond the analysis of date and emperor in order to examine more closely the religious symbolism associated with the cult. The inscriptions, coins, sculpture, architecture, and occasional literary text, once gathered and ordered, reveal a great deal about the religious traditions and values which this institution embodied.

The final chapter includes several conclusions about the significance of the Cult of the Sebastoi for the lives of the inhabitants of the Roman province of Asia. A great deal of diversity can be found in any human society, and this fact must be born in mind in the interpretation of this cult. The actions of some individuals from various strata of Asian society are examined. This is followed by a concluding statement that deals with the role of Domitian in this cult.

Mercifully, for reader and author alike, there is little history of research on this cult. Several of its aspects—dating, dedication, architecture, and the like—have been addressed in various studies devoted to other topics, but no monograph on this topic has been produced up to this time. The articles and notes of scholars that are related to this study will be duly noted in the chapters to which they are relevant. No rehearsal of these works is necessary at this point.

More urgent is the task of providing some definitions and explanations for some of the vocabulary that will be used. Above all, a few words are in order about the word "cult."[1] I have tried to avoid the

---

[1] The modern pejorative connotations associated with the term "cult" should not be imported into the word's usage in this study.

abstract noun "religion" in this study because it so often connotes a system of beliefs or an impersonal pattern of ritual actions.[2] Instead, I have chosen to write of "cults," i.e., specific institutions devoted to sacrificial activities. Occasionally, "cult" will be used to indicate a collection of such local phenomena, but this broader category will not be the focus of the discussion. The related adjective "cultic" is used to describe events, institutions, officials, actions, etc. which have to do with sacrificial activity. "Religious" also occurs at times in this study as a rough equivalent of "cultic." It does not necessarily imply emotional involvement or dogmatic content, though these may be involved; it refers primarily to phenomena which are implicated in the imaging and promotion of proper relationships through sacrificial activity.

Most modern studies of provincial imperial cults use the term "neokoros" for such cults. In chapter three it will be demonstrated that this term is only appropriate in reference to a province's imperial cult beginning in the late first century CE. Before that date, it is anachronistic to call such a cult neokoros and so we will refer to them as "provincial" (i.e., related to a province) rather than neokoros. "Neokoros" turns up quite often, nevertheless, and I have chosen to Anglicize it rather than to italicize every occurrence. When there is a particular reason, "neokoros" is rendered in Greek. Its English adjective is "neokorate."

There are other Greek words which occur often enough to be freed from their italicized existence. One such word is "koinon," an adjective meaning "common" that came to be one of the terms for the provincial council of Asia. It appears in this study as the English name of the provincial council.

Another difficult word is the English rendering of Σεβαστός. Its normal English translation is "Augustus," but this is not appropriate in one crucial context: the official designation of the temple whose cult is under examination. I have chosen to refer to the cult as the "Cult of the Sebastoi" rather than "of the Augusti" because "Augusti," a transliteration from Latin, would detract from the fact that this is a thoroughly Greek institution. "Cult of the Emperors" would also have been a possible title, but it would have been less

---

[2] For an interesting, though not always convincing, discussion of "religion" in modern usage, see Wilfred Cantwell Smith, *The Meaning and End of Religion* (New York: Harper & Row, 1962) 15-50.

exact and would have caused confusion with the word normally translated as "emperor" (αὐτοκράτωρ). Furthermore, "emperor" does not retain the reverent quality of "sebastos." It would have been impractical to translate every example of σεβαστός as "sebastos," though, as this would have required the renaming of the Augustus who is credited with founding the Roman Empire. In general, I have used "sebastos" (without italics) except when pragmatic considerations overcame my obsession with consistent usage.

The geographic focus of this study is the Roman province of Asia, that included the western section of Asia Minor and the nearby Aegean islands. The area came under the control of the Romans after it was willed to them by Attalos III of Pergamum in 133 BCE and after they put down the resistance led by Aristonikos. Asia finally became a province in 126 BCE but was reorganized by Octavian in 29 BCE. In the north the province extended to the Propontis and Bithynia; its eastern flank was bordered by Galatia (also a Roman province after 25 BCE), and its southeast border was shared with Lycia. In the Imperial period, Phrygia was included in the province. These are the boundaries referred to in this study by the terms "province of Asia" and "Asia."

Discussions of methodology will be found at various places in the study as the need arises. A somewhat longer statement dealing with broader issues of interpretation can be found at the beginning of the last chapter. At this point a few statements should be made about my conceptual model of society and the methods I use in the analysis of social phenomena.

One assumption that I hold is that societies are always in transition. At any given time a group may reconfirm or reshape its received traditions. The forces involved in such developments can be thought of in three general categories: social organization, ideology, and individuals. Social organization encompasses the constituent subgroups within the larger society, as well as the patterns of interaction between subgroups or persons. Ideology articulates the values which a society's form of social organization is thought to embody. Individuals are the sometimes predictable actors who shape, and are shaped by, their social relationships and ideology. Each of these three categories affects the others, but none is simply a dependent expression of another. Each must be reckoned an active player in the negotiations involving new situations and inherited solutions.

This view of society is integrative and is particularly helpful in analyzing social groups that are not suffering severe disruption. The model, however, also presupposes the continual waxing and waning of tension within a given society and within its subgroups. No social organization completely matches its attendant ideology, no ideology ever satisfies fully the individuals who make up a social group, and no individual incorporates his or her social setting in the same fashion. These discrepancies result in conflicts and shortages that are felt to a greater or lesser degree by various individuals or subgroups. Changes and rationalizations are thus attempted or implemented at various levels of society with varying degrees of success. Occasionally the dissonance becomes so great that a breakdown occurs in the society's ability to function.

What I find interesting is the way in which problems are denied or redressed in the ongoing life of a social group by means of religious institutions and rhetoric. Religious institutions are often involved in social developments, sometimes conserving and sometimes challenging the status quo of the time. This is especially true of certain types of religious institutions, and in the Roman Empire, provincial imperial cult was the type of religious phenomenon which was most overt in its involvement with the issues of supralocal organization and ideology.

It is important to note that all three categories—social organization, ideology, and individual—are modern constructs for the analysis of a complex society. The accurate description of ancient society through the use of such constructs is a goal which can never be accomplished fully, for the process of studying the past seems to me to be dialogical. The modern analyst brings questions and methods to bear on the data that remain from antiquity. These data can be construed and misconstrued in many ways, for our intentions and abilities always influence our perception of the evidence. My experience, however, leads me to the conclusion that the ancient data can also affect modern analysis, and change the way we understand the past. Words, coins, sculptures, buildings, inscriptions, and even erasures all were created to communicate. Our task is to learn to understand those communications as best we can, and to evaluate critically our ability to understand them.

This process of dialogue with the past is made more difficult in this sort of study by the fact that much of the information from antiquity comes from one particular segment of the population. Our ancient informants tend to be wealthy, educated, and male. We hear from others as well, but the bias of the data in favor of the interests of the elite must be continually evaluated.[3]

Because of these biases, both ancient and modern, I have adopted a method that gives primacy to detailed description of particular pieces of ancient evidence. The attempt to give as full and accurate a description as possible of selected data does not produce "objective" results; rather, it forces me to place my biases next to those of the ancients in the hope that they will illuminate each other and illustrate each other's shortcomings.

Another feature of my method is the deliberate attempt to describe any piece of evidence in its local context. At several points in my research I have encountered vague or mistaken scholarly interpretations that were due not to a lack of evidence but rather to improper context. All too often, evidence from distant locations or from other historical periods has been employed to explain the data from late first century CE Asia. Whenever possible, I have tried to interpret the Ephesian or Asian evidence locally before using other data. Outside data is informative and necessary for comparison and contrast, but it must be treated as a distinct category of evidence.

By employing this approach, I have become convinced that the existing data will yield much more information than we have yet won from it if the evidence is subjected to close scrutiny by a variety of interpreters, all with their own concerns. I hope that this study adds in its own way to that process.

The resonance of some of the themes in the preceding paragraphs with the work of anthropologist Clifford Geertz is due to his influence on my thinking about social analysis.[4] Less apparent in

---

[3] In this study, the general term "elite" refers to the wealthy, influential segment of society. I have avoided the term "class" in referring to this and other social subgroups because such terminology is more accurately applied to groups involved in a capitalist economy; see Keith Hopkins, "Introduction," in Peter Garnsey, Keith Hopkins, and C. R. Whittaker, eds., *Trade in the Ancient Economy* (Berkeley and Los Angeles: University of California Press, 1983) esp. xiii-xiv. "Aristocracy" could have been used also, but I prefer "elite" because it is not so closely associated with modern European nobility.

[4] See especially, "Thick Description: Toward an Interpretive Theory of Culture," "Religion as a Cultural System," and "Ritual and Social Change: A Javanese Example," in Clifford Geertz, *The Interpretation of Cultures* (New York: Basic Books, 1973) 3-30, 87-125, 142-69. A helpful critique of Geertz's proposals regarding the definitions of religion and culture can be found in Talal Asad, "Anthropological Conceptions of Religion: Reflections on Geertz," *Man* 18 (1983) 237-59.

these paragraphs, but more apparent in the chapters that follow, are the influences of three other individuals. Historian of religion Helmut Koester has taught me many things, including the necessity of searching out the distinctive features and signs of change in ancient religious phenomena. Archaeologist David Mitten has demonstrated to me, in the personal and the academic realms, the humane task of the archaeologist: the recovery of human voices that were nearly lost from the record of our species' search for meaning. Finally, from author Dorothy L. Sayers I have learned the value of the "clue," the piece of evidence that does not fit into an inaccurate scenario. There are many mysteries left to us by antiquity, and it seems to me that a methodology that crosses disciplinary boundaries holds the most promise for understanding at least some of them.

CHAPTER ONE

EARLY PROVINCIAL CULTS IN ASIA

The purpose of this chapter is to survey the three provincial cults of
Asia that were established before the cult in Ephesus. The various
institutions related to the cults and the historical circumstances of
the inaugurations of the cults will be examined as a way of developing an understanding of provincial worship in Asia. Following this,
comparative material will be introduced from the growing number
of provincial cults outside of Asia. In this way it will be possible to
place the cult in Ephesus into the historical context of provincial imperial cults in Asia and throughout the empire.

Pergamum

In 32 BCE Mark Antony controlled the eastern Mediterranean. He
and Cleopatra VII spent that winter in Ephesus where Antony had
been received earlier as the New Dionysos, perhaps as early as 41
BCE.[1] A group of senators who had opposed Octavian met them in
Ephesus and the city became a temporary center of resistance to
Octavian.

In the naval battle off the coast of Actium in 31 BCE, Octavian
defeated Mark Antony. Antony's flight and suicide in the following
year left the province of Asia in a difficult position. Now that the
former ruler had been eliminated, how would Asia greet his suc-
cessor?

The province lost no time in declaring its allegiance to the man
who was consolidating his control over the entire Mediterranean
world. In the winter of 29 BCE, the koinon of Asia[2] requested permission to establish a cult in Pergamum for Octavian.[3]

---

[1] Plutarch, *Ant.* 24.4; also 60.3-5 (Athens). Regarding divine honors for
Cleopatra, see *Ant.* 26.5; 54.9.

[2] The koinon was the provincial council of the cities of Asia.

[3] Dio Cassius 51.20.6. Tacitus (*An.* 4.37) agrees with Dio that the initiative for
establishing the cult was taken by the province. The emperor did not stop them
(*divus Augustus. . . non prohibuisset*) from building a temple for him and for Rome.
Bithynia also requested and received such a cult at the same time, which was located
in Nikomedia.

Given the political events of the time, a new cult for Octavian in an eastern province in the year 29 BCE was a particularly sensitive issue. Octavian had used religious propaganda quite effectively against Antony, whom he had accused of accepting the divine status accorded to an eastern monarch. It was by no means certain that Octavian would allow such a cult, and if he did, what particular form it might take.

While the cult was established before Octavian took the name Augustus in 27 BCE, all extant evidence comes from after that date. Thus, we do not know what the original title of the temple was, but numerous inscriptions and coins indicate that Asia's cult came to be known as one dedicated to Rome and Augustus, and Tacitus confirms this identification.[4] It is not clear whether the koinon requested that Rome be included in the cult, or whether Octavian insisted upon it.[5] Whatever the individual roles of the various parties might have been, it is sufficient for our purposes to recognize what kinds of cultic models were being used in order to construct this new cult of the emperor.

Deininger argued for direct continuity between the cult of Rome and Augustus and the cults that the koinon offered to Hellenistic monarchs such as Antiochos I Soter. Deininger's interest in this was to show that the function of the koinon of Asia changed little from the Hellenistic to the Roman periods.[6] If we examine the format of the two cults rather than the function of the koinon, it becomes clear that there are important distinctions between the cult for Antiochos and that for Rome and Augustus.

---

[4] *An.* 4.37.

[5] Most modern interpreters of the provincial cult in Pergamum theorize that Asia requested only a cult of the emperor but that Octavian required the inclusion of Rome. The basis for this opinion is Suetonius's characterization (*Aug.* 52) of Augustus as refusing all cults for himself if Rome was not also worshipped. While it is true that Asia showed much less interest in the figure of Rome than that of Augustus, the passage from Suetonius may or may not be accurate. The Pergamene cult was the first precedent for an Augustan policy on worship of the living emperor. It may even have been the point at which that policy was determined, but that still leaves open the question of who suggested the inclusion of Rome. It is possible that the Asians promoted the inclusion of the goddess Rome, for the provincial elite was not unaware of the various sentiments in the city of Rome regarding the worship of rulers (see Glen Bowersock, *Augustus and the Greek World* [Oxford: Clarendon Press, 1965] 115). Furthermore, a close reading of Tiberius's speech, as rendered by Tacitus (*An.* 4.37), implies that the province and not the emperor included Rome in the cult, for Augustus is said to have allowed both.

[6] Jürgen Deininger, *Die Provinziallandtage der römischen Kaiserzeit von Augustus bis zum Ende des dritten Jahrhunderts n. Chr.* (Munich: Beck, 1965) 10, 17.

According to an inscription found in Klazomenai, the cult for Antiochos I was decreed by the koinon between 268 and 262 BCE.[7] Sacrifices were offered to all the gods and goddesses, to Antiochos I, his wife Stratonike, and their son Antiochos II (l. 32-34). A temenos was to be built at the site of Antiochos's choosing (l. 20-24), but the place in the inscription that would have designated precisely to whom the precincts were dedicated is damaged and cannot be restored with certainty (l. 23). The one reference to a temple building is also a restoration (l. 29), but there is a secure reference to an "altar of the kings" in the temenos (l. 42-43). Thus, the cult included the royal family of the Seleucid dynasty.

The cult for Rome and Augustus, however, was not for a dynasty; it centered on one political leader and the city of Rome. This was not a new pattern; it had been used in a related situation less than twenty years earlier. Publius Servilius Isauricus had been consul with Julius Caesar in 48 BCE and two years later served as proconsul of Asia. His proconsulship lasted two years (46-44 BCE) during which time he became known as a benefactor and protector of the traditions of the cities in the province.[8] Isauricus gave statues and was honored by statues in several places in the province, but was known especially for restoring the right of asylum to several sanctuaries.[9] After Caesar's death, Isauricus sided with Octavian. Octavian married his daughter Servilia but the marriage did not last long. Octavian was able to assuage his former father-in-law by having Isauricus appointed consul again in 41 BCE, and he remained loyal to Octavian in the ensuing years.[10]

In gratitude for the actions of Isauricus on behalf of the province, a cult was established for this prominent Caesarean that is known to us through two inscriptions from Ephesus that refer to priests of Rome and Isauricus.[11] The exact nature of the cult is not attested,

---

[7] *OGIS* 222. For a brief discussion of this inscription and the cult, see Christian Habicht, *Gottmenschentum und griechische Städte* (Zetemata 14; Munich: Beck, 1956) 91-93.

[8] *IGR* 4.433 (Pergamum) calls him σωτῆρα καὶ εὐεργέτην τῆς πόλεως καὶ ἀποδεδωκότα τῇ πόλει τοὺς πατρίους νόμους καί τὴν δημοκ[ρα]τίαν ἀκούλωτκν, "saviour and benefactor of the city, and the one who has given back to the city the ancestral customs and unenslaved democracy."

[9] The inscriptions which mention Isauricus are conveniently gathered together by Jeanne and Louis Robert in "III. Hierocesaree," *Hellenica* 6 (1948) 38-42, where the identity of P. Servilius Isauricus is discussed, and where a summary of his activities in Asia can also be found.

[10] *Kl.P.* 5.143 #30; *OCD* s.v. "Servilius (2)."

[11] *IvE* 7,1.3066 l. 6-7: ἱερέα Ῥώμης καὶ Ποπλίου Σερουειλίου Ἰσαυρικοῦ. See

but the connections of the two priests in these inscriptions with gymnasia suggest that the cult of Rome and Isauricus was located in such an institution rather than in a temple.

Asia's first provincial imperial cult in Pergamum drew upon this pattern of combining the cult of a prominent Roman with that of the city of Rome, and so used an accepted format from the late Republican period. As such, Asia's cult for Rome and Augustus signalled a desire to follow approved institutions of the Republic rather than the eastern models used by Antony. The cult of Rome and Augustus was on a grander scale than any cult for a proconsul,[12] but the very name of the cult indicated that it was organized in a manner consistent with accepted norms.[13]

Dio Cassius recorded an unusual complementary component to the cults in Asia and Bithynia for Augustus and Rome: a cult for Rome and Divus Julius was also established in both provinces.[14] The cults for Rome and Julius had not been requested by the provinces; Octavian ordered that they be set up, one in Ephesus and one in Nicea.[15] The two parallel types of cults (i.e., Rome-Augustus, Rome-Julius) were designed for two kinds of worshippers. The cult requested by the provinces was to be for local inhabitants, or "foreigners" as Dio Cassius called them.[16] The cult involving Julius was specifically for Romans living in the provinces.[17]

Octavian apparently decided that the inclusion of Rome in his cult was not a strong enough statement of fidelity to Roman religious practice.[18] Thus, another cult was established that clearly dis-

---

also *IvE* 3.702. The latter inscription comes from the mid-first century CE while the former is dated to about 100 CE, so the cult continued for more than a century.

[12] The koinon initiated a pentaeteric festival for the proconsul Q. Mucius Scaevola in the early first century BCE; *AvP* 8,2.268 (= *OGIS* 437) and commentary. There were also games at Mylasa for C. Marcius Censorinus, another early first century BCE proconsul; *CIG* 2698b.

[13] Habicht's argument (*AvP* 8,3, p. 165) that a cult of Rome and Salus became a cult of Rome and Augustus might be correct, but the inscription he cites does not refer to the provincial cult of Rome and Augustus. The priesthood in the inscription was hereditary, and the term θεός was used of Augustus. Neither of these would be unusual in a municipal cult of Rome and Augustus, but they would hardly be appropriate for Asia's provincial cult.

[14] Dio 51.20.6-7.

[15] Dio wrote that Augustus allowed (ἐπέτρεψε) his own cult with Rome, but required (προσέταξε) that of Rome and Julius.

[16] ...τοῖς δὲ δὴ ξένοις, Ἕλληνας σφας ἐπικαλέσας...

[17] ...τοῖς Ῥωμαίοις τοῖς παρ' αὐτοῖς ἐποικοῦσι...

[18] For a discussion of Greek and Roman systems of thought about the veneration of deities, see S. R. F. Price, "Gods and Emperors: The Greek Language of the Roman Imperial Cult," *JHS* 104 (1984) 79-95.

tinguished between religious practice appropriate for Greeks and that appropriate for Romans in regard to the worship of political figures.[19] In this way, Octavian recognized the existence of two distinct religious systems and signaled his intent to preserve both of them within their appropriate spheres, rather than to legitimize one at the expense of the other.[20] When confronted with the choice between Roman traditions of ruler cult and acceptable eastern traditions, he recognized both as proper for their respective peoples.

The cult for Rome and Divus Julius never became significant for the religious life of the province of Asia. It is not mentioned in any surviving inscriptions nor on any coins.[21] This is not surprising, for the cult was not the responsibility of the koinon nor was it designated for the use of the majority of the residents. Furthermore, the reasons for the establishment of this sort of cult were tied directly to the political and religious situation of the years just after Actium. There was no reason to replicate the cult in later imperial cult institutions, whether local or provincial.

The site of the temple for Rome and Augustus in Pergamum has never been located nor have any architectural pieces been found.[22]

---

[19] At this same time, Octavian was consciously redefining proper Roman practice in Rome as well. Upon returning to Rome from Samos in 29 BCE, he celebrated a triple triumph and participated in the dedication of the completed temple of Divus Julius that dominated the Forum Romanum. It may have been his intention to extend this development from Rome to the provinces. See Heidi Hänlein-Schäfer, *VENERATIO AUGUSTI: Eine Studie zu den Tempeln der ersten römischen Kaisers* (Archaeologica 39; Rome: Giorgio Bretschneider, 1985) 99-102.

[20] The way that the figure of Rome was understood also shows that two differing religious systems were involved. According to the Greek inscriptions of Asia, the cult was for the goddess Rome (Θεὰ 'Ρώμη). Latin writers like Tacitus, however, viewed the cult as one for the city of Rome (*An.* 4.37.3; *urbi Romae templum*). A Latin inscription from Pergamum suggests the same distinction when it refers to games *in honorem Romae* (*AvP* 8,2.269 l. 12; Trajanic period).

[21] Foundations of a double cella temple have been found in Ephesus which are probably to be identified as those of the temple for Rome and Julius (Fig. 1). The building techniques and architectural details are those of the late first century BCE; the building occupied a strategic location in an administrative area next to the prytaneion (an institution for the regulation of the city's official religious life); and, the podium temple that is backed up near the wall of a small peribolos courtyard is the first known example of this typical Italian temple design in Asia. Wilhelm Alzinger, "Das Regierungsviertel," *ÖJh* 50 (1972-75) Beib. 249-53; and Anton Bammer, *ÖJh* 51 (1976-77) Haupt. 57-58. Hänlein-Schäfer 1985, 264-65.

[22] A copy of a decree of the city of Mytilene found on the island of Lesbos shows that the temple was not finished before 27 BCE, for the inscription uses the name "Augustus" when referring to the temple that was under construction for him in Pergamum (note the present participle in line A 12: [ἐν τῷ ναῷ τῷ κατασ]κευαζομένῳ α[ὐ]τῷ ὑπὸ τῆς 'Ασίας ἐν Περγάμῳ). The decree is discussed in Conrad Cichorius, *Rom und Mytilene* (Leipzig: Teubner, 1888) 30-41. The text of the decree can also be found in *IGR* 4.39; *IG* 12,2.58; and *OGIS* 456.

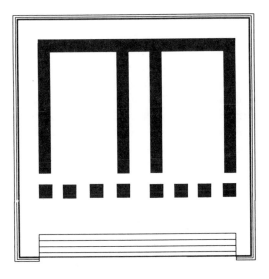

Fig. 1. Plan of double cella temple at Ephesus.
(after Bammer, ÖJh 51 [1976–77] H. 58).

This lack of evidence for the building is alleviated somewhat by the
depiction of the temple on several different coins. One particular
group of Augustan cistophori, issued in Asia between June, 20
BCE, and June, 18 BCE, are particularly valuable in this regard.[23]
The obverse design of these cistophori is constant: a bareheaded
bust of Augustus facing right with a linear border and official titulature (Pl. I).[24] This obverse appeared with three different reverses:

Plate I. One of the Augustan cistophoroi showing the Temple of Augustus and
Rome, Pergamum. *BMCRE* 1.114 #705. Courtesy of the Trustees of the British
Museum.

---

[23] C. H. V. Sutherland, *The Cistophori of Augustus* (London: Royal Numismatic
Society, 1970) 36, 103.
[24] Sutherland 1970, pl. 12-14.

a triumphal arch, a round temple of Mars, and a hexastyle temple.[25]

The temple with six Corinthian columns in front is a representation of the first provincial temple in Pergamum: on its architrave is written *ROM.ET.AUGUST*, and the words *COM(mune) ASIAE* are found in the open fields on either side of the temple. The building, viewed frontally, rests on five monumental steps. Palmette acroteria are visible on the top and on the corners of the pediment.[26] While the coins give us no idea of the exact size of the temple nor of the cella arrangement, they do indicate that the basic design of the temple was Greek rather than Italian.[27]

A second type of coin provides information about the temple statue of Asia's cult in Pergamum. Starting already in the lifetime of Augustus, some coins in Asia depicted the temple in Pergamum but omitted the two central columns in order to show a statue inside.[28] The obverse of a bronze coin of Pergamum from approximately 4-5 CE uses this convention to reveal a statue of Augustus in military garb with spear in right hand, standing in the provincial temple.[29] The same image reappears on the reverse of a Pergamene bronze from the later Tiberian period (29-35 CE).[30]

---

[25] Sutherland 1970, pl. 31-36.

[26] The temple of Rome and Augustus in Nikomedia was similar to the temple in Pergamum but also had several distinctive features. The Bithynian temple was a Corinthian octastyle on a three-step crepidoma. The akroterion on the top was palmette, but those on the sides each included a Nike with battle trophy. Some figures are depicted in the tympanon reliefs but the nature of the temple's external sculpture is not known because the coins are not consistent in this respect. *BM Pontus* 105, #10-27, pl. 24; *BMCRE* 3.232-33, #1096-1100, pl. 75 (Nerva-Hadrian); Hänlein-Schäfer 1985, 70.

[27] Sutherland (1970, 36) noted that the arch and the Temple of Mars were both built in 20 BCE, just before the issuing of the coins with their likeness. Since these cistophori commemorate the completion of two building projects, it may be that the appearance of the Rome and Augustus temple on the coins indicates that it too was finished in the previous year (20 BCE). It is also possible, however, that the temple was finished a few years earlier without appearing on the cistophori until this series was issued, perhaps from a provincial mint in Pergamum.

[28] Behrendt Pick ("Die Neokorie-Tempel von Pergamon und der Asklepios des Phyromachos," in *Festschrift Walther Judeich zum 70. Geburtstage* [Weimar: Hermann Boehlaus, 1929] 30) discussed this temple in particular, and the way temples were sometimes modified on coins to depict the temple statue. It has sometimes been assumed that such coins did not show the statue but rather the emperor reigning at the time the coin was issued. See S. R. F. Price, *Rituals and Power: The Roman imperial cult in Asia Minor* (Cambridge: Cambridge University Press, 1984) 178 n. 37, for bibliography on both sides of the issue.

[29] *BM Mysia* 139, #242, pl. 28.

[30] *BM Mysia* 140, #256, pl. 28.

Plate II. Tetradrachma of Asia showing temple with the statue of Rome crowning the statue of Augustus (Claudian). *BMCRE* 1.196 #228. Courtesy of the Trustees of the British Museum.

Later coins show both Augustus and a personified Rome in this temple (Pl. II). To do so, two more columns were omitted leaving only the two outer columns to represent the front colonnade. The same statue of Augustus in military dress stands inside the temple. To the right stands a female figure in a long belted chiton who personifies Rome. She holds a cornucopia in her left hand; the right arm is extended and raised, with the hand holding a crown above the emperor's head.[31] The image occurs again under Nerva, though the figure of the emperor is holding something in his left hand and may be clothed differently.[32]

Thus, the temple statues for Asia's first provincial cult were well-known throughout the province and beyond.[33] The imagery of the statues focussed attention on Augustus. The cuirassed emperor was honored by the figure of Rome, and when only one statue was depicted on coinage, that of Augustus was the obvious choice. The emperor was memorialized as a military conqueror.

The text from Dio Cassius mentioned earlier[34] concludes with the note that Pergamum received the right to hold sacred games associated with the temple.[35] The name of these games is known

---

[31] A silver cistophoric tetradrachma from Asia: *BMCRE* 1.196, #228, pl. 34 (Claudius). A silver tetradrachma from an unknown mint: *BMCRE* 2.94, #449, pl. 43 (Vespasian).

[32] Silver tetradrachma: *BMCRE* 3.12, #79, pl. 3 (Nerva).

[33] The statue from the Rome and Augustus temple in Nikomedia is more difficult to reconstruct because there is no tradition of depicting the statue on coins. The only evidence is a group of coins that were minted during a relatively short period of time at a later date (ca. 128-138 CE). They are not completely consistent, but the same two figures (Augustus being crowned by Rome) seem to be indicated. See Hänlein-Schäfer 1985, 83 regarding the numismatic evidence.

[34] See above, p. 7.

[35] Dio 51.20.9.

through the many references to them in inscriptions of successful athletes and of agonothetes.[36] The games could be fully described as ['P]ωμαῖα Σεβαστὰ τὰ τιθέμενα ὑπὸ τοῦ κοινοῦ τῆς 'Ασίας ἐν Περγάμῳ[37] or simply referred to as τὰ μέγαλα Σεβαστὰ 'P[ω]μαῖα.[38]

To summarize, Asia's cult of Rome and Augustus was established at a time of political and religious transition. The cult reflected a desire to maintain continuity with religious practices of the Republican period while promoting allegiance to Augustus and his adoptive father Julius Caesar. Because of its particular historical setting in the early years of Augustus's reign, some of the cult's aspects were not replicated in later developments of Asia's provincial worship. For fifty years, however, the cult in Pergamum was Asia's only provincial cult, and decrees from the time of Hadrian show that it was flourishing in the second century CE.[39] Because of its longevity and because of Augustus's legacy, the cult set a precedent which had to be taken into account in later decisions regarding provincial imperial cult in Asia and throughout the empire.

Smyrna

The institution of a Tiberian cult in Smyrna was the result of a long series of events that constitute a significant chapter in the development of provincial imperial worship. This development can be examined because the cult is one of the few provincial cults whose origins are described in some detail in an extant literary text.

Tacitus recorded that charges were brought against two Roman officials by the province of Asia during the reign of Tiberius. In 22 CE, the province's best lawyers accused their former proconsul Gaius Silanus, a man with many enemies in the Roman aristocracy as well, of extortion.[40] The trial was held before the Senate, but Tiberius made it clear by his involvement in the proceedings that he was seeking a guilty verdict. The prosecution was successful. Silanus was relegated to the island of Gyarus and part of his family's property was confiscated.

---

[36] These were benefactors who sponsored and sometimes organized competitions. *Kl.P.* 1.140-41.

[37] "The Romaia Sebasta established by the koinon of Asia in Pergamum." *IGR* 4.1064 = *SIG* 3.1065 (Kos, reign of Caligula).

[38] "The great Sebasta Romaia." *IGR* 4.498 (Pergamum).

[39] *AvP* 8,2.374 (= *IGR* 4.353).

[40] *An.* 3.66-9.

In 23 CE, the province of Asia also brought charges against Lucilius Capito, who had been the procurator in charge of imperial holdings in that province.[41] He was accused of usurping the praetor's responsibilities and using military force against the provincials. Tiberius approved of the decision of the Senate to hear the case, and the prosecution was again successful.

In response to these two judicial decisions, the cities of Asia decreed a temple for Tiberius, Livia (his mother, the widow of Augustus), and the Senate.[42] Permission to build it was forthcoming, but later on, Tiberius was faulted by some for not opposing the request for the temple.[43]

Tacitus reported that the province of Hispania Ulterior presented a request in 25 CE for permission to build a similar temple in honor of Tiberius and Livia, without the inclusion of the Senate.[44] Tiberius used the occasion to defend himself against charges of self-glorification that arose from his approval of Asia's cult, and to lay out a policy for future provincial cults.

According to Tacitus, Tiberius explained in a speech to the Senate that he had granted the request of the cities of Asia because of the precedent set by Divus Augustus in allowing a cult to be founded in Pergamum. A further consideration which made the province's second request more palatable to the emperor was that the worship of Tiberius was linked to that of the Senate. The request of Hispania Ulterior, however, was to be rejected because a proliferation of such cults to Tiberius would be arrogant and would diminish the significance of the veneration of Augustus.[45]

---

[41] Tacitus *An.* 4.15.

[42] Tacitus *An.* 4.15. P. A. Brunt pointed out that united fronts by an entire province such as that presented by the koinon of Asia under Tiberius were unusual, and not without risks. Repeated accusations by a particular koinon might produce a negative reaction against the province, and any accusation would inevitably create enemies among the defendant's supporters. If the defendant was acquitted and remained in a position of power, the province might be left especially vulnerable. "Charges of Provincial Maladministration under the Early Principate," *Historia* 10 (1961) 189-227, esp. 217, 220, 224-25

[43] Tacitus *An.* 4.37. While the speech in this text was crafted by Tacitus, his claim to have had access to the speeches of Tiberius seems to have been accurate. Furthermore, the historian apparently took care not to misrepresent the content of the speeches. Ronald Martin, *Tacitus* (Berkeley and Los Angeles: University of California Press, 1981) 120, 133-34.

[44] Tacitus *An.* 4.37.

[45] Suetonius implied that Tiberius never allowed cultic honors for himself when the historian reported that the emperor prohibited temples, flamens, and priests to

Asia's provicial cult came to the Senate's attention again in 26 CE.[46] In the three years since the cult had been approved, no agreement had been reached as to which city would be given the privilege of providing the site for the temple. The Senate, with Tiberius in attendance, spent several days listening to representatives from eleven cities of the province of Asia. Each representative presented the arguments for the respective city's claim to be the most appropriate site for the temple, after which the Senate was to decide the matter.

The arguments in this case provide a unique record of the factors which were considered important in the choice of an appropriate site for an imperial temple.[47] Tacitus recorded that, in general, all eleven cities based their arguments on the antiquity of their people,[48] and on the support (*studium*) which they had offered the people of Rome in time of war. Along with these came arguments based on longstanding cultic honor for Rome (Smyrna) or for Augustus (Pergamum), and on wealth of natural resources (Sardis).[49]

In the deliberations which ensued, several cities were eliminated

---

be decreed for him (*Tib.* 26). The text from Tacitus (*An.* 4.37) shows that Suetonius was correct in stating that Tiberius decided not to accept divine honors for himself from the provinces. Suetonius neglected to record, however, that this policy was formulated only after the cult of Tiberius, Livia, and the Senate had been approved. We cannot be certain about whether Suetonius was unaware of the cult in Smyrna, or whether he intentionally omitted reference to it in his writings. As a proponent of the traditional Roman view toward the glorification of the emperor (*Aug.* 52, 97; *Gaius* 22; *Dom.* 13), Suetonius may have suppressed the exceptional cult in Smyrna to make Tiberius's general policy more commendable. Moreover, Suetonius was probably aware of provincial cult procedures involving Asia for he was a prominent scholar in Rome who served in three secretarial posts under Trajan and Hadrian, the latter of whom made an unprecedented grant of three provincial cults to Asia (Kyzikos, Smyrna, Ephesus).

[46] Tacitus, *An.* 4.55-56

[47] Tacitus's account of these discussions is based on historical sources and is not his own creation. The conditions which are described in the arguments (e.g., the exclusive hold of Artemis on Ephesus) are those of the first half of the first century CE and not of Tacitus's own time.

[48] For example, Ilium claimed to be the parent of Rome through Troy. Sardis, on the other hand, recounted their mythic history in such a way as to show that Sardis and Rome traced their lineages back to Tyrrhenus and Lydus, the sons of Atys, which made the two peoples "brothers."

[49] Halikarnassos is reported to have received some consideration due to their claim to be free from earthquakes. While this is a rarity in Anatolia, the claim would have been especially impressive during the time of Tiberius. A severe earthquake struck the province in 17 CE and occasioned one of the few examples of major imperial largesse from Tiberius. Suet. *Tib.* 48.

from the competition because they were considered to be too insignificant to receive the honor of providing a home for the cult.[50] The argument of the Pergamenes that their cult for Augustus qualified them to host the new cult as well turned against them; the cult of Augustus was considered to be sufficient honor for the city and their claim was rejected. The requests of Ephesus and Miletus were refused because they already had renowned cults (of Artemis and of Apollo, respectively) which dominated the cities.

In the end, only Sardis and Smyrna were left as serious contenders. The representatives from Sardis emphasized their city's ancient, mythic ties with Rome, produced documentation of treaties and agreements, and praised their own rich rivers and land. Smyrna's advocates reviewed their own city's mythic past (in three variants!) but emphasized their early support for Rome both in battle[51] and through cult.[52] The senators voted and Smyrna was granted the right to build the temple. The Senate also decided to send a *legatus super numerum* to oversee construction.[53]

From the writings of Tacitus it is clear that while this cult was sponsored by the whole province, it also was an occasion for intense competition between the cities of the province. While the motives of the cities are not made explicit, we can extrapolate that the presence of such a cult would enhance a city's development in many ways. It would enrich the cultic life of the city; it would increase the city's status in relation to other cities; it would create new offices for wealthy individuals to demonstrate their commitment to the city's well-being; it would bring these individuals and the city in closer contact with the Senate and the emperor; and, it would improve the city's economy through a building program partially funded by outside sources and through periodic festivals.

---

[50] Hypaipa, Tralles, Laodikeia, Magnesia on the Meander, Ilium, and Halikarnassos were disqualified for this reason.

[51] Smyrna could boast of helping Rome with naval reinforcements both in her foreign wars (such as against Antiochos III, 191-88 BCE) and at home (Social Wars, 90-87 BCE). They also noted that they had sent supplies to Sulla at a crucial point in his campaigns.

[52] Smyrna claimed to have built the first temple to Rome in Asia (ca. 195 BCE) at a time when Carthage was not yet vanquished and when there were still rival kings ruling large areas of Asia Minor.

[53] Valerius Naso was chosen by lot from among the ex-praetors for this position. The exact nature of his responsibilities is unknown since Tacitus, our only source on the matter, is not precise in his description (*qui templi curam susciperet*).

In developing their arguments, the cities were in some respects sailing on uncharted seas, for no province had previously received a second provincial cult and the factors that would determine the choice were not clear. Thus, Pergamum gambled on the presence of the first provincial cult in their city, and lost. The cities were not without guidelines, however, in presenting their cases. They could look to former negotiations of alliances with Rome and, more specifically, to earlier discussions in the provincial koinon about the site of the cult.

The record of Tacitus suggests that the presence of such a cult in a city at the time of Tiberius involved three conditions. The first was the wealth and status of the city where the cult was founded. No matter what other arguments might be presented, a relatively insignificant city without a distinguished heritage would not be considered as a possible site.

Second, a city had to have room in its cultic life for this major, new cult. Ephesus and Miletus were excluded from consideration because each city's religious ethos was already dominated by a cult of international renown. Pergamum also had at least one cult—that of Rome and Augustus—which would certainly have dominated the new one.[54]

Third, the presence of a provincial cult in a city was supposed to commemorate an established relationship between two specific peoples: the demos of the city and the *populus Romanus*. The claims of mythic consanguinity, the references to old cults of Rome, and the records of military assistance all were used to demonstrate this point. It appears that in the final analysis, the factors of cultic and military fidelity decided the case among the more prestigious cities of Asia.

The ancient city of Smyrna is mostly covered by the modern city of Izmir and this has hampered excavations of the ancient remains. Thus, no architectural pieces from the provincial temple in Smyrna have been found. A bronze coin of Smyrna (Pl. III), issued while P. Petronius was proconsul of Asia (29-35 CE) remedies that problem to some extent by depicting the temple.[55] The obverse of

---

[54] This factor was to change significantly in the future. The cult of Artemis was no longer a hindrance for Ephesus in the late first century CE, and by the end of Hadrian's reign, three Asian cities had received a second provincial cult. The case of Miletus is discussed below (p. 21-30).

[55] *BM Ionia* 268, #266-68; pl. 28. Another bronze coin of Smyrna (*BM Ionia* 268, #263-65) might portray an altar associated with the temple.

Plate III. Bronze coin of Smyrna (29-35 CE). Obverse: Livia and Senate; reverse: Tiberius sacrificing in temple. *BM Ionia* 268 #267. Courtesy of the Trustees of the British Museum.

the coin bears two draped heads: that of Livia on the right and that of a youth (on the left) who symbolizes the Senate. Around them is the inscription Σεβαστή Σύνκλητος Ζμυρναίων Ἱερώνυμος "Hallowed Sebaste (and) Senate; (coin) of the Smyrnians." The temple itself is shown on the reverse. There are four columns, probably Corinthian, with a statue of Tiberius in the center wearing a toga and with his head covered in priestly fashion. The inscription reads Σεβαστὸς Τιβέριος, ἐπὶ Πετρωνίου: "Sebastos Tiberius, when Petronius (was proconsul)."

This coin yields significant information about the cult established in Smyrna after the senatorial decision of 26 CE. First, it confirms the unusual combination of Tiberius, Livia, and the Senate recorded by Tacitus as the recipients of cultic honors. The coin, by depicting only Tiberius in the temple, confirms that he was the most important member of the triad. Second, the temple appears to have the same basic design, to the extent that this can be determined from coins, as that of Rome and Augustus in Pergamum.[56]

Third, we note that the temple statue portrayed Tiberius not in the cuirass of a general, but in the robes of a priest. Such a portrayal does not necessarily remove Tiberius from the realm of the divine; gods were sometimes shown in priestly garb offering sacrifices.[57] In the context of imperial cult in Asia, however, it places Tiberius in a different role than that of the well-known image of the cuirassed Augustus. Whereas Augustus was the military conqueror who brought security to Asia and to the empire, Tiberius was portrayed as one who venerates, one who carries on a sacred tradition.

---

[56] The temple of Tiberius, though shown with four columns, was probably a hexastyle temple whose middle two columns were left out on the coin in order to show the temple statue.

[57] On this issue, See Price 1984b, 184-85 and notes.

An inscription from Sardis gives the standard phrase for referring to this temple while mentioning one of the offices created by the new cult: ἀρχιερεὺς τῆς Ἀσίας ναοῦ το[ῦ ἐν] Σμ[ύρ]νῃ, "highpriest of Asia of the temple in Smyrna."[58] Other offices related to the cult and attested epigraphically include highpriestess,[59] hymnodes,[60] and neokoros.[61]

In the Smyrna cult, then, several similarities with the cult in Pergamum are apparent: the initiative of the province in requesting the cult; the necessity of including figures other than the emperor in the cult; and the use of Greek architectural designs in the construction of a temple. In addition, the nature of our sources about the cult in Smyrna make clear the ways in which the siting of a provincial cult occasioned intense competition between the cities of a province. Finally, we note that no separate cult for Romans, nor one dedicated to Divus Julius or to Augustus accompanied the provincial cult in Smyrna.

Miletus

Very little evidence for the third provincial cult of Asia has survived the centuries; we possess only two witnesses that refer to it. This relative lack of information is due to the fact that the cult, established in Miletus under Caligula, lasted no more than a few years. The two extant witnesses do, however, provide some valuable data on the organization of this provincial cult, and suggest that it included some unique aspects in comparison to its predecessors.

An inscription concerning the cult was found near the southwest corner of the temple of Apollo at Didyma. The inscription is on a statue base of marble and has been published most recently by Louis Robert.[62] His edition of the text is printed below.

---

[58] *IGR* 4.1524. A discussion of the responsibilities of this office can be found in chapter four.

[59] *IvSm* 2,1.727. This inscription comes from the period when Smyrna had two provincial cults (ca. 123-214 CE).

[60] *IvSm* 2,1.594.

[61] *IvSm* 2,1.594; 596; 639 l. 6-7.

[62] Louis Robert, "Le cult de Caligula a Milet et la province d'Asie," *Hellenica* 7 (1949) 206-38. The statue base measures 0.95 m. high, ca. 0.75 m. wide, and ca. 0.75 m. deep. The letters are 0.02 m. high (p. 206 n. 3).

[Αὐτοκράτορα Γάϊον Κα]ίσαρα Γερμανικὸ[ν]
[Γερμανικοῦ υἱ]ὸν θεὸν Σεβαστὸν νεοπο-
ιοὶ οἱ πρώτως νεοποιήσαντες αὐτοῦ
4   ἐπὶ ἀρχιερέως Γναίου Οὐεργιλίου Καπίτωνος
τοῦ μὲν ἐν Μειλήτῳ ναοῦ Γαίου Καίσαρος τὸ πρῶτον, τῆς δὲ ᾿Ασίας τὸ τρίτον, καὶ Τιβερίου ᾿Ιουλίου,
Δημητρίου νομοθέτου υἱοῦ, Μηνογένους, ἀρχιερέως
8   τὸ δεύτερον καὶ νεωκόρου τοῦ ἐν Μειλήτῳ ναοῦ, καὶ
Πρωτομάχου τοῦ Γλύκωνος ᾿Ιουλιέως τοῦ ἀρχινεοποι-
οῦ καὶ σεβαστονέῳ καὶ σεβαστόλογου ἐκ τῶν ἰδί-
11   ων ἀνέθηκαν,
[lines 12-20: a list of thirteen names]
21   οἱ φιλοσέβαστοι,
γραφέντων τῶν ὀνομάτων κατὰ κλῆρον.

The neopoioi, the first ones to serve him in this capacity, dedicated (this statue of) Emperor Gaius Caesar Germanicus, son of Germanicus, God Sebastos, from their own funds, when Gaius Vergilius Capito was highpriest of the temple in Miletus of Gaius Caesar for the first time, but highpriest of Asia for the third time; and (when) Tiberius Julius Menogenes, son of Demetrios the nomothete, was highpriest the second time and neokoros of the temple in Miletus; and (when) Protomachos Julieus, son of Glykon, was leader of the neopoioi and sebastoneos and sebastologos, [Thirteen neopoioi are listed with the cities they represent], those devoted to Sebastos, the names being written (in order, chosen) by lot.

The base once supported a statue of the emperor Gaius, which dates the inscription to the years 37-41 CE. Several officials are named and reference is made to the temple. From the way in which the temple is mentioned, it is clear that this cult differed from the previous provincial cults in Asia in its glorification of the living emperor, for the temple was dedicated to a single emperor without including any other individual or collective (e.g., Rome, Livia, the Senate).[63]

Furthermore, the word θεός is used in the name of Gaius. While θεός was used for the living emperor in various contexts, provincial cults tended to be more conservative in this than were the municipal or private imperial cults. This was due to the closer contact of provincial cults with Rome and its traditions. Local imperial cults were subject to local custom; provincial cults, on the other hand, needed to be cognizant of the traditions in Rome in order to secure the approval of the Senate and emperor.[64] For these reasons,

---

[63] Line 5.
[64] This difference in practice between provincial imperial cults and local

provincial cults in Asia usually reserved the designation of θεός for an officially divinized emperor, while local cults were less restrictive in their use of the label.[65]

An equally significant aspect of the inscription, though, is the unprecedented glimpse it provides into the organization of the cult. As one would expect, highpriests are mentioned. One of these, Gaius Vergilius Capito,[66] was serving for the first time as highpriest of the temple in Miletus, and we are told that he had already served twice as highpriest for another provincial cult or cults. Another highpriest, Ti. Julius Menogenes, was also the neokoros of the provincial temple.[67] The third official, Protomachos son of Glykon, had three positions. He was the sebastoneos, the sebastologos, and the head of the group of neopoioi (l. 9-10).

Individuals who served as neopoioi normally were part of a commission whose responsibility it was to administer temple finances. In some cases, groups of neopoioi functioned as a building committee for a new temple, but the normal responsibilities for such a group in Asia in the Roman period was the maintenance of buildings and oversight of a temple's income.[68] The neopoioi in this inscription are given credit for setting up the statue of Gaius in the Didymeion precincts. They are also listed by name in lines 12-21, and we are told that they were the first ones to serve in this way. Since these are

---

imperial cults is demonstrated by Hänlein-Schäfer's systematic examination of temples to Augustus from his lifetime and throughout the empire in *VENERATIO AUGUSTI*, esp. p. 80.

[65] For example, during the lifetime of Augustus (specifically, 2 BCE–14 CE) an eponymous local official in Kyme is referred to in the phrase ἐπὶ ἱερέος τᾶς Ῥώμας καὶ Αὐτοκράτορος Καίσαρος Θέω υἵω Θέω Σεβάστω "when (he was) priest of Rome and of Emperor Caesar Augustus, God, Son of God;" *IGR* 4.1302, l. 55-56. A provincial high priest, however, was ὁ ἀχιερεὺς θεᾶς Ῥώμης καὶ Αὐτοκράτορος Καίσαρος θεοῦ υἱοῦ Σεβαστο[ῦ], "the highpriest of Goddess Rome and of Emperor Caesar Augustus, Son of God;" *IGR* 4.1756, l. 75-76 (Sardis, 4 BCE). In the Tiberian period, an official of the same provincial cult is called τὸν νεωκόρον θεᾶς Ῥώμης καὶ θεοῦ Σεβατοῦ Καίσαρος, "neokoros of Goddess Rome and of God Augustus Caesar;" *IGR* 4.454 (Pergamum). Augustus was a θεός in local cults and in provincial cults after his death, but not in a provincial cult during his lifetime.

[66] Lines 4-6. At some time after the reign of Augustus, a cult was established for Capito in Miletus which is, according to Bowersock (*Augustus*, 120), the last known cult for a Roman official other than an emperor.

[67] The neokoros was an official whose responsibilities are discussed below in chapter three.

[68] Otto Schulthess, "*Neopoioi*," PW 16 (1935) 2433-39.

specifically denoted as the first group of neopoioi, they probably
supervised the building of the temple to Gaius. The designation
"first" implies that the office is to continue, though. The major responsibility of the office, therefore, was probably administration of
the temple.

The list of names includes the city of Asia from which each neopoios came. Robert's study has shown that the cities listed on the
inscription were not chosen arbitrarily.[69] The cities were chosen to
represent their district (known as *conventus iuridi* or διοίκησις) within
the province. All areas of the province were thus represented in the
organization of the cult and responsible in part for its operation.[70]

In the first half of the third century CE, Dio Cassius wrote about
the provincial cult for Gaius in Miletus in a section of his *Roman History* which dealt with the events of 40 CE.

> Gaius ordered that a sacred precinct should be set apart for his
> worship at Miletus in the province of Asia. The reason he gave for
> choosing this city was that Artemis had pre-empted Ephesus,
> Augustus Pergamum, and Tiberius Smyrna; but the truth of the mat-
> ter was that he desired to appropriate to his own use the large and
> exceedingly beautiful temple which the Milesians were building to
> Apollo.[71]

Dio's account must be read with caution for Gaius did not find a
sympathetic audience among the Roman historians. It would appear from this passage, however, that the initiative for establishing
this cult did not come from Asia, as was the case in the two earlier
provincial cults, but rather from the emperor. This is not an im-
probable scenario, and it does accord with what is known about
Gaius's other actions in connection with religious institutions.[72]

A second point of interest in Dio's account is the issue of choosing
a city for the cult. Gaius is reported to have chosen Miletus because
the three major cities of the province already focussed their piety on
other deities. This was the same argument used in 26 CE by the

---

[69] See esp. 226-38

[70] Competition within the province surfaces in this inscription in the last line
that notes that the ordering of the names in the list was determined randomly; i.e.,
the order of the names does not reflect individual or municipal status.

[71] Dio 59.28.1. Based on the translation by Earnest Cary in *Dio's Roman History*, vol. 7 (Loeb Classical Library; Cambridge, Mass.: Harvard University Press,
1924).

[72] See, for example, Suet. *Gaius* 22 and 52.

Senate in their decision to site the cult of Tiberius, Livia, and the Senate in Smyrna. Gaius's use of the argument is not convincing, though, since Miletus was also dominated by the ancient and respected cult of Didymeian Apollo.[73] Dio then goes on to say that Gaius's actual intention was to take over the precincts and temple of Apollo at Didyma.

Dio was probably not accurate when he linked the Didyma precincts to the provincial cult of Gaius. Provincial cults did not normally convert existing facilities for the use of the new cult. Rather, a new temple accompanied the new cult.[74] Moreover, an attempt by Gaius to replace Apollo in a famous eastern sanctuary like Didyma would probably have come to the attention of Suetonius and would have been noted by him.[75] Suetonius does mention that Gaius planned or tried to complete unfinished work on the Didymeion.[76] Dio probably has connected, or even confused, these two separate projects related to Miletus: a provincial cult for Gaius; and, Gaius's support for the continuing construction of the Apollo sanctuary.[77]

With the death of Gaius, the provincial cult in Miletus disappears from the archaeological record. No temple has been identified for the cult,[78] and no other inscriptions mention either officials or fes-

---

[73] In the deliberations of 26 CE, the argument may have been in part a matter of convenience as well. The need to decrease the number of cities under consideration may have caused the argument about other major cults to have taken on exaggerated significance.

[74] Two exceptions to this general rule may have occurred, both of which come from a later period when provincial cults were much more easily acquired. In the middle of the second century CE, Sardis may have used its Artemis temple for a provincial cult involving Antoninus Pius and Faustina (Price 1984b, 260). It has also been argued that Smyrna's third provincial cult, granted in the early third century CE, was housed in the temple of the goddess Rome. See Barbara Burrell, "*Neokoroi*: Greek Cities of the Roman East" (Ph.D. diss., Harvard University, 1980) 342-44 for a discussion of Smyrna's third provincial cult.

[75] We cannot consult Tacitus on this matter because his account of the reign of Gaius has not survived.

[76] Suet. *Gaius* 21.

[77] J. P. V. D. Balsdon, *The Emperor Gaius* (*Caligula*) (Oxford: Clarendon Press, 1934) 162; Burrell, 327. Gaius is known to have promulgated the placement of statues of himself in venerable sanctuaries like the temple of Yahweh in Jerusalem (Tacitus, *Hist.* 5.9), and Gaius may have tried to do this at the temple of Apollo in Didyma as well.

[78] There is a bronze coin issued by Miletus with a head of Gaius on the obverse and a hexastyle temple of uncertain identity on the reverse; *BM Ionia* 198, #143. This could be a representation of the provincial temple, though Haussoullier (*Études*

tivals related to the cult. The reason for the silence is that this cult, like all others dedicated to the adopted son of Tiberius, was discontinued after Gaius's assassination. The emperor was not deified; in fact, Gaius's memory barely escaped the *damnatio* of the Senate.[79] The cult had to be terminated for it would immediately have become a problem for the province of Asia in its relations with Rome, and it would have been of little benefit to the city of Miletus.

Imperial Cults of Other Provinces

Not long after the inauguration of cults for Rome and Octavian in Asia and Bithynia, Galatia was incorporated into the Roman Empire as a province. The Temple of Rome and Augustus in Ankyra was built for this cult, probably around 25 BCE when Galatia became a province.[80] In 12 BCE an altar for Rome and Augustus was dedicated by the three Gallic provinces at Lugdunum, and within three years the province of Germania also had an altar. The latter was built in *Oppidum Ubiorum* (modern Cologne) but its significance was greatly reduced after 9 CE when Varus and the Roman troops were defeated in the Teutoburgerwald.[81]

Noricum's cult may have been instituted during the Augustan period, but the next datable provincial cult was established for Divus Augustus in Hispania Citerior in 15 CE, the year after his death.[82] Britain's Temple of Claudius probably served a provincial cult, and while Deininger suggests that the cult of the province of Lusitania may have been from the Claudian period, it is first attested under Vespasian.[83] The reign of Vespasian is also the possible starting point for cults of Narbonensis, Africa, Baetica and Lycia.[84] Macedonia's provincial cult is attested under Nerva, but it may be somewhat earlier.[85]

---

sur l'histoire de Milet et du Didymeion [Paris: Émile Bouillon, 1902] 277-78) thought the temple on the coin was the Didymeion which Gaius helped complete. His identification is questionable; the Didymeion was an octastyle temple at that time and such an important shrine would probably have been depicted more accurately.

[79] Suet. *Claudius* 11; Dio Cassius 60.4.5.

[80] Deininger 1965, 20. Note, however, Heidi Hänlein's argument that the cult was established only after the death of Augustus in "Zur Datierung des Augustustempels in Ankara," *AA*, 1981, no.3:511-13.

[81] Hänlein-Schäfer 1985, 14-15.

[82] Hänlein-Schäfer 1985, 152-54; Deininger 1965, 25-27.

[83] Deininger 1965, 29, 31-32.

[84] Deininger 1965, 28-30, 31.

[85] Burrell 1980, 6; *contra* Deininger 1965, 21.

Summary

This brief review of Asia's early provincial imperial cults has explored a variety of patterns and institutions. A cult for Rome and Octavian, granted in 29 BCE, soon became known as that of Rome and Augustus, and was accompanied by a corresponding cult of Rome and Julius at Ephesus for resident Romans. The Rome and Julius cult made little impression on the province, while that of Augustus and Rome developed into a venerable cult of wide renown, serving as Asia's only provincial cult for over 50 years.

The new province of Galatia followed the lead of the cults of western Asia Minor by establishing a cult for Rome and Augustus as early as 25 BCE. There is no evidence that a cult of Rome and Julius was initiated in Galatia, though. The western provinces of the empire, on the other hand, proceeded more slowly in the establishment of provincial cults, inaugurating two altars and perhaps a temple for Rome and Augustus in his lifetime.

Tiberius allowed Hispania Citerior to honor Augustus with a temple in 15 CE and he followed Augustus's precedent, set some fifty years earlier, by approving a provincial cult for Asia in 23 CE that was dedicated to Tiberius, Livia, and the Senate. This cult was occasioned by two successful prosecutions of Roman officials by Asia before the Senate. After three years another hearing was required before the Senate in Rome in order to settle the dispute between the cities of Asia as to which one would serve as the site for the cult's temple. After criticism resulted from his approval of the cult, Tiberius initiated a new policy of not sanctioning similar petitions for provincial cults like the request that came from Hispania Ulterior.

Around the year 40 CE, Gaius promulgated a provincial cult for himself in Miletus, but his downfall brought down the cult as well. The small amount of surviving information about the cult indicates that it departed from the tradition of including figures other than the emperor (e.g., Rome, the Senate, Livia) in a provincial cult. The cult had a clearly defined, province-wide organization and it was more explicit in the use of divine terminology for the emperor.

Even though Claudius seems to have received cultic honors in Britain, neither he nor Nero received provincial worship in Asia. In fact, after Gaius there was no other provincial imperial cult established in Asia for over 40 years. In the next chapter it will be shown

that no such cult was inaugurated for either Vespasian or Titus in
Asia during their lifetimes. Thus, it seems that the later policy of
Tiberius (i.e., no provincial cults for the living emperor), was soon
suspended by Gaius (ca. 40 CE), and that later emperors of the first
century CE followed Gaius's policy rather than that of Tiberius. No
emperor, however, is known to have granted any other province a
second imperial cult even though Asia had two such cults. For nearly
sixty years—from 26 CE until the reign of Domitian in the late first
century CE—Asia had two provincial cults but was not successful in
establishing a third.

CHAPTER TWO

THE TEMPLE INSCRIPTIONS FROM EPHESUS

Discovery of the Inscriptions

Several inscriptions with similar texts have been found during the last 125 years that are related to the provincial temple in Ephesus.[1] They are all dedications from various cities in Asia, set up for display in Ephesus. All but one of them are carved into rectangular marble blocks, the exception being inscribed into an unfluted marble column. The rectangular blocks are of a standard type that was used for statue bases in Asia in the imperial period (Pl. IV).

The total number of inscriptions in this group now stands at thirteen. The first one to come to light, a dedication from the people of Makedones Hyrkanioi, was found in the early 1870's during the British excavations.[2] A second inscription of the same general type, this one from the people of Aphrodisias and found near the Church of St. John on Ayasoluk Hill, was first published in 1880.[3]

When the Austrian Archaeological Institute began excavating in and around Ephesus during the late nineteenth century, several more temple inscriptions were discovered. In the mid-1890's six inscriptions were found built into a late bridge northwest of the village of Selçuk. These six were dedications from five cities: Tmolos, Stratonikeia, Silandos, Aizanoi (2 copies), and one unidentified locale.[4] Within a few years, an inscription from Synaos was also unearthed in the theater.[5]

---

[1] The inscriptions have appeared in various publications with different numbering systems. In the text of this chapter, they will be referred to by their city of origin. The *IvE* publication numbers that correspond to the city names may be found in the notes and in the Chronological Chart on p. 46-47.

[2] E. L. Hicks, *IBM* 3.498 (no inventory number listed) = *IvE* 5.1498. The white marble stele is 3 ft., 11 in. high and 2 ft. wide.

[3] *Mouseion Smyrna* 3 (1878-80) 180; *IvE* 2.233.

[4] *IvE* 2.241, 237, 238, 232, 232a, and 242, respectively.

[5] *IvE* 6.2048. Found in 1898-99, according to *FiE* 2, #48. The bottom half of the white marble block is missing so that its present height is only 0.46 m. Its width is 0.55 m. and the depth 0.56 m. The extant letters vary in height from 4 to 2.5 cm.

Plate IV. Statue base with inscription commissioned by the city
of Keretapa for the dedication of the Temple of the Sebastoi.
IvE 2.234.

The remaining four inscriptions were found in more recent excavations. Miltner's campaigns from 1955 to 1958 near the Varius
Baths uncovered the dedicatory inscription of Keretapa that had
been reused as a roof support.[6] Klazomenai's inscription was found

---

[6] *IvE* 2.234. Also of white marble, the block measures 1.205 m. high, 0.595 m.
wide, and 0.59 m. deep. The letters vary in height from 5 cm. (l. 1) to 3 cm.
(l. 11-15). J. Keil and G. Maresch, "Epigraphische Nachlese zu Miltners Ausgrabungsberichten aus Ephesos," *ÖJh* 45 (1960) Beib. 83-84.

Plate V. Text of the Keretapa inscription. Note erasure of Domitian's personal names. This inscription was not reinscribed with a dedication to Vespasian.

west of the Trajan Fountain on Kuretes Street in 1955.[7] The other two, from Teos and Kyme, were recovered near the Pollio Fountain and the Hydrekdochion, respectively.[8]

---

[7] *IvE* 2.235. The blue-white marble block is 0.9 m. high, 0.58 m. wide, and 0.59 m. deep. Its largest letters are 8 cm. high, its smallest 2 cm. Anton Bammer, Robert Fleischer, Dieter Knibbe, *Führer durch das archäologische Museum in Selcuk—Ephesos* (Vienna: Österreichisches Archäologisches Institut, 1974) 115-16.

[8] *IvE* 2.239, 240. The Teos dedication was discovered in 1964. It consists of two

Many of the thirteen inscriptions are no longer available for examination. The six inscriptions from the bridge over the Kaystros have disappeared since they were discovered and recorded. The fragmentary Teos and Kyme inscriptions are stored on site at Ephesus. One inscription, that of Klazomenai, can be viewed in the courtyard of the Ephesus Museum in Selçuk, and the Aphrodisias inscription is on display just inside the Gate of Persecution that serves as the entryway to the site of St. John's Church. The Synaos inscription remains in the orchestra of the theater in Ephesus and the Keretapa inscription is in the cryptoporticus west of and below the Scholastikia Baths where it was reused as a structural support in antiquity. The Hyrkanioi inscription is in the British Museum, London. The published descriptions and the available examples, along with squeezes where they exist, make the texts of the inscriptions very reliable.

The Texts of the Inscriptions

The thirteen inscriptions related to the imperial temple at Ephesus represent one basic pattern in two versions. The long version is found in the two inscriptions from the free cities Aphrodisias and Stratonikeia. The inscriptions commissioned by other cities use an abbreviated version (above, Pl. V).

The inscription from Aphrodisias provides an example of the long version that was used by the free cities.

	Αὐτοκράτορι [[Δομι-
2	τιανῶι]] Καίσαρι Σε-
	βαστῶι [[Γερμανικῶι]]
4	ἐπὶ ἀνθυπάτου Μάρκ[ου]
	Φουλουίου Γίλλωνο[ς]
6	ὁ φιλοκαῖσαρ Ἀφροδεισι[έων]
	δῆμος ἐλεύθερος ὢν κα[ὶ αὐ-]
8	τόνομος ἀπ᾽ ἀπχῆς τῆι τῶν Σε[βασ-]
	τῶν χάριτι ναῶι τῶι ἐν Ἐφέσ[ωι]
10	τῶν Σεβαστῶν κοινῶι τῆς Ἀσί[ας]
	ἰδίᾳ χάριτι διά τε τὴν πρὸς τοὺς [Σε-]
12	βαστοὺς εὐσέβειαν καὶ τὴν π[ρὸς]
	τὴν νεωκόρον Ἐφεσίων [πό-]
14	λιν εὔνοιαν ἀνέστησαν
	ἐπιμεληθέντος Ἀρίστω[νος τοῦ]

fragments of an unfluted column shaft (Inv. no. 3353-54) whose diameter is 0.64 m. Fritz Eichler, "Die österreichischen Ausgrabungen in Ephesos im Jahre 1964," *AnzWien* 102 (1965) 103-4, #2.

```
16        Ἀρτεμιδώρου τοῦ Καλλι.[    ]
          ὡς ἱερέως Πλούτωνος [καὶ]
18        Κόρης καὶ νεοποιοῦ θεᾶ[ς]
          Ἀφροδείτης, ἐπὶ ἀρχιερ[έως]
20        τῆς Ἀσίας Τιβερίου Κλαυδ[ίου]
          Φησείνου [[                        ]]
          [[                                 ]]
          [[                                 ]]
          [[                                 ]]⁹
```

To Emperor [[Domitian]] Caesar Sebastos [[Germanicus]] when the proconsul was Marcus Fulvius Gillo.

The demos of the Aphrodisians, devoted to Caesar, being free and autonomous from the beginning by the grace of the Sebastoi, set up (this statue) by its own grace because of its reverence toward the Sebastoi and its goodwill toward the neokorate city of the Ephesians, (because of) Asia's common temple of the Sebastoi in Ephesus. (This was) accomplished by Aristo[son] of Artemidoros of Kalli.[   ]os, priest of Pluto and Kore, and neopoios of the goddess Aphrodite, when the high priest of Asia was Tiberius Claudius Pheseinos [[three and one half line erasure]].

The elements of the pattern of these inscriptions can be listed as follows, with the line numbers of the inscription from Aphrodisias indicated for reference.

1. Dedication to Domitian (lines 1-3);   stable element.[10]
2. Proconsul (l. 4-5);   stable element.
3. Dedicating city (l. 6-7);   stable element.
4. City's free status (l. 7-9);   long version.
5. Reference to provincial temple (l. 9-10);   stable element.
6. Motivations for dedication (l. 11-13);   long version.
7. Main verb: ἀνέστησαν (l. 14);   long version.
8. Representative(s) from dedicating city (l. 15-19).[11]
9. Highpriest of Asia (l. 19-21);   stable element.
10. Neokoros of the temple.[12]
11. Erasure (l. 21-24).[13]

---

⁹ Personal examination of the inscription showed that the published text (*IvE* 2.233), recording a two and one half line erasure, is incorrect.

10 "Stable element" is defined as a feature which occurs in all examples of the extant long and short inscriptions.

11 The inclusion of officials from the dedicating city occurs in some long and in some short inscriptions.

12 This does not occur in the Aphrodisias inscription, but is included here so that all elements can be examined together.

13 Three other inscriptions, all of which are of the short version, have such erasures. Chapter five includes a discussion of the reasons for the erasures and a proposed reconstruction of the original readings.

The pattern of these inscriptions can be summarized by noting that elements 1, 2, 3, 5, and 9 appear in all thirteen inscriptions. The inscriptions from Aphrodisias and Stratonikeia (i.e., those representing the long version) also include elements 4, 6, and 7. Elements 8, 10, and 11 appear occasionally in short and in long inscriptions.

The opening dedication to Domitian in the dative (lines 1-3) may indicate that a statue of the emperor once stood upon this base. A dative dedication, however, was a standard way of opening an honorary inscription and did not necessarily coincide with the identity of the statue.[14] When a statue is identified in an inscription, it normally appears in the accusative. While a statue of Domitian or of another member of the imperial family would have been appropriate, we cannot be completely certain about the kinds of statues which these bases would have supported.

The content of the dedicatory phrase has implications for our understanding of the cult. The original inscription began Αὐτοκρά-τορι Δομιτιανῶι Καίσαρι Σεβαστῶι Γερμανικῶι, "To Emperor Domitian Caesar Sebastos Germanicus." This is normal nomenclature for Domitian after he adopted the title "Germanicus" in 83/84 CE. The term θεός was not used of Domitian in these inscriptions. Domitian was identified as a Sebastos, though, which makes him an object of worship in this particular temple. Thus, the vocabulary of the dedication as well as the numerous dedications themselves indicate that Domitian was central to the cult. With respect to the divinization of the emperor, however, the language of the dedications does not deviate from normal practice in the provincial cults. The use of Θεός in reference to a living emperor was not unusual in Asia at this time,[15] but the term was studiously avoided in provincial cults. Thus, there is no suggestion of extraordinary cultic honors for Domitian or for any other imperial figure in this inscription.

---

[14] *IvE* 7,2.3272 is an inscription from near Ephesus which begins with a dative dedication to Ephesian Artemis and to the κατοικία of the Lareisians, but explicitly states that the donors set up statues of two deer. An Ephesian inscription (*IvE* 3.858) from the year 104/105 CE dedicated a statue group to Ephesian Artemis, Trajan, and the neokorate demos, but left the statue group unidentified, referring to it simply as τὸ σύνπλ[ε]γμα ("the group"). Artemis, Trajan, and the demos would hardly have been the subjects of the statues; this was simply a standard, threefold dedicatory formula from the decades around the year 100 CE. For other examples of the formula, see *IvE* 4.1124 (Nerva); 2.424a (Street Fountain, Trajanic); and 2.429 (so-called Hadrian Temple).

[15] S. R. F. Price, "Gods and Emperors: The Greek Language of the Roman Imperial Cult," *JHS* 104 (1984) 82.

The text of the inscription from Aphrodisias illuminates the nature of the cult in several other ways. The reader of the text is immediately informed by the naming of the proconsul that this cult had provincial, rather than just civic, importance (lines 4-5). Inscriptions dealing with matters of local interest or with municipal concerns normally included the name of the highest municipal official, the city secretary (γραμματεὺς τοῦ δήμου) as a dating device. Here, the presence of the proconsul's name both dates the inscription and indicates the regional significance of the monument.

One of the most significant aspects of the inscription for our understanding of the cult is that it contains the official title of the temple (l. 9-10). The temple is described in two ways. First, the temple is "in Ephesus" but "common to Asia." The implication is that it is not a temple dedicated only by Ephesus; it is rather a temenos of the whole province. Ephesus was the caretaker (or "neokoros," according to l. 13) for the cult.

Secondly, the temple is described as one for the Sebastoi, rather than for an individual. Who was included in this group of Sebastoi? One possibility is that Domitian and his wife Domitia were signified by this term. She and the imperial household are mentioned as part of a local cult in the Tmolos inscription,[16] and she is depicted on at least one Ephesian coin that commemorated this provincial cult.[17] This would require an unusual, although not unprecedented, use of the term "Sebastoi." In other inscriptions of western Asia Minor, "Sebastoi" usually indicates emperors, even though a wife of a given emperor is regularly called Σεβαστή. It seems that the customary way of referring to the imperial couple was as they appear in the Tmolos inscription: Δωμιτιάνος Καίσαρ καὶ Δομιτία Σεβαστή ("Domitian Caesar and Domitia Sebaste"),[18] or as part of the imperial household.[19] There are a few examples which do seem to

---

[16] *IvE* 2.241.

[17] Josef Keil, "Die erste Kaiserneokorie von Ephesos," *Numismatische Zeitschrift* N.F. 12 (1919) 118 no. 12.

[18] When the living wife of an emperor is referred to using divine or cultic terminology without reference to the emperor, there seems to be a tendency to assimilate her to a goddess. For example, the base for a statue of Domitia was found in 1979 in Stratonikeia with the inscription, Δομετίαν νέαν ῞Ηραν τὴν γυναῖκα τοῦ Σεβαστοῦ ὁ δῆμος καθιέρωσεν "The demos erected (a statue of) Domitia, New Hera, wife of Sebastos" (*IvStr* 2,1.1008). Livia was honored as the new Hera in Pergamum (*AvP* 8,2.385; 14-29 CE) and as Sebaste Demeter Karpophoros in Ephesus (*IvE* 7,2.4337; the nephews of Tiberius are also mentioned as the new Dioskoroi).

[19] *IvE* 4.1393; *MAMA* 3.449 (Aphrodisias).

use "Sebastoi" for Augustus and Livia, and so it is not impossible that Domitia was included in the Cult of the Sebastoi in Ephesus.[20]

Since the temple continued to be called the "Temple of the Sebastoi" after the death of Domitian,[21] the original cult must have included more individuals than just Domitian and Domitia. What other emperors would have been included? If the emperors who suffered the *damnatio memoriae* or who were already objects of provincial cultic activity in Asia are eliminated from consideration, only Gaius,[22] Claudius, Vespasian, Titus, and Domitian remain. Gaius could not have been included in such a cult after his assassination and the termination of plans for his cult in Miletus. There is no evidence that there was ever a cult of Claudius in Ephesus, and it would have been highly unusual to start one for him some 35 years after his death.

We are left, then, with the Flavians. Domitian, as the reigning emperor, would necessarily have been included in the cult. Vespasian, whose name replaced the erased name of his son in the temple inscriptions, would also have been included as the founder of the new line of emperors, and cultic activity for Titus is also probable.[23] Thus, on the basis of the description of the cult in the temple inscriptions, it is clear that the provincial cult of the Sebastoi in Ephesus was a cult for the emperors of the Flavian family, and perhaps included Domitia.

The dedications to Domitian on the statue bases lasted only a few years. After the assassination of Domitian in 96 CE, his name was to be stricken from all public records throughout the empire by order of the Senate in Rome. In Ephesus, nearly all references to him were changed through the removal of the names "Domitian" and "Germanicus."[24] The two names were systematically removed

---

[20] Two inscriptions from Ankyra (*IGR* 4.555-56) and three from Aizanoi (*IGR* 4.582-84) testify to cults for the θεοὶ Σεβαστοὶ θέοι ὁμοβώμιοι ("the new gods Sebastoi who share an altar"). These gods Sebastoi were apparently Augustus and Livia.

[21] The name of the temple was not changed on any of the thirteen inscriptions from which Domitian's names were removed.

[22] Claudius prevented the Senate from voting the *damnatio* for Gaius. Dio Cassius 60.4.5

[23] Even if Suetonius's depiction of Domitian's hatred for Titus (*Tit.* 9; *Dom.* 2) is factual, it would not necessarily have been a factor in the decision to include or exclude his deceased older brother from the family cult in Asia.

[24] The erasure of "Germanicus" has puzzled some scholars since several emperors carried this title. Reinhold Merkelbach ("Ephesische Parerga 26:

from the statue bases in the Temple of the Sebastoi precincts as well. On all but one of the extant inscriptions,[25] the stonemasons inscribed θεῷι in place of "Domitian," and Οὐεσπασιανῷι in place of "Germanicus." In this way the statues were given a new dedication to the God Vespasian.

Cultic activity for Domitian would have been terminated in Ephesus as a result of the *damnatio memoriae*. The temple was not immediately renamed, however, for the phrase describing the cult (l. 9-10 in the Aphrodisias inscription) was not modified in any of the inscriptions,[26] indicating that "Temple of the Sebastoi" was still an appropriate name for the building. By the end of the second century CE, however, the emperor Titus seems to have become insignificant, for the cult was apparently referred to as that of Vespasian.[27]

An examination of the content of the Aphrodisias inscription shows that the cultic vocabulary is intertwined with the language of political discourse. Terms such as ἐλεύθερος καὶ αὐτόνομος ("free and autonomous"), δῆμος, πόλις, Ἀσία and (repeatedly) Σεβαστός indicate that the provincial cult raised issues of political relationships at several levels.

One prominent issue in the inscriptions is the relationship of the cities of Asia to the emperor. The fact that all of these statues were dedicated to the living emperor has already been mentioned. In comparison with the other cities, the Aphrodisians emphasized their

---

Warum Domitians Siegername 'Germanicus' eradiert worden ist," *ZPE* 34 [1979] 62-64) argued that Domitian used the title like a proper name because he was the first emperor to gain the title through a military victory rather than as an inherited family name. The title was not erased, however, from at least one inscription—a fragment of a statue base dedication (*IvE* 6.2047) found in the Ephesian theater.

25 The inscription donated by the Keretapaians (*IvE* 2.234) had Domitian's names erased but no reinscription took place. This was perhaps an accidental omission.

26 Unfortunately, an inscription from 104/5 CE which refers to the temple by name is missing about a dozen characters at the crucial point (*IvE* 1a.27 l. 458) and so provides no evidence for the name of the temple in the next decade.

27 *IvE* 3.710 b and c speak of the "temple of Vespasian." *IvE* 7,1.3038 refers to someone who inherited the office of neokoros of the temple of Vespasian. The absence of a reference in these inscriptions to the temple's provincial status is unusual, though. It is possible that these inscriptions might be related to a different, otherwise unknown, temple for a local cult of Vespasian.

alignment with imperial authority by describing their demos as φιλοκαῖσαρ ("devoted to Caesar").[28]

More germane, however, is the series of phrases that outlines a reciprocal relationship of the free cities to the emperor. The first statement on the subject is an assertion of the free status of the city (1. 7-8), but this is immediately defined as a status which has from the beginning depended upon the grace (χάρις) of the emperors. The freedom of the cities is due to the actions of the emperors.

The cities can act with their own grace as well. In this case the action entailed the erection of a monument dedicated to the current emperor in the temenos of the Sebastoi. This was done because of εὐσέβεια toward the Sebastoi (1. 11-12), the proper response of the cities to the emperors who have protected their ancient rights from the beginning.

The inauguration of the cult in Ephesus raised another issue that this inscription formula addressed: the relationships among the cities of Asia. The new cult and its related institutions changed the status of Ephesus among the cities of the province. Ephesus would henceforth be more prominent in provincial assemblies, it would have more claim to imperial favor, its wealthy citizens would have greater access to more distinguished offices, delegations from various cities would make annual trips to her festivals, and new sources of revenue would become available. How would the cities respond to this challenge to the status quo?

Here again, the inscriptions describe a complex relationship. The honor bestowed upon Ephesus is recognized by the reference to her as neokoros,[29] "caretaker" (of the Temple of the Sebastoi). The reference is long delayed, though, occurring only in line 13, after several positive statements about the donor city Aphrodisias.

---

[28] This is not a normal expression in inscriptions from Aphrodisias. Louis Robert ("Inscriptions d'Aphrodisias," *AntCl* 35 [1966] 410-11) understood the whole phrase, "The demos of the Aphrodisians, devoted to Caesar, being free and autonomous from the beginning by the grace of the Sebastoi," to be a special statement of fidelity to Caesar by the Aphrodisians for his role in procuring their free status. Since most of this phrase occurs in the inscription from Stratonikeia, and presumably in the (lost) inscriptions of the other free cities, it is possible to be more precise in describing the text. The role of the Sebastoi in establishing and maintaining the cities' freedom was part of the standard formula for these dedications for the Temple of the Sebastoi. The Aphrodisians added φιλοκαῖσαρ to emphasize Caesar's role in their acquisition of free status. The addition is unusual in a late first century CE inscription honoring a Flavian emperor.

[29] The development and significance of this term is discussed in chapter three.

Furthermore, the reference to Ephesus is couched in standard phrases from the language of benefaction. Εὐσέβεια ("reverence") and εὔνοια ("goodwill") are terms with a long history in the inscriptions of Asia. One or both of these two terms appear often with other terms[30] in praise of individuals, with certain phrases being favored in some regions[31] or by particular cults.[32] In all the varieties of specific usage, a distinction is generally maintained between these two words. Εὐσέβεια is an attitude or disposition which one ought to have toward deity[33] while εὔνοια is an honorable way to relate to a city, demos, homeland, or parents.[34]

The significance of the benefaction language in the inscription from Aphrodisias is not that concepts regarding individual benefactors have been attributed to whole cities. These concepts were already used in the Hellenistic period for relations between cities, primarily in inscriptions thanking another city for sending one or more judges to deliver decisions.[35] Rather, the importance of the benefaction language is found in the particular way in which it is used in the inscriptions of the free cities. In the longer inscriptions about the Temple of the Sebastoi, laudatory comportment is not ascribed to others; it is the donor cities who commend themselves for their own virtues. Instead of praising Ephesus, the cities honor themselves by portraying themselves as the benefactors of Ephesus,

---

30 For example: ἀρετή ("virtue"), *IvE* 4.1451, *IvMyl* 2.866 (Olymos); καλοκαγαθία ("noble character"), *IvPr* 108 l. 328; προθυμία ("eagerness"), *IvE* 5.1466.

31 In Iasos, the phrase ἀρετῆς ἕνεκεν καὶ εὐνοίας ἧς ἔχει [π]ερὶ τὸν δῆμον ("because of the virtue and goodwill which s/he has for the demos") and variants appeared often in Hellenistic honorary decrees; *IvI* 1.41; 51 l. 24; 59; 62. The combination was also used elsewhere (*IvE* 2.203; 5.1457; *OGIS* 472 [Didyma]).

32 Priestesses of Athena Polias and Athena Nikephoros in Pergamum were honored "because of reverence for the goddess and the goodwill of the parents toward the demos" (διά τε τὴν πρὸς τὴν θεὸν εὐσέβηαν καὶ τὴν τῶν γωνέων αὐτῆς πρὸς τόν δῆμον εὔνοιαν; *AvP* 8,2.489; 515) while in Smyrna other priestesses (of Demeter Karpophoros?) are praised for zealously providing all the things necessary "for reverence toward the goddess and for the feast of the initiates" (περὶ τὴν εὐσέβειαν τῆς θεοῦ καὶ τὴν τῶν μυστῶν ἑορτήν; *IvSm* 2,1.653; 654).

33 Along with the examples in the previous note, see *AvP* 8,3.23; *IvSm* 2,1.639; *IvPr* 117 l. 63. An inscription from Iasos (*IvI* 1.122 l. 15) is an interesting exception which actually confirms the generalization; a widow commemorates her εὐσέβεια for her deceased husband who is now within the divine realm.

34 See *IvI* 1.56 l. 10; 153 l. 9 (Samothrake); *IvE* 7,1. 3049; *IvPr* 109 l. 34.

35 For example, Iasos praises Priene (*IvI* 1.73; 74); Kalymna praises Iasos (*IvI* 1.82); Bargylia honors Samos (*IvI* 2.609); Magnesia on the Meander honors Priene (*IvPr* 61).

toward whom they display εὔνοια.[36] Thus, the longer inscriptions
tend to minimize the significance of the cult for Ephesus, while em-
phasizing the role of the other cities of the province.

The language of benefaction also confirms the tendency observed
earlier of focusing the cult on the Sebastoi rather than on the living
emperor,[37] for εὐσέβεια, a term used in relation to deity, is directed
in the inscriptions toward the Sebastoi rather than toward Domitian
alone. This accords with the name of the temple ("of the Sebastoi")
and with the reference to the Sebastoi as the protectors of the free
status of the cities. The inscriptions make clear that the public
rhetoric of this provincial imperial cult acclaimed the emperors, not
a single ruler, as the reason for its establishment.

The inscriptions of the cities without free status are much shorter,
containing none of the elements that deal with inter-city relationships except the reference to the temple. After the dedication to
Domitian and the naming of the proconsul, the shorter inscriptions
include the donor city, the reference to the provincial temple, local
officials from the donor city (usually), and officials related to the
temple (highpriest, neokoros). Although the pattern of these shorter
inscriptions relates them to the free city inscriptions, a distinction is
maintained throughout. The brevity of their texts and the specific
omissions placed the cities in a position of lesser status than the free
cities.[38]

These temple inscriptions are located at a turning point in the
rhetoric of status among the cities of the province of Asia. In the inscriptions of the second century, the prominence of free city status
decreased. The term "neokoros" that appeared only in the middle
of some of these temple inscriptions, became one of the most coveted

---

[36] The use of benefactor language for the cities may be an indication that the
cities contributed to the funding of the new temple and cult.

[37] Page 34.

[38] The pattern and content of the inscriptions related to the Temple of the
Sebastoi in Ephesus are unparalleled in the inscriptions from Asia. Where did the
formula originate? The establishment of a provincial cult could involve many
"players," most notably municipal leaders, the provincial koinon, the proconsul,
the Roman Senate, and the emperor. Given the preoccupation of the inscriptions
with intercity relationships, the concern for the status of the cities with respect to
the emperor, the absence of any statements about proconsular administrative
issues, and the reticent attitude toward Ephesus, the most likely source for the texts
of the inscriptions is the provincial council of Asia. The long and short versions of
the formula were probably crafted in the koinon by the representatives of the cities
of the province.

titles for elevating a city's public standing. This topic will be explored further in chapter three, after further examination of the inscriptions from the Temple of the Sebastoi.

The Date of the Cult of the Sebastoi

For nearly a century, arguments have been proposed for the various dates at which the province of Asia might have received permission to build the first provincial temple for the emperors in Ephesus. Since Keil's article in 1919 disproved the theory that Ephesus had a temple of Claudius,[39] three proposals have been suggested. In all three, the completion of the temple under Domitian is affirmed, but there is disagreement as to when the grant was made. Some have argued that Vespasian approved the request to build the temple,[40] while others have suggested that Titus may have been responsible for initiating the cult.[41] Keil's conclusion that Domitian founded the cult has found supporters as well.[42]

The main reason for the confusion on the dating of the temple was that L. Mestrius Florus, one of the proconsuls of Asia mentioned in the inscriptions, was previously thought to have served in 83/84 CE[43] while the other two proconsuls were dated late in the eighties

---

[39] Josef Keil, "Die erste Kaiserneokorie von Ephesos," *Numismatische Zeitschrift* N. F. 12 (1919) 115-20.

[40] See David Magie, *Roman Rule in Asia Minor* (Princeton: Princeton University, 1950) 1.572; 2.1434, for the outline of the argument. Barbara Burrell ("*Neokoroi*: Greek Cities of the Roman East" [Ph.D. diss., Harvard University, 1980] 255) tends to agree with him but concedes that Titus might have approved the request.

[41] In Georg Daltrop, Ulrich Hausmann, and Max Wegner, *Die Flavier: Vespasian, Titus, Domitian, Nerva, Julia Titi, Domitilla, Domitia* (Berlin: Mann, 1966) 26, 38, the authors argued that statue fragments from the temple were part of an image of Titus, not of Domitian as is commonly thought. They implied, without clearly stating the conclusion, that the temple should also be identified with a cult of Titus. The temple is labeled as the "Temple of Titus?" on a few maps of Ephesus; e.g., *ÖJh* 50 (1972-5) Beib. 391-92.

[42] E.g., S. R. F. Price, *Rituals and Power: The Roman Imperial Cult in Asia Minor* (Cambridge: Cambridge University, 1984) 178, 255.

[43] The 83/84 date apparently goes back to William H. Waddington (*Fastes des provinces asiatique de l'Empire romain* [Paris: Firmin-Didot Freres, 1872] 155-56, #102) who argued that Mestrius Florus must have been proconsul when Domitian acquired the name Germanicus in the year 83 CE, because some Smyrniote coins minted while Mestrius Florus was proconsul do not call Domitian "Germanicus" and others do. This interpretation appears in many standard references works, e.g., *PIR* 1,2 M 380; PW 15 (1932) 1293; *Kl.P.* 3 (1969) 1256.

of the first century CE. Werner Eck has shown, however, that
Florus was proconsul of Asia in 88/89.[44] With the incorrect dating
of Florus's proconsulship, these inscriptions seemed to have been
scattered about at various times during the ninth decade of the first
century CE. It is now clear, however, that the three succeeded each
other as proconsuls: L. Mestrius Florus (88/89), M. Fulvius Gillo
(89/90 CE), and L. Luscius Ocrea (90/91 CE). These inscriptions
form a group, having been inscribed between the years of 88 and 91,
and perhaps within as short a span of time as 89-90.

The reason for the commissioning of this group of inscriptions can
be deduced from the reference to the temple in the thirteen temple
inscriptions.[45] Specifically, we must consider why the temple is
mentioned in the dative case. An honorary inscription like this normally uses the dative for the person or deity to whom the monument
is dedicated, as is the case with Domitian in these inscriptions. We
are not dealing with a double dedication ("to Domitian and to
Asia's temple. . . .") for there is a standard method for multiple dedications in which the objects of the dedication are listed in the dative
and linked with καί at the beginning of the inscription.

An examination of other inscriptions from Asia shows that this
particular use of the dative with the verb ἀνίστημι is unusual. Other
epigraphic attestations of the verb from Ephesus provide no parallel
for this construction.[46]

The meaning of the construction can be discerned from the text
of the inscription, though. The immediate context suggests that we

---

[44] Werner Eck, *Die Senatoren von Vespasian bis Hadrian* (Vestigia 13; Munich:
Beck, 1970) 85-86, 236; idem, "Prokonsuln von Asia in der Flavisch-Traianischen
Zeit" *ZPE* 45 (1982) 151; and, idem, "Jahres- und Provinzialfasten der senatorischen Statthalter von 69/70 bis 138/139," *Chiron* 12 (1982) 315-18. One of the
factors in his argument was the way in which the offices overlapped in these temple
inscriptions. His conclusions are now accepted as standard dates in the scholarly
discussion (e.g., Brian Jones, *Domitian and the Senatorial Order: A Prosopographical
Study of Domitian's relationship with the Senate, A.D. 81-96* [Philadelphia: American
Philosophical Society, 1979]; *IvE* 2, p. 26, 38, 44).

[45] Lines 9-10 in the Aphrodisias inscription.

[46] The most common use of the verb is in a genitive absolute construction
which concludes an inscription. This type of formula begins with the statue (the
direct object) in the accusative case (usually τὴν τειμὴν [e.g., *IvE* 3.644] or τὸν
ἀνδριάντα [e.g., *IvE* 3.642]) followed by the genitive participle ἀναστήσαντος (e.g.,
IvE 3.634) or ἀναστησάσης (e.g., *IvE* 3.637). The person who erected the statue
is then named in the genitive at the end of the formula. Other cities used much the
same formula, though the word order could vary; see *IvI* 1.91; 118.

are dealing here with either a dative of location[47] or a dative of cause; the other Ephesian inscriptions help us at this point by narrowing the range of possibilities. Honorary inscriptions rarely mention the location of a dedication for the reader is normally standing in that location.[48] In an inscription using some form of ἀνίστημι, the location of a dedication (if mentioned at all) comes in a prepositional phrase. In fact, there is a mid-second century CE Ephesian inscription which mentions putting up statues in the provincial emperor temples in this way.

ἀνδριάντας ἀναστῆ[σαι]
ἐν τε τοῖς ἱεροῖς τῆς Ἀσίας τῶν αὐτοκρατόρ[ων]
ναοῖς ἐν τε τῇ φιλοσεβάστῳ Νύσῃ πατρίδι τ[οῦ Ἀλ-]
κιβιάδου στήλλην τε ἐν τῷ ἱερῷ τοῦ Ἀπόλλων[ος]
ἀναγράψαι τῶν ψηφισμάτων...[49]

> ...statues shall be set up in Asia's holy temples of the emperors, and a stele of (these) decrees shall be inscribed in the native city of Alkibiades, Nysia, devoted to Sebastos, in the temple of Apollo...

Thus, the reference to the temple in the inscription from Aphrodisias must be a dative of cause which could be translated, "(The Aphrodisian people set this up) because of Asia's temple..." or "on the occasion of Asia's temple..." The exact meaning of this might still be unclear, were it not for analogous groups of inscriptions related to the inauguration of the Olympieion at Athens and the third neokorate temple at Ephesus. In both cases, various cities participated in the commemoration of the opening of newly-built temples and this participation was recorded in inscriptions.[50] Therefore, the inscription from Aphrodisias and the other twelve inscriptions related to the Temple of the Sebastoi must have been

---

[47] This is how Joyce Reynolds translated the phrase in *Aphrodisias and Rome* (Journal of Roman Studies Monographs 1; London: Society for the Promotion of Roman Studies, 1982) 167-68, document 42.

[48] Decrees or edicts will often include instructions as to the specific location where the inscription is to be exhibited; e.g., *IvE* 1a.6 l. 35-37 (second century BCE); *IvPr* 105 l. 67 (9 BCE); *IvE* 1a.21 I l. 34-35 (138 CE).

[49] *IvE* 1a.22 l. 46-48.

[50] For the inscriptions related to the opening of the Olympieion in Athens under Hadrian, see Anna S. Benjamin, "The Altars of Hadrian in Athens and Hadrian's Panhellenic Program," *Hesperia* 32 (1968) 57-86. A similar phenomenon is attested by four inscriptions from Ephesus (*IvE* 6.2053-56) on statue bases set up by the city of Ephesus to honor cities who participated in the celebration of its third neokoria (211 CE).

commissioned for the inauguration of the provincial imperial temple in Ephesus.

This conclusion provides us with a date between 88 and 91 CE for the dedication of the precincts of the Temple of the Sebastoi.[51] The inscriptions, however, allow us to be even more precise. Each of the inscriptions originally mentioned the proconsul and the high-priest of Asia who were in office at the time the inscription was executed. Both of these offices lasted one year, but they did not begin at the same time. The proconsul of Asia took office sometime in mid-summer,[52] perhaps in July,[53] and it is generally agreed that a provincial highpriesthood began with Augustus's birthday, 23 September.[54] This overlap in terms of service of the two offices enables us to construct a chronology of the relative order in which the inscriptions were made, and the known dates of the proconsuls give the chronology a high degree of accuracy.[55]

The chart on p. 46-47 places the inscriptions in their relative chronological order. Four of the thirteen inscriptions are missing the name of either the proconsul or the highpriest because of damage to the stones. Since these four each contain the name of one of the officials, they are included in the chart in their approximate (although not necessarily precise) position.

---

[51] Four separate events must be distinguished here: the date of the approval for Ephesus to establish the cult; the beginning of construction of the precincts; the dedication of the precincts; and the completion of all building activities related to the precincts. The last two events could have been separated by a considerable span of time. The argument here is that construction had progressed at least to the point that cultic functions and related festivals were feasible by September of 90 CE at the latest.

[52] Richard J. A. Talbert, *The Senate of Imperial Rome* (Princeton: Princeton University Press, 1984) 497-98.

[53] Timothy D. Barnes, *Tertullian: A Historical and Literary Study* (Oxford: Clarendon Press, 1971) 260-61.

[54] Rossner, "Asiarchen," 103 n.11. From 9 BCE, the new year in Asia began on Augustus's birthday (*IvPr* 105) and this seems to be the origin of the highpriestly year. The attempts of Aristides to avoid election to the provincial highpriesthood in the autumn of 147 CE appear to confirm this. Aristides *Or* 50.100-104.

[55] With only a few of the temple inscriptions at his disposal, William Ramsay realized that such a chronological ordering could be constructed (*The Social Basis of Roman Power in Asia Minor* [Aberdeen: Aberdeen University Press, 1941] 211-14) but his intention was to discover the order of the proconsuls and highpriests. He was not able to reconstruct an accurate chronology because some of the proconsuls were still incorrectly dated at that time. The small number of the inscriptions available to him also prevented any analysis of the other features of the inscriptions that affect the dating of the Cult of the Sebastoi.

The first column of the chart contains the name of the respective
donor city. In this column the nine securely ordered inscriptions
(i.e., those with the names of both officials still legible) are listed with
uppercase letters. The four cities whose inscriptions are less securely
ordered are entered with lowercase letters. The second column gives
the name and date of the proconsul, and the name of the highpriest
is found in the third column. In several cases, the inscription does
not end with the highpriest, and the fourth column notes such
circumstances: fragmentary ending, erasure, or the name of the
neokoros of the temple. In the fifth column can be found the date
of the inscription and in the sixth is the inscription's number in *IvE*.

Once the inscriptions are placed in chronological order, one feature stands out as significant for dating the temple and the cult: the
two references to the neokoros of the temple are not optional elements that occur randomly. The neokoros is listed only in the last
two inscriptions. There are only two possible explanations for this
phenomenon: either the neokoros of this temple was a new office
created in 89/90 CE; or, the office existed earlier but was left out of
the other inscriptions. The latter possibility is highly unlikely because once the office is included, it appears at an especially significant point in the inscription, namely, at the end, next to the reference to the highpriest. The significance of the office is underscored
by the first known holder: Tiberius Claudius Aristio, the most influential citizen of Ephesus from the late first century CE through
the first quarter of the second century. Had such an important office
existed before 90, it surely would have been included in the earlier
inscriptions.[56]

The reason for the sudden appearance of the neokoros in these inscriptions is to be found in the responsibilities which the position entailed.[57] The office of neokoros is often overlooked in modern treat-
ments of Greek religion,[58] but it was an essential and widespread

---

[56] It should be noted that the four inscriptions before those which mention a neokoros end in erasures. It is possible that a neokoros could have been mentioned
and erased in these earlier inscriptions and so the office could have been attested
as early as September, 89 CE. In chapter five, however, I will argue that the
erasures had a completely different motive and did not mention a neokoros of the
temple. In fact, the erasures suggest the possibility of a more precise dating of the
temple's inauguration.

[57] The responsibilities of a neokoros are described in more detail in chapter
three, below.

[58] The term is not indexed in Martin Nilsson's *A History of Greek Religion*

CHRONOLOGICAL CHART OF THE INSCRIPTIONS
FROM THE TEMPLE OF THE SEBASTOI

The inscriptions are listed in the relative order of their execution. The order of the inscriptions whose cities' names appear in capital letters is exact. Inscriptions executed under the same proconsul and highpriest are given in alphabetical order by city. The order of the inscriptions whose cities are listed with lower case letters is approximate because the name of only one of the two officials is extant. A proconsul took office in mid-summer; provincial highpriesthoods began on September 23.

CITY	PROCONSUL	HIGHPRIEST OF ASIA	FINAL FEATURE if not highpriest	DATE OF INSCRIPTION	*IvE* NUMBER
Synaos	L. Mestrius Florus (88/89 CE)		(unknown)	summer 88-summer 89	6.2048
KERETAPA	L. Mestrius Florus	Ti. Cl. Aristio		23 Sept 88-summer 89	2.234
Teos		Ti. Cl. Aristio		23 Sept 88-22 Sept 89	2.239
KLAZOMENAI	M. Fulvius Gillo (89/90)	Ti. Cl. Aristio		summer 89-22 Sept 89	2.235
MAKEDONES HYRKANIOI	M. Fulvius Gillo	Ti. Cl. Aristio		summer 89-22 Sept 89	5.1498

(unknown)	M. F[ulvius Gillo]		(unknown)	summer 89-summer 90	2.242
Kyme	[M. Fu]lvius Gill[o]	[Tib]erius [Cl. Aristio]; or, [Cl. Pheseinos]		summer 89-summer 90	2.240
AIZANOI	M. Fulvius Gillo	Ti. Cl. Pheseinos	4 line erasure	23 Sept 89-summer 90	2.232
AIZANOI	M. Fulvius Gillo	Ti. Cl. Pheseinos	3 1/2 line erasure	23 Sept 89-summer 90	2.232a
APHRODISIAS	Marc[us] Fulvius Gillo	Ti. Claud[ius] Pheseinos	3 1/2 line erasure	23 Sept 89-summer 90	2.233
SILANDOS	M. Fulvius Gillo	Ti. Claud[ius] Pheseinos	3 1/2 line erasure	23 Sept 89-summer 90	2.238
STRATONIKEIA	L. Luscius Ocrea (90/91 CE)	Ti. Cl. Pheseinos	Neokoros of temple: Ti. Cl. Aristio	summer 90-22 Sept 90	2.237
TMOLOS	L. Luscius Ocrea	Ti. Julius Dama Claudianus	Neokoros of temple: Ti. Cl. Aristio	23 Sept 90-summer 91	2.241

institution in antiquity. As will be shown in chapter three, the actual responsibilities of the neokoros could vary quite a bit from one cultic setting to another. In general, he or she assisted the priestly officials in the overall administration of a temple cult. This might involve caring for the facilities of a small shrine (Sikyon),[59] assisting the priests and guarding the precincts (Delos),[60] or witnessing legal transactions (Delphi).[61] The Artemision of Ephesus was a significant banking center and the neokoros received money deposited there.[62]

While we lack direct testimony about the nature of the office of neokoros for the Temple of the Sebastoi in Ephesus, we can conclude that this official dealt with administrative matters related to the finances or facilities of the Cult of the Sebastoi. It is also possible that in this case the neokoros did not actually execute these responsibilities but rather financed such services for a certain period of time.

The reason a neokoros was needed for the Temple of the Sebastoi by 90 CE is because that is the date when the temple and cult became fully functional. Before the temple was completed, the office was unnecessary. Once the temple began to operate, the office was crucial.

The temporal distribution of the extant temple inscriptions supports the conclusion that the temple was inaugurated in 89/90 CE. Only two of the thirteen inscriptions were late (i.e., executed after the naming of a neokoros). The majority of the inscriptions (8 or 9, 61% or 69%) were made under proconsul Gillo during the last year before the temple was opened. Two or three of the thirteen cities appear to have made their dedications early under proconsul Florus.[63]

(2d ed.; Oxford: Clarendon, 1949), nor in Walter Burkert's *Greek Religion* (Cambridge, Mass.: Harvard University, 1985).

[59] Pausanias 2.10.4.

[60] Philippe Bruneau, *Recherches sur les cultes de Délos a l'époque hellénistique et a l'époque impériale* (Paris: E. de Boccard, 1970) 502.

[61] G. Colin (ed.), *Épigraphie*, vol. 3,2 of *Fouilles de Delphes* (Paris: Fontemoing, 1909) 128 l.15; 215 l.15, etc.

[62] Xenophon *Anab.* 5.3.4-6.

[63] The excessive punctuality of the Keretapeians perhaps explains the short, unpublished inscription on the back side of the same block used for their official inscription. The back of the block is roughly dressed, but across its width stretches an inscription in which the top of the letters are approx. 18 cm. from the top of the block. The letters are approx. 5 cm. in height. The inscription reads: ΚΕΡΕ-ΤΑΠΕΩΝ, "of the Keretapeians." This inscription appears to have reserved the marble block between the time when the representative of Keretapa (perhaps the Glykon mentioned in l. 11-12) selected it and the time when the work was actually executed.

Since the provincial Temple of the Sebastoi in Ephesus began to function by 90 CE (nine years after Domitian became emperor), there is no longer any reason to suppose that the privilege of instituting the cult was granted before the reign of Domitian. Nine years was more than enough time to send embassies to Rome, secure approval, and build the temple complex near the southwest corner of Ephesian upper agora.[64] In fact, it would be unusual for a project of this size to last as long as nine years.

Summary

This examination of the temple inscriptions has produced several conclusions about the cult. First, the inscriptions allow us to date the cult precisely since they indicate that the temple was dedicated in 89/90 CE. This in turn leads to the conclusion that the right to establish the provincial cult in Ephesus was granted by Domitian, in the early to mid-eighties of the first century CE.

Second, the inscriptions provide insight into the nature of the cult. While the dedications indicate that Domitian was the predominant figure in the cult, he was not the only recipient of worship at the temple. The inscriptions show that the temple was dedicated to the Sebastoi, of whom Domitian was one. The repeated use of the plural ''Sebastoi'' indicates that undue emphasis ought not to be placed on one or the other of these rulers.

As to the identities of the Sebastoi, it appears that cultic honors were offered to the three Flavian emperors (Vespasian, Titus and Domitian), and perhaps to Domitia. This original dedication to an imperial group allowed the cult to survive the ignominious demise of Domitian. After Domitian's downfall, the cult shifted its focus to Vespasian and flourished for at least another century.

Finally, the inscriptions reveal that the provincial cult of the Sebastoi in Ephesus occasioned concerns about the relationships among the cities of Asia. The free cities and the others used the opportunity of the temple dedication to make a statement about their role in the cult, their reverence for the emperor, and their relationship to Ephesus.

---

[64] The coin from Smyrna which depicts Livia and the Senate on the obverse and Tiberius in the provincial temple on the reverse (see Pl. III; *BM Ionia* 268 #266-68, pl. 28 #8; discussed above in chapter one) probably indicates that the temple was completed by the time the coin was minted. The coin records that it was minted while Petronius was proconsul. Since he served in that office from 29-35 CE, we can conclude that the temple was finished within a maximum of nine years after Smyrna received the right to build it in 26 CE.

CHAPTER THREE

DEVELOPMENTS IN CULTIC TRADITIONS

The provincial Cult of the Sebastoi in Ephesus provides us with an example of a Graeco-Roman cult whose inauguration in a given location can be dated precisely. This chapter examines the ways in which religious traditions were appropriated in the creation of this new cult. The use of the traditions in the media of inscriptions, architecture, and sculpture illuminates the religious significance of the cult for the city of Ephesus and for the province of Asia.

Ephesus, Neokoros of the Emperors

The term "neokoros" has become a standard part of the modern interpretation of provincial cults for the emperors. It is sometimes used adjectivally, as in "neokorate temple," to specify provincial cults. Very few interpreters have noted, however, that the term neokoros was not used as a city title related to imperial cults until the establishment of the Sebastoi cult in Ephesus.[1] Why was this particular title chosen? What religious significance did it have?

The word neokoros was the title for certain officials associated with many different cults. The official, as suggested by the presence of the word νεώς in the title, was always associated with temple cults. In contrast to offices like the νεωποίοι,[2] there was rarely more than one neokoros at a temple. Also, there was a tendency for goddesses to have a female neokoros, while male deities usually had a male neokoros.[3]

---

[1] Burrell ("*Neokoroi*: Greek Cities of the Roman East" [Ph.D. diss., Harvard University, 1980] 204, 253-54) noted that the term does not appear in relationship to cities until the late first century CE, but she still used the term to refer to earlier provincial cults. S. R. F. Price (*Rituals and Power* [Cambridge: Cambridge University Press, 1984] 64-65, esp. n. 47) clearly recognized that the cult in Ephesus was a turning point in the use of the term, but did not analyze the significance of the imagery. He continued to use "neokorate" as a label for provincial cults prior to the one founded in Ephesus.

[2] See above, chapter one.

[3] E.g., Pausanias recorded that a small temple of Aphrodite at Sikyon near Corinth could be entered only by the celibate female neokoros and the annually

The responsibilities of a neokoros were seen as complementary to those of priests and priestesses. In Plato's recounting, Sokrates required two types of officials to care for the temple cults in his ideal state: priests or priestesses, and neokoroi.[4] This connection of priestly officials and neokoroi can be seen in the epigraphic evidence as well. For example, an inscription on a marble stele from Skepsis lists the various exemptions (tax, military, etc.) for the priest of Dionysos Bambyleios, and then notes that they apply also to the neokoros.[5]

It is not surprising, therefore, that the neokoros often seems to be an official who assists in the performance of priestly duties. An inscription from Pergamum describing how the proceeds of sacrifices to Athena Nikephoros are to be distributed includes the neokoros among the other cultic officials: the annually elected ἱερονόμοι received the skins of the sheep and lambs, while the neokoros, the flute player, and the ὀλολύκτρια (crier) were all entitled to a small amount of money (two obols or a half obol, depending on the kind of sacrifice).[6] In Delphi, the neokoros was often included with the priests and others as a witness in manumission decrees.[7] Philo also used the term in a way which implies both cultic involvement and a distinction from priestly office when he described the tribe of Levites as being comprised of priests and neokoroi,[8] and when he called the Levitical cities of refuge "cities of neokoroi" (πόλεις νεωκόρων).[9]

On some occasions, the neokoros functioned as a guard for a precinct or for the possessions of the deity. A fourth century BCE inscription from Arkesine on Amorgos indicates that the neokoros of the local Heraion was ordered to ensure that no strangers (ξένοι)

---

elected *parthenos*; Pausanias 2.10.4. Ephesian Artemis, however, had a male neokoros, and Pausanias also mentioned (12.5) that a sibyl named Herophile served as the neokoros of Apollo Smintheus in Alexandria in the Troad.

[4] Plato, *Laws* 6.759. Sokrates mentioned later that exegetes and treasurers should also be appointed, but these are clearly of secondary importance.

[5] Z. Taşliklioglu and P. Frisch, "New Inscriptions from the Troad," *ZPE* 17 (1975) 106-9. The inscription probably comes from the second century BCE. It is now in the museum of Çanakkale.

[6] *AvP* 8,2.255.

[7] G. Colin (ed.), *Épigraphie*, vol. 3,2 of *Fouilles de Delphes* (Paris: Fontemoing, 1909) e.g., 128; 215; 223.

[8] *De fuga* 93.

[9] *De fuga* 94.

were brought into the sacred area.[10] In a very different situation, Xenophon entrusted a large amount of booty to the neokoros of Artemis at Ephesus. The treasure was to be used for a votive offering to the Ephesian Artemis, but Xenophon had to leave on another military campaign before he could arrange for the offering.[11] The status of the neokoros of Ephesian Artemis was considerably higher than that of a mere watchman, for he later traveled to Olympia to attend the games. There, the neokoros met Xenophon and returned the deposit.[12]

The island of Delos presents an interesting case: there are at least four different neokoros offices attested in a given locale during the third and early second centuries BCE. The different cults paid different salaries and seem to have required different services. The neokoros of the Asklepieion had his own building where he probably stayed and perhaps kept watch over votive offerings for the god. The neokoros of Sarapis also seems to have resided at a sanctuary and may have assisted the priests in their duties. Three neokoroi—of the Asklepieion, of the Archegesion, and of the island—are known to have held their offices for more than one year in the mid-third century BCE.[13]

There are also examples, primarily in the Roman period, where the neokoros becomes an office which is more or less a *leitourgia*, a responsibility taken on for the civic good. In the third century CE, for example, three decrees commended Aurelius Hermodoros (neokoros of the goddess Archegetis of Chalkis) for rebuilding the precinct walls, putting up stoas, building a triclinium, and providing trees and plants for the sacred area. In return, he was made neokoros for life, and the office became hereditary.[14]

To sum up, then, the responsibilities of a neokoros were not necessarily the same in every locale nor at every time. In general, the neokoros was charged with the care of sacred facilities, equip-

---

[10] *SIG* 3.981.

[11] Xenophon, *Anab.* 5.3.4-6.

[12] *Anab.* 5.3.7-13. The money was used to buy a plot of wooded land near Olympia. Xenophon built an altar and a small temple modeled on the Artemision in Ephesus, and had a statue of the Ephesian Artemis placed in the temple. He also endowed annual festivals for the goddess there.

[13] Philippe Bruneau, *Recherches sur les cultes de Délos a l'époque hellénistique et l'époque impériale* (Paris: E. de Boccard, 1970) 500-504.

[14] *SIG* 2.898, discovered in Chalkis.

ment, or funds. He or she might also assist priestly officials in their sacrificial duties. The needs of a small cultic institution were usually different from those of larger ones, and it seems that the nature of a particular cult also affected the duties of its neokoros. The office sometimes lasted a year; other times it was granted for life.

At some point, certain cities began to call themselves neokoros in relation to a deity. This shift from individual office to municipal self-designation is difficult to trace because there are so few references to it. In fact, there are no literary, epigraphic, or numismatic references to a city as neokoros before the first century CE, although the concept may have been in popular use for some time before this without becoming an official designation. This unofficial use accounts for the three known examples from Asia during the first century or early second century CE where a city uses the title for itself.[15] Two of the references are related to Ephesus.

An Ephesian coin from the reign of Nero portrays the emperor on the obverse.[16] The reverse names the proconsul of Asia Marcilius Acilius Aviola, whose service in 65/66 CE provides the date for the coin. The reverse also depicts a temple with four columns in front and six on the side, and bears the words Ἐφ(εσίων) νεωκόρων ("of the neokorate Ephesians"). Pick interpreted the coin to be a reference to an otherwise unattested provincial cult of Claudius at Ephesus,[17] but Keil pointed out the problems with Pick's reasoning and argued that the coin referred to Ephesus as the neokoros of Artemis.[18] Keil's conclusion is the most reasonable solution, although the temple on the coin is not a faithful representation of the Artemision.

---

15 One inscription from Beroia in Macedonia (*SEG* 17 [1960] 315) honors a certain Q. Popillius Pytho who requested from Nerva the right of his native city Beroia to retain sole use of the titles "neokoros" and "metropolis." This sole right pertained to the province of Macedonia, since Ephesus was already neokoros. The inscription might have been erected after the death of Nerva, but the request of Pytho would certainly have been made in the years 96-98 CE. The date of Macedonia's first provincial cult is not known since this is the first attestation of the cult. It may be that Beroia, like Ephesus, became neokoros of the Sebastoi under Domitian, or they may have had a provincial cult because of which the city later became known as neokoros.

16 Mionnet 3.93 #253; B. Pick, "Die Neokorien von Ephesos," in *Corolla Numismatic. Essays in Honour of Barclay V. Head* (London: Oxford University Press, 1906) 234-44.

17 Pick 1906, 235-36.

18 Josef Keil, "Die erste Kaiserveokorie von Ephesos," *Numismatische Zeitschrift* N. F. 12 (1919) 115-20.

The other neokoros reference related to Ephesus gives Keil's argument weight. At some time later than the Neronian coin, the author of the book of Acts recorded the fact that the city of the Ephesians was known throughout the world as the neokoros of Artemis.[19] This element in the narrative—the appellation for the city—seems to reflect accurately the situation in the last half of the first century CE, for the speaker's argument rested on the assumption that the idea was common knowledge.

One epigraphic reference is earlier than either of the two Ephesian examples, however. In the year 38 CE, the boule and the demos of the Kyzikenes published a decree honoring Antonia Tryphaina for her benefactions toward the city and her piety toward Augustus and the imperial house.[20] The inscription, although interesting for several reasons, is important to this study because it provides the first known attestation of a city called "neokoros." Furthermore, the city calls itself neokoros of the family of emperor Gaius: ἀρχαίαν καὶ προγονικὴν τοῦ γένους αὐτοῦ νεωκόρον ἐπανακτωμένη πόλιν.[21]

The use of the term neokoros in the Kyzikos inscription was not yet an official city title. The term is not attested in any other contemporary inscriptions or coins, and even in this inscription it occurs but once in the midsection of the text. Rather, the Kyzikenes took the popular notion of a city as neokoros and applied it to their multifaceted relationship to the imperial family line of Gaius.

Tryphaina, who had assisted Kyzikos in many ways, had manifold connections to Gaius. She and Gaius were descendants of Mark Antony by different wives (she through Antonia, he through Octavia). As the wife of Cotys II, king of Thrace (12-19 CE),

---

[19] Acts 19:35. This reference could well be later than the Cult of the Sebastoi in Ephesus. According to Werner Kümmel (*Introduction to the New Testament* [rev. ed.; Nashville: Abingdon, 1975] 186), "The most likely assumption . . . is a date for Acts between 80 and 90, but a date between 90 and 100 is not excluded." Helmut Koester (*Introduction to the New Testament* [Philadelphia: Fortress, 1982] 2:310) prefers a date around 135 CE.

[20] *SIG* 2.799 = *IGR* 4.146. Note the improvements of the text by F. W. Hasluck in *ABSA* 12 (1905-06) 183. See also *AthMitt* 7 (1891) 141-44; and Andre Joubin, "Inscription de Cyzique," *REG* 6 (1893) 8-22. The stone, found in 1889, measures 0.90 m. high, 1.25 m. wide, and 0.20 m. deep.

[21] ". . .(she) restoring the ancient and ancestral city, (which is) neokoros of his [i.e., Gaius's] family . . ." (l. 9-10). The emperor is referred to as μέγιστος καὶ [ἐ]πιφανέσ(τα)τος θεός [[Γαῖος]] Καῖσαρ, "(the) great and most eminent god [[Gaius]] Caesar" (l. 8-9).

Tryphaina bore three sons. These three boys were taken to Rome after their father was assassinated in 19 CE. There they became close friends of their cousin Gaius. Not long after Gaius became emperor, he appointed the three sons of Tryphaina to be kings of Thrace, Pontus, and Armenia Minor. Thus, there were biological and emotional, as well as political, ties between Tryphaina and Gaius.

Kyzikos could claim yet another way in which it was related to Gaius. The city lost its free status in 20 BCE but regained it from Augustus in 15 BCE through the assistance of Marcus Vipsanius Agrippa.[22] Agrippa, Gaius's maternal grandfather, is likened in lines 6-7 of the inscription to the city's legendary founder king Kyzikos.

In this inscription, then, the city used the neokoros terminology to emphasize the many aspects of their affiliation with the branch of the imperial family that gained ascendancy when Gaius came to power. This shift in dynastic power was especially significant to Kyzikos, for the city had lost its free status once again in 25 CE under the previous emperor Tiberius.

The Kyzikos inscription, the Ephesian coin, and the situation reflected in Acts 19 are the only extant examples of a city calling itself neokoros prior to the establishment of the Cult of the Sebastoi in Ephesus. The ambiguity of the coin makes it of little value for understanding the significance of the neokoros imagery. In the case of Kyzikos, however, the term describes a relationship of interdependence and fidelity: the city was refounded, and later renovated, by Gaius's line and had remained faithful to that family over the years. While Augustus's role is not slighted,[23] the more intimate relations with the Agrippan and Antonian lines are emphasized.

Acts 19 emphasizes a different aspect of the neokoros relationship between a city and a deity. While the Kyzikos inscription reflects the benefits for the faithful city, the Ephesian situation suggests the responsibilities of the city. According to the usage of the author of Acts, the concept of the city as neokoros implies that the Ephesians

---

[22] Dio Cassius 54.7.6; 54.23.7.

[23] See l. 3-4 (Tryphaina's performance of acts of εὐσέβεια toward Augustus), l. 6 (the votive is for Augustus), and l. 8 (the peace of Augustus).

were responsible for guarding the goddess's honor when it was endangered by the work of the Christian apostle Paul.[24]

These different portraits of the role of the neokoros city grow out of the situations of the respective cities. Kyzikos had been beset by a series of problems in relationship to Roman authority. Ephesus, on the other hand, was prospering under the aegis of its civic deity. Both aspects of the role of the neokoros, however, were consistent with the source of the neokoros imagery—the temple official who assisted in the sacrificial duties and who kept watch over that which belonged to the deity.

This concept was taken up in the Ephesian Cult of the Sebastoi and elevated to the status of an official title for the city. In Ephesus, however, the adoption of this title for the Cult of the Sebastoi had special import. Ephesian Artemis was the preeminent deity of her neokoros Ephesus. The use of this term for the Cult of the Sebastoi immediately raised the cult's status to that of the most significant cult in the city and the region.[25]

The Ephesians went one step further to confirm the high esteem they sought for the Cult of the Sebastoi. On at least two coins of the Domitianic period, the Ephesians called themselves "twice neokoros," i.e., of Artemis and of the Sebastoi.[26] One coin has the head of Domitian, crowned with a laurel wreath, on the obverse and his titles Δομιτιανὸς Καῖσαρ Σεβασ(τὸς) Γερμανικὸς Αὐτοκράτ(ωρ). The reverse of this coin shows a temple front with two columns on either side of the statue of Ephesian Artemis, around which is the phrase Ἐφεσίων Β Νεοκόρων. The second coin depicts a bust of Domitia with the legend Δομιτία Σεβαστή on the obverse; on the reverse is an eight-columned temple front with Ephesian Artemis in the middle and the phrase Ἐφεσίων Δ[ὶς Νε]οκόρων.[27] These two coins present a vivid visual image of the city's new religious

---

[24] Acts 19:27, 37. Verse 34 might imply that Jews in general, not just those who claimed allegiance to Jesus, were viewed as denigrating the dignity of the goddess. For a review of source-critical theories on the reference to Alexander, and on the relation of this story to the tradition of Jewish requests for toleration, see Robert F. Stoops, Jr., "Riot and Assembly: The Social context of Acts 19:23-41," *JBL* 108 (1989) 73-91.

[25] Robert Fleischer, *Artemis von Ephesos und verwandte Kultstatuen aus Anatolien und Syrien* (EPRO 35; Leiden: Brill, 1973) 391-93.

[26] Pick 1906, 236; Keil 1919, 118.

[27] Pick 1906, 236; Keil 1919, 118; and *CollWadd* 1628. Pick noted that the Δ of *Dis* was difficult to read.

situation. The city now had two dominant cults of equivalent significance: that of Ephesian Artemis, and that of the Emperors.[28]

Ephesus apparently had more freedom to create city titles on its coinage than in its inscriptions. The "twice neokoros" slogan is not known in the epigraphic record of this period. Rather, the inscriptions used "neokoros" without any numbers until the city received its second provincial cult under Hadrian (ca. 130 CE). After the two exceptional "twice neokoros" coins, the numismatic evidence matches what appears to have been the epigraphic practice of Ephesus.

The neokoros concept was corporate rather than individual, for the term normally occurs in reference to the demos or polis as the party involved in the Cult of the Sebastoi.[29] The adjective "neokoros" appears in the plural modifying "Ephesians" on the "twice neokoros" coins mentioned above, but "neokoros" never modified βουλή.[30] Thus, the entire city, and not just its representative council, was included in the imagery of the Cult of the Sebastoi.

While commentators have occasionally noted that the use of neokoros as an official, municipal self-designation began in Ephesus with the cult of the Sebastoi, it has not been recognized before that this constituted the starting point for the proliferation of city titles in Asia in the second century CE. Before the granting of the Cult to Ephesus, inscriptions of the cities simply referred to the boule and the demos. With the advent of the neokoros title, however, a process began that changed the epigraphic and numismatic record of the eastern Roman Empire.

For example, in 89/90 CE when the cult of the Sebastoi was inaugurated at Ephesus, Smyrna had already possessed a provincial cult for over 60 years and Pergamum for nearly 120 years. Neither city had previously called itself neokoros of an emperor, though. City titles begin to show up in a few of the inscriptions from Smyrna after the late first century CE, but that city's reaction to Ephesus's

---

[28] This coin might suggest that Domitia was one of the recipients of worship in the Cult of the Sebastoi (see above, chapter two). It is not unusual, however, for the wives of emperors to appear on the obverse of coins from western Asia Minor. Domitia appears on the obverse of a coin from Smyrna (*BM Ionia* 274 #309), as does Julia Titi (*BM Ionia* 275 #311-14).

[29] E.g., *IvE* 1a.27 l. 132; 2.236; 2.264.

[30] See *IvE* 1a.27, l. 4; and 2.266.

new status is difficult to trace because of the small number of Smyrniote inscriptions known from this period.[31]

The evidence for Pergamum, however, clearly documents the importance of such titles for the inhabitants of Asia's cities.[32] In the early years of Trajan's reign, the city of Pergamum stopped using the simple title ἡ βουλὴ καὶ ὁ δῆμος in its inscriptions and replaced it with ἡ βουλὴ καὶ ὁ δῆμος τῶν νεωκόρων Περγαμηνῶν "the boule and the demos of the neokorate Pergamenes."[33] In a matter of a few years, the Pergamenes amended their official title to show that they were the first city of Asia to receive a provincial cult and so the inscriptions from about 102-114 CE read ἡ βουλὴ καὶ ὁ δῆμος τῶν πρώτων νεωκόρων Περγαμηνῶν.[34] In 114 CE, the city received a second provincial cult from Trajan and initiated the title ἡ βουλὴ καὶ ὁ δῆμος τῶν πρώτων καὶ δὶς νεωκόρων Περγαμηνῶν.[35] In 120 CE the title appears with the addition of the term μητρόπολις.[36]

Thus, the innovation at Ephesus that took a religious concept with local significance and turned it into an official city title related to the Cult of the Sebastoi spread quickly throughout the province, and then beyond. By the mid-third century CE, the title was in use from Beroia in Macedonia to Neapolis (modern Nablus) in Samaria. An inscription from Sardis of the fifth century CE preserves the last known occurrence of the title.[37]

Such an expansion of the use of city titles in the eastern Mediterranean could hardly have been envisioned when Ephesus became the neokoros of the Sebastoi in the late first century CE. This innovation, however, developed into the primary means by which the

---

[31] Smyrna received its second provincial cult around the year 123 CE from Hadrian. The beginning of a list of contributors for a harbor project (*IvSm* 2,1.696) appears to refer to the city as having only one provincial cult ἡ νεοκόρος Σμυρναίων πόλις), but it cannot be dated with precision. Other inscriptions use the same wording but are known to have come from the time when Smyrna had two provincial cults (e.g., *IGR* 4.1388). *IvSm* 2,1.594 (124 CE) might be an inscription about the organization of the second provincial cult. An early third century CE inscription (*IvSm* 2,1.640) mentions three provincial cults in Smyrna.

[32] The development of Pergamum's official titles is outlined and documented in *AvP* 8,3 p. 158-61. See also Burrell 1980, 248.

[33] See *AvP* 8,2.461. See also *AthMitt* 32 (1907) 330, #62; 331, #63; 35 (1910) 472, #58; 473, #59.

[34] E.g., *AvP* 8,1.438; 431.

[35] *AvP* 8,1.395; 397; 520.

[36] *AvP* 8,3.20; 23; 37; 38.

[37] Burrell 1980, 382, 405 #11.

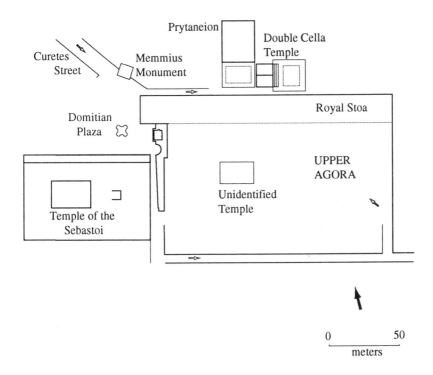

Fig. 2. Plan of Upper Agora and Temple of the Sebastoi.
(after Bammer, ÖJh 50 [1972-75] B. 391-92).

larger cities asserted their status in relation to one another. The use of city titles constituted a fundamental development in the political and religious propaganda of the Empire.

Architecture, Sculpture, and the Emperors

In 1930, Josef Keil conducted an excavation on top of an artificial terrace built in the Roman imperial period near the southwest corner of the Ephesian upper agora (Fig. 2). Prior to that time, the function of the terrace had been unclear. Earlier discoveries of several large marble friezes in different sections of Ephesus had revealed the existence of a large "Parthian Monument" that was yet to be found, and there was an expectation that the remains of this monument would be uncovered atop the terrace. As the excavation progressed, it became clear that the terrace supported the foundations of a temple. The identification of the temple was unknown until the

Plate VI. Statue fragment: Head of Titus. Archaeological Museum,
Izmir. Courtesy of Helmut Koester.

excavators uncovered the head and left forearm of a colossal,
akrolithic male statue in the 3.9 meter wide barrel-vaulted cryptoporticus under the terrace (Pl. VI-VII).[38]

The statue fragments found in the cryptoporticus were immediately identified by Keil as a likeness of Domitian, which in turn

---

[38] Josef Keil, "XVI. Vorläufiger Bericht über die Ausgrabungen in Ephesos,"
ÖJh 27 (1931) Beib. 53-61.

Plate VII. Statue fragment: Arm of Titus. Archaeological Museum, Izmir. Courtesy of Helmut Koester.

was used as an argument for the identification of the temple on the terrace.[39] Later excavations below the northeast corner of the precincts confirmed Keil's hypothesis about the identification of the temple by dating the building of the terrace to the late first cen-

---

[39] Keil 1931, 59-60.

tury.[40] Keil's team had found the site of the provincial temple built
in Ephesus during Domitian's reign.

The identification of the statue as an image of Domitian, however, has been questioned by Georg Daltrop and Max Wegner, who
argued convincingly that the features of the face are those one finds
on portraits of Domitian's older brother Titus (emperor, 79-81
CE).[41] They implied that the identification of the temple with a cult
of Domitian was tenuous as well,[42] but the discussion about the
identification of the temple and the statue has been hampered by the
lack of clarity regarding the nature of the provincial cult established
in Ephesus. The arguments in the previous chapter of this study
showed that the cult was dedicated to several emperors. Therefore,
the existence of a statue of Titus can now be understood properly as
one of at least three statues related to the Cult of the Sebastoi, not
as an argument that the cult began in the time of Titus.[43] Similar
statues of Vespasian and Domitian, and perhaps of Domitia, would
also have been present in the temple.[44]

The features of the head of Titus are a little unusual and do not
reflect the standard portrait of Titus in the city of Rome. Rather,
Wegner noted that the head was an especially interesting example
of Asian workmanship that he called "das 'asianische' Barock."[45]
The left forearm, now standing upright next to the head of Titus in

---

[40] These excavations, dealing with the situation in the area before the construction of the terrace, are discussed below, p. 69-70.

[41] Georg Daltrop, Ulrich Hausmann, and Max Wegner, *Die Flavier: Vespasian,
Titus, Domitian, Nerva, Julia Titi, Domitilla, Domitia* (Berlin: Mann, 1966) 26, 38, 86,
and pl. 15b. The more general study by Jale Inan and Elisabeth Rosenbaum
(*Roman and Early Byzantine Portrait Sculpture in Asia Minor* [London: Oxford University Press, 1966] 67, and pl. 16 #1) accepts the identification as Domitian.

[42] Georg Daltrop et al. 1966, 38, 100.

[43] Wegner suggested that the unusual size of the statue and the provincial workmanship might account for certain irregularities, and that the sculpture might have
been executed posthumously. Daltrop et al. 1966, 86.

[44] Bammer's suggestion ("Römische und byzantinische Architektur", *ÖJh* 50
[1972-75] Beib. 386-89) that this statue stood outside above the terrace's monumental north entrance cannot be correct. The back of the statue's head is hollowed
out to decrease its weight. This was done because the statue was designed to be
placed near a wall where the back would not be seen. Also, an akrolithic statue cannot be left outside in the elements because its wooden torso would deteriorate
rapidly.

[45] Daltrop et al. 1966, 26. The head (inv. #670) measures 0.740 m., chin to
crown, and is made of course-grained white marble. Inan and Rosenbaum 1966,
67.

the Archaeological Museum in Izmir, Turkey, is as tall as an adult. The left hand has a groove in which a spear was held, which agrees with Ephesian coins depicting this temple with a statue in a standing position and holding a spear.[46]

Colossal statues in Asia were normally smaller than the Titus statue.[47] A pair of over lifesize statues was found in 1966 in the eastern end of the Royal Stoa of the Ephesian upper agora[48] that were not a part of the Cult of the Sebastoi. The pair of seated statues from the Royal Stoa are about one and one third lifesize and have been identified as statues of Augustus and Livia. They probably were placed in the set of rooms known as the "Chalcidicum" at the east end of the Royal Stoa, probably no later than the death of Livia (26 CE).[49] It is unknown whether cultic activities took place in the Chalcidicum. The statues of Augustus and Livia nevertheless provide comparative material on the size of the temple statutes in the Cult of the Sebastoi.

There were also a few other statues of deities and of rulers in Asia of approximately the same magnitude as the statue of Titus. Apollo, Artemis, and Leto were portrayed at Claros by statues approx. eight m. tall.[50] At Sardis, pieces from the head of a colossal Zeus have been found as well as the lower part of the head of Antoninius Pius, who seems to have moved into the temple occupied by Zeus.[51] Both colossals from Sardis were of approximately the same proportions as the statue of Titus from Ephesus.

During Keil's excavation in 1930, recognition of the temple floor-plan was slowed by the presence of a later wall—part of a Byzantine cistern—that covered the temple foundations (Fig. 3). Underneath this rubble wall lies the 34 × 24 m. base of the temple. The cella

---

[46] *BM Ionia* 91, #305, and pl. 14, #6; Fernand Chapouthier, "La Coiffe d'Artémis dans Éphèse trois fois neocore," *REA* 40 (1938) pl. 3, #3 and 4.

[47] See Price 1984b, 187 and 255, for a discussion of colossal statues in Roman Asia Minor.

[48] The find site is roughly 200 meters east of the temple terrace's northeast corner in the Royal Stoa (see Fig. 2).

[49] Fritz Eichler, "Die österreichischen Ausgrabungen in Ephesos im Jahre 1966," *AnzWien* 104 (1967) 18-20; Wilhelm Alzinger, "Das Regierungsviertel," *ÖJh* 50 (1972-75) Beib. 260-64.

[50] Price 1984b, 187.

[51] George M. A. Hanfmann and Nancy H. Ramage, *Sculpture from Sardis. The Finds through 1975* (Cambridge, Mass.: Harvard University Press, 1978) #79 (Antoninus Pius); #102 (Zeus).

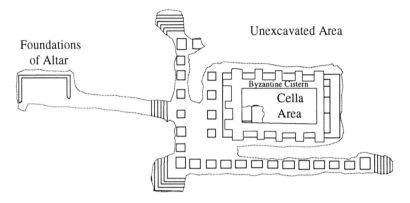

Fig. 3. Temple of the Seḅastoi Excavations.
(after ÖJh 27 [1932] B. 55-56).

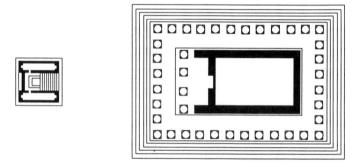

Fig. 4. Reconstructed Plan of the Altar and Temple of the Sebastoi.
(after ÖJh 27 [1932] B. 55-56).

had an interior measurement of about 7.5 × 13 m.[52] The preserved clamp holes and foundations show that the tetraprostyle
temple was surrounded by a pseudodipteral colonnade (8 × 13
columns). The temple sat upon a crepidoma with six steps on all
sides (Fig. 4).

---

[52] The size of the temple cella raises the question of how many statues would
have fit inside the temple. A statue like that of the colossal Titus would require a
base approximately 3.5 meters wide and 2 meters deep. A maximum of five such
bases, one in back and two on each side, could have fit in the temple cella. Proof
of the actual number of statues and of their disposition in the temple will perhaps
be available if further excavations are carried out in the cella area. For an example
of another imperial cult temple with multiple statues, see Shelley C. Stone, III,
"The Imperial Sculptural Group in the Metroon at Olympia," *AthMitt* 100 (1985)
377-91; Georg Treu, *Die Bildwerke von Olympia in Stein und Thon* (Olympia 3; Berlin:
Ascher, 1897) 232-35.

Plate VIII. Ephesian coin showing Temple of the Sebastoi (right?), Temple of Hadrian, and Temple of Artemis (center). *BM Ionia* 83 #261. Courtesy of the Trustees of the British Museum.

Reconstruction of the superstructure of the medium-sized temple has not been possible because only a few fragments of the building itself have been found. The temple appears on the reverses of several Ephesian coins alongside the temple of Artemis, and sometimes with other later provincial temples from Ephesus as well (Pl. VIII-IX).[53] While these are not always accurate regarding details, they do provide a general description. The coins depict an octastyle temple but the order appears to be Ionic rather than the Corinthian order that was normally employed in early imperial temple building. Bluma Trell has suggested that this was simply a convention by which the Ionic order of the Artemision influenced the way the other temples were depicted on a given coin.[54] Thus, the original order was probably Corinthian.

The temple was set within a precinct that occupied the entire area

---

[53] *REA* 40 (1938) pl. 3.3-6. *BM Ionia* 92 #306; pl. 14 #6.). Examples are conveniently assembled in Bluma Trell, *The Temple of Artemis at Ephesus* (New York: American Numismatic Society, 1945) pl. 6 #3-5; and pl. 7 #1-3.

[54] Trell 1945, 58-59. The Temple of the Sebastoi is shown with three doors in the pediment, but this may also be an assimilation to a known feature of the Artemision. Trell's suggestion that the so-called Sarapeion was the second neokorate temple built for Hadrian is no longer tenable. The argument that the "Sarapeion" was a temple for the Egyptian deities has been supported by recent discoveries (Günter Hölbl, "Die ägyptische Wasseruhr aus Ephesos. III. Die ägyptische Wasseruhr Ptolemaus' II," *ÖJh* 55 [1984] Beib.21-68; Steven Friesen, "Ephesus A" *ARNTS* 2, forthcoming). Recent excavations have begun to unearth massive temple foundations north of the basilica/Church of Mary that appear to have been laid for the second neokorate temple. Stefan Karwiese, "Der Numismatiker-Archäologe," *ÖJh* 56 (1985) Haupt. 105-8; Hermann Vetters, "Ephesos: Vorläufiger Grabungsbericht 1983," *AnzWien* 121 (1984) 210-11, Abb. 1.

Plate IX. Ephesian coin showing Temple of the Sebastoi (lower right?), Temple of Hadrian, Temple of Caracalla, Temple of Artemis (uppper left). *BM Ionia* 91 #305. Courtesy of the Trustees of the British Museum.

Plate X. Overview of temple terrace from Mt. Pion, facing south.

on top of the 85.6 × 64.6 meter artificial terrace (Pl. X). The precinct was lined by stoas on three sides, leaving the north side open to the plaza and to the intersection of streets below. The front of the temple was near the center of the precinct, with its back approximately twenty meters from the precinct's west end.[55]

[55] Fritz Eichler, "Die österreichischen Ausgrabungen in Ephesos im Jahre 1961," *AnzWien* 99 (1962) 47-48.

In the middle of the east end of the precinct was a U-shaped platform for an altar. The platform's east-west axis aligned with the
temple and its north-south axis with the monumental entrance on
the north side of the precincts. The altar's platform measured about
9 meters square, but only about half of the foundations and some of
the orthostats have survived.[56] A flight of steps would have ascend-
ed on the open west side that faced the temple[57] to a raised platform
where an altar would have stood.[58]

   The layout of the temple precincts draws on Hellenistic traditions
from western Asia Minor in several ways. First, the temple was built
in a Greek style rather than in an Italian style. Instead of a high podium temple near the back wall of the precincts with one flight of
steps in front, the temple of the Sebastoi was placed closer to the
center of the precincts and had monumental steps on all sides.
Italian temples were not unknown to the builders, for the double cella temple in the Italian style that was probably devoted to the cult
of Rome and Divus Julius occupied a small courtyard on the north
side of the Ephesian upper agora (Fig. 1-2). A Greek design was considered more appropriate for the Temple of the Sebastoi.[59]

---

[56] Three friezes that once decorated the external faces of the altar orthostats
were found in the 1930 campaign. The workmanship is very poor and they do not
seem to have been part of the original building phase. Keil (*ÖJh* 27 [1930] Beib.
57) dated them to the early third century CE; Alzinger (*ANRW* 2.7.2 [1980] 820)
noted that the style of the ornamentation could not be earlier than the mid-second
century CE. Because the concern of this chapter is in the religious imagery used
in this cult's institutions in the late first century CE, these altar reliefs will not be
included in the analysis.

[57] Anton Bammer proposed a reconstruction that oriented the altar not toward
the temple but toward the monumental entrance to the north. He also suggested
that the colossal statue stood or sat above the monumental entrance. "Römische
und byzantinische Architektur," *ÖJh* 50 (1972-75) Beib. 386-92; "Wo einst ein
Weltwunder stand," *Das Altertum* 21 (1975) 33-34. His interpretations of the archaeological remains have not found wide acceptance. See above, n. 44.

[58] Wilhelm Alzinger, "Ephesos. B. Archäologischer Teil," *PWSup* 12 (1970)
1649.

[59] A previously unidentified temple on a coin from Smyrna (Mionnet 6.319
#1564) probably depicts the Temple of the Sebastoi. On the obverse is a woman
who was incorrectly identified as a hitherto unknown "Demeter Horia" by A. v.
Sallet ("Demeter Horia auf Münzen von Smyrna," *ZfN* 4 [1877] 315-17). B. Pick
corrected the error ("Die tempeltragenden Gottheiten und die Darstellung der
Neokorie auf den Münzen," *ÖJh* 7 [1904] Haupt. 2). The woman is Asia personified, for the obverse inscription reads: Δομιτιανῷ Καίσαρι Σεβαστῷ Ζμυρναῖοι
Ἀσίαν, "the Smyrnians (dedicated) Asia to Domitian Caesar Sebastos [assuming
a verb such as καθιέρωσαν]." The reverse carries an image of a temple surrounded
by the words: Ἐπὶ Λουκίου Μεστρίου Φλώρου Ἀνθυπάτου, "When Lucius Mestrius

Second, the floorplan of the temple itself was modeled on traditional forms from Asia. The pseudodipteral style was often said to have been developed by Hermogenes of Teos,[60] and the premier example of his work was the second century BCE temple of Artemis Leukophryene at Magnesia on the Meander.[61] While Hermogenes did not create the pseudodipteral style, his widely-accepted codification of the design is reflected in the Temple of the Sebastoi.[62]

Finally, the U-shaped altar platform was a common feature associated with major temples in Asia. For example, it was used in the Artemision at Ephesus, the temple of Artemis at Sardis, the temple of Athena in Priene, and the temple of Artemis Leukophryene at Magnesia on the Meander. The form was also found on a grander scale in the great altar of Zeus and Athena on the Pergamene akropolis.

The construction of the temple terrace for the Cult of the Sebastoi significantly affected this central area of the city of Ephesus. The impact is difficult to assess precisely because our knowledge of that area

---

Florus was proconsul [i.e., 88/89]." This is an unusual coin: the obverse has Asia rather than the emperor; the emperor is mentioned in the dative and Asia in the accusative; and a temple seems to provide the occasion for the design. The only reason for Smyrna to mint such a coin in honor of a temple dedication that involves Asia in the year 88/89 CE would be the inauguration of the Temple of the Sebastoi. This was not realized before because the temple was not precisely dated. Unfortunately, the coin is not a reliable source for details of the temple architecture (Martin Jessop Price and Bluma L. Trell, *Coins and their Cities* [Detroit: Wayne State University Press, 1977] 32 fig. 326 for a plate showing the reverse with the temple image). The temple on the coin is octastyle with six steps, but it is a podium temple with a statue on each parastasis. The statues have the pose one would expect for statues like that of Titus, but they are standing outside the temple. Since the temple terrace excavations uncovered evidence of a pseudodipteral design and since die-cutters occasionally needed to introduce inaccurate features in order to show temple statues, this coin should probably be considered to be an approximate representation of the Temple of the Sebastoi, executed by an artisan in Smyrna who probably did not intend to portray the temple accurately, or who did not have accurate information about actual appearance of the temple in Ephesus.

[60] Jerome J. Pollitt, *Art in the Hellenistic Age* (Cambridge: Cambridge University Press, 1986) 244-46.

[61] Built ca. 150 BCE, the temple was pseudodipteral (8 × 15 columns) on a seven-step crepidoma. The pronaos was relatively larger than that of the temple of the Sebastoi with two columns *in antis*, front and back. Arnold W. Lawrence, *Greek Architecture* rev. R. A. Tomlinson (Pelican History of Art; New York: Penguin, 1983) 282-84.

[62] Wilhelm Alzinger, "Ephesos vom Beginn der römischen Herrschaft in Kleinasien bis zum Ende der Principatszeit. B. Archäologischer Teil," *ANRW* 2.7.2 (1980) 820.

of the city is incomplete. No systematic investigation has been undertaken yet in the areas south, west, or north of the terrace, and very little is known about the area covered by the terrace structures.

Some things, however, can be affirmed. The terrace was situated near the upper agora and not far from the main artery now known as "Curetes Street." Excavations in the general vicinity, such as those in the slope houses to the northwest of the terrace, have demonstrated that large dwellings of wealthy inhabitants lined the blocks surrounding Curetes St. The temple terrace for the Cult of the Sebastoi was built on valuable land in the city center.

In 1960 and 1961, some probes were carried out at points along the east side of the terrace to gather evidence about the history of this area. Small trenches were excavated in the shops at the bottom of the terrace's east side and one trench was dug across the street (now called "Domitiangasse") that runs up the slope between the terrace and the upper agora. These probes revealed an earlier street from the Augustan period following the same route at a level about 0.75 m. below the Domitianic paving. Under the shops near the terrace's southeast corner, parts of a pre-Roman wall were discovered that was once the east front of an unidentified building. Under the pre-Roman wall were smaller walls of individual dwellings. Another earlier wall was used as a foundation near the northeast corner of the terrace. In this area, early imperial pottery was found in the fill that supports the terrace. Below this was another layer of fill from the Hellenistic period.[63]

The evidence gathered by these probes suggests that at least part of the terrace covered an area that had been a residential area in Hellenistic times. A larger building of some sort succeeded the houses, perhaps as a part of the Hellenistic terracing effort that is known from the fill. The street below Domitiangasse was paved in the Augustan period at which time there were already shops on the agora side. The street was repaved when the terrace was constructed during the reign of Domitian. Thus, the temple terrace seems to have constituted a major building project in an area that was already well-developed. It did not create a new district of the city, but rather redefined an existing one.

The construction of the terrace was part of a larger redevelopment

---

[63] Hermann Vetters, "Domitianterrasse und Domitiangasse," *ÖJh* 50 (1972-75) Beib. 323-30.

of the area. The new and remodeled shops, and the repaved
Domitiangasse were discussed above. More significant were the
changes below the northeast corner of the terrace. Here a large plaza
was redesigned in relation to the temple. The plaza was paved, the
Pollio Fountain (an Augustan period monument) was renovated
and expanded,[64] and an apsidal monument was raised in the middle of the plaza.

The multi-leveled redevelopment of the area around the terrace
appears to have been a part of the same plan that included the temple
and its terrace.[65] The precincts were not closed off by adding a
fourth stoa to the top of the terrace on the north side. The planners
chose, rather, to create a precinct open on the long side toward the
lower plaza. In so doing, they drew on Hellenistic precedents for
creating dramatic contexts for religious architecture. The Asklepieion of Kos and the Athena Lindia precincts on the island of
Rhodes are the aesthetic ancestors of the general layout of the area
around the Temple of the Sebastoi in Ephesus.[66] The examples
from Rhodes and Kos are more dramatic in their location, but the
Cult of the Sebastoi is a reasonable translation of these same ideas
into an urban context.

One important function of the plaza was the creation of free space
in front of the terrace from which the viewer could see the open north
side of the precinct and the terrace's north facade. The visual impact
of this architectural setting was a crucial aspect of the whole
complex.

The practical function of the temple terrace was to create a level
area above the descending slope of Mt. Koressos. The distance between the top of the terrace and the ground level was greatest
(10.4 m.) on the north side of the precincts by the plaza. At the level
of the plaza, the entire length of the north terrace contained vaulted
shops behind a colonnaded hall approximately 5 meters wide
(Pl. IX). In front of the hall stood a three-story facade reaching to
the top of the terrace. This north facade was broken only by a 4.3
meter wide monumental stairway (on axis with the temple's altar)

---

[64] See Anton Bammer, "Das Denkmal des C. Sextilius Pollio in Ephesos," *ÖJh*
51 (1976-77) Beib. 77-92; and idem, "Elemente flavisch-trajanischer Architekturfassaden aus Ephesos," *ÖJh* 52 (1978-80) Haupt. 67-81 for a detailed examination
and reconstruction of the fountain.
[65] Alzinger 1980, 820.
[66] Alzinger 1980, 820.

Plate XI. Remains of stairway and stoa on north side of temple terrace opening onto plaza. Facing southwest.

a little over twenty meters from the northeast corner. The stairway provided the main access to the top of the terrace; at least one other entrance, at the southeast corner, is known.[67]

The first story of the facade was executed in Doric half columns. Above the first story architrave was an area decorated with palmette, lotus, and rosette designs, that supported columns with engaged figures of deities along the length of the facade, interrupted only by the staircase entrance near the northeast corner. The Corinthian order may have been used for the third story.[68]

Use of the figures on the columns of the north facade's second story is an unusual feature. Hilke Thür suggested that this feature indicates western influence, since analogous figured supports are found in Corinth (the Captives Facade) and in the Forum of Augustus in Rome.[69] The argument for western influence is not

---

[67] Vetters 1972-75, 311-15.

[68] Hilke Thür, "Ephesische Bauhütten in der Zeit der Flavier und der Adoptivkaiser" in *Lebendige Altertumswissenschaft. Festgabe zur Vollendung des 70. Lebensjahres von Hermann Vetters dargebracht von Freunden, Schülern und Kollegen* (Vienna: Verlag Adolf Holzhausens, 1985) 184.

[69] Thür 1985, 184.

Plate XII. Engaged figures of Attis and Isis on facade of temple terrace stoa.

strong, though. The columns in the Forum of Augustus are not engaged figures but female figures serving as columns. Moreover, they are copies of the karyatids from the Erechtheum in Athens and show Athenian influence on Rome.[70] While the Captives Facade in Corinth is closer to the Ephesian example in style, it is dated to the late second century CE and therefore is much later than the Ephesian terrace facade. Furthermore, the Ephesian facade does not portray bound figures but standing deities.[71]

The two figures from the Ephesian column facade that have been recovered are both eastern deities: Attis and Isis (Pl. XII). This led Bammer to the conclusion that the entire facade contained eastern deities. He interpreted their appearance as an attempt by the emperor to coopt these "salvation religion" figures for imperial propaganda.[72]

[70] John B. Ward-Perkins, *Roman Imperial Architecture* (Pelican History of Art; 2d integrated ed.; New York: Penguin, 1981) 25.

[71] James Wiseman, "Corinth and Rome I: 228 B.C.–A.D. 267" *ANRW* 2.7.1 (1979) 525; Richard Stillwell, "The Facade of the Colossal Figures," in idem, Robert L. Scranton, and Sarah Elizabeth Freeman, *Architecture* (Corinth 1,2; Cambridge, Mass.: Harvard University Press, 1941) 55-88.

[72] Anton Bammer, *Architektur und Gesellschaft in der Antike* (2d ed.; Vienna:

The assumption that the emperor, or someone else in Rome, designed or approved the facade is groundless, though. There is no extant evidence for the assumption, and the architecture shows little Italian influence. Furthermore, the facade originally had 35-40 engaged figures, of which only two have been identified. It would not have been easy to find enough eastern deities with recognizable iconographies to use in the colonnade. It is more likely that the colonnade figures included gods and goddesses from east and west. But even if eastern deities were the only figures on the columns, the salvation religion interpretation is inadequate. It is based on a discredited interpretation of the role of religions in the imperial period that credited eastern traditions, and especially the mystery cults, with supplying the hope of salvation for individuals in an otherwise hopeless world.[73]

More recently, Simon Price has tried to elucidate the significance of architecture and sculpture in a temple precinct as one way of defining the relationship of the emperors and the gods.[74] There are numerous examples from the Roman imperial period where statues of emperors have been placed in temples of other deities, or where a separate building has been dedicated to the emperors in the precincts of a temple. Price took the point made by Nock that an emperor rarely shared fully in a temple of a traditional god,[75] and enlarged upon it in a specific fashion. After careful examination of situations where the emperor or members of the imperial family were represented in the temple of a traditional god in Ephesus, Athens, Pergamum, Priene, Sardis, and elsewhere, Price noted that

> there was generally concern to avoid elevating the emperor too high. His statues did not rival or displace those of the traditional deities.[76]

Hermann Böhlaus Verlag, 1985) 124-25. Another weakness in his argument is his description of Isis and Attis as deities that appealed primarily to the lower classes. Both Ephesus and Pergamum built large, and therefore expensive, sanctuaries for the Egyptian gods in the second century CE.

[73] See Walter Burkert's *Ancient Mystery Cults* (Cambridge, Mass.: Harvard University Press, 1987) for a more recent interpretation; and, Jonathan Z. Smith, *Drudgery Divine: On the Comparison of Early Christianities and the Religions of Late Antiquity* (Chicago: University of Chicago Press, 1990) 116-143 for a critique of modern soteriological interpretations of ancient mystery cults.

[74] Price 1984b, esp. 146-56.

[75] A. D. Nock, "Σύνναος Θεός," *HSCP* 41 (1930) 1-62.

[76] Price 1984b, 147.

Thus, the evidence from the precincts where gods and emperors were present was interpreted as a deliberate attempt to classify the emperors in the divine category without equating them with the gods. This in turn became a crucial part of Price's larger argument that the imperial cult carefully distinquished the emperors from the gods.[77]

The Temple of the Sebastoi in Ephesus, however, presents a problem for Price's theory. Why would the temple of the emperors tower above the ranks of the gods? Why would statues of the emperors be depicted so much larger than the gods? This apparent contradiction is generated by a mistaken premise that underlies Price's interpretation. The placement of the emperor in any given precinct should not be understood as a statement about the general status of emperors and gods. It is, instead, a much more modest statement about the emperor's place in that particular precinct which is dedicated to someone else. The question is not so much divine ontology as hospitality and protocol.

To put my point another way, it was not only unusual for emperors to share fully in the cult of a traditional god. It was also unusual for a god to share fully in the cult of another god. Greco-Roman religions included certain predictable combinations such as Asklepios and Hygeia, Isis and Sarapis, Demeter and Kore, or the Dioscuri. Other gods might be included in the cult in an exceptional instance, but they would seldom "share fully" in the cult.

It was not unusual to have statues of divinities in the precincts of another god. Large precincts or sanctuaries with important periodic festivals were often littered with statues of gods, humans, even animals. If Apollo was depicted in an Asklepieion with a smaller statue than that of his son, this was not a general statement about their relative status. It only indicated that the Asklepieion was dedicated to Asklepios. The implications of these suggestions for an understanding of the relationship of the gods to the emperors will be laid out in the concluding chapter. At present, the significance of the iconography of the temple precincts in Ephesus deserves more consideration.

In the case of the facade in front of the Temple of the Sebastoi at Ephesus, the symbolism was indeed related to the relative positions

---

[77] E.g., Price 1984b, 231-32.

of the gods and the emperors. The entire complex was not an attempt to articulate a comprehensive hierarchy of the divine world. Rather, we should take the position of a viewer standing on the plaza below the facade, who would have looked up to see a host of divine beings lined up across the length of the massive terrace. Behind this row of deities was the temenos of the Sebastoi. The message was clear: the gods and goddesses of the peoples supported the emperors; and, conversely, the cult of the emperors united the cultic systems, and the peoples, of the empire. The emperors were not a threat to the worship of the diverse deities of the empire; rather, the emperors joined the ranks of the divine and played their own particular role in that realm.

In this way, the architecture of the temple terrace communicated the same basic message implied by the neokoros imagery initiated for the Cult of the Sebastoi in Ephesus. In both instances, the emperors were associated with symbols from the upper realms of the pantheon. The city recognized the benefits received from the emperors and acknowledged its cultic responsibilities toward them. The argument that reverence for Artemis might crowd out reverence for the emperors that was used earlier in the century[78] was no longer persuasive in the late first century CE. The emperors and the (other) gods and goddesses each had their proper, complementary places in the life of the city, the province, and the empire.

This imagery, used to articulate the significance of the Cult of the Sebastoi, was not imposed from Rome. The concept of the neokoros city, the design of the temple, the sculptural figures, and the architectural program all originated in the Greek east. The symbolic systems employed in the cult show that the institutions were part of the Asian heritage. As such, the religious imagery reflected local values. The developments in the religious traditions of western Asia Minor that have been the subject of this chapter were conscious, creative transformations by participants in those traditions who sought to express a new situation using the received symbolic vocabulary.

---

[78] This claim about Ephesus was also made in the deliberations regarding the choice of a site for the provincial cult that was finally granted to Smyrna (26 CE), as well as the one founded in Miletus (40 CE). See above, chapter one.

CHAPTER FOUR

PROVINCIAL HIGHPRIESTHOODS

In chapter one, many of the known offices of three different provincial cults of Asia were examined. In chapters two and three, several offices related to the cult of the Sebastoi in Ephesus have already been mentioned. The goal of this chapter is to describe in detail the priesthoods of Asia's Cult of the Sebastoi in Ephesus, and to discuss the issue of whether Asiarchs were related to provincial imperial cult.

The parameters of the scholarly discussion of these offices have been relatively stable since the early years of this century. Occasional refinements have been suggested or deviations proposed, but little attempt has been made to reevaluate the topic systematically in the light of the growing body of archaeological data.

One of the reasons that the discussion has progressed so little is that tentative conclusions about one office are frequently used as evidence to support conclusions about other offices. For this reason, this chapter will deal with each office separately, making every attempt to assess the data on its own merits, and will examine the interpretations of prominent, representative scholars.

One other problem has plagued the scholarly debates. Because the available evidence is not complete, interpreters often seek far and wide across the Roman Empire for analogous situations. Often, decisions about a specific issue are made on the basis of an inscription or coin from a distant province. While it is true that the evidence for the province of Asia is not complete, there are nevertheless hundreds of sources pertinent to the question of sacerdotal offices in Asia. Evidence from the province of Asia must be given priority; the significance of data from another province must be carefully evaluated, for there is no reason to think that the provinces were uniform either in governance or religiosity.

It would be impossible to cite all the coins and inscriptions that provide the evidence for this discussion. The reader may consult Appendix I where the known epigraphic and numismatic references to provincial highpriests, highpriestesses, and to Asiarchs are listed.

The attestations are arranged in chronological order with personal names, complete titles, and bibliographic information. An index to the appendix has also been provided.

Provincial Highpriests

The provincial highpriests were leading figures in the affairs of the province. They often appear in inscribed texts of koinon documents, as well as in other inscriptions from many cities. In fact, extant coins and inscriptions contain over 140 references to highpriests of Asia.

In spite of this abundance of data, there has been no agreement on the number of provincial highpriests in Asia at a given time. Late in the nineteenth century, a general scholarly consensus seemed to be forming, of which William Ramsay was a representative. He argued that there was only one highpriest of the province (ἀρχιερεὺς Ἀσίας) but this highpriest of Asia had several deputies, each of whom was called a "highpriest of the temple(s) in (a given city):" ἀρχιερεὺς ναῶν τῶν ἐν κτλ. These deputies were appointed to service the provincial temples in the various cities and formed a sacerdotal hierarchy within the province.[1]

Magie challenged this position, which he characterized as "the generally accepted view."[2] He argued that the phrases "highpriest of Asia" and "highpriest of the temple(s) in (a given city)" were variants of the same title for the same office. According to Magie, there was only one such highpriest in the province of Asia at any given time. The references to cities in the titles of highpriests did not indicate a plurality of highpriests. Rather, the naming of cities in the titles were determined by the location of the koinon's meeting during that highpriest's tenure in office.[3]

In order to evaluate Magie's position, we need to consider the number of known highpriests in relationship to the total number of highpriestly terms of office during the approximately three centuries of Asia's provincial cult for Roman emperors. Approximately

---

[1] "The distinction between the titles...is clearly drawn, and is of course known to all accurate writers," according to William Ramsay, "The Province of Asia" *ClRev* 3 (1889) 175. See also Victor Chapot, *La province romaine proconsulaire d'Asie* (Paris: Emile Bouillon, 1904) 470.

[2] David Magie, *Roman Rule in Asia Minor* (Princeton: Princeton University Press, 1950) 2.1297-98 n. 59.

[3] Magie 1950, 2:1297-98 n. 59.

eighty different names of provincial highpriests are known from the coins and inscriptions of Asia and its environs, and a few of these served more than one term. In addition, there are eighteen other references to highpriests of Asia for which no name has been recorded.[4] If Magie's view is correct, there were only about 320 highpriestly terms of office in Asia between the establishment of the first provincial cult in Pergamum in 29 BCE and the reforms of Diocletian which apparently entailed the demise of the koinon of Asia as well as those of other provinces.[5] This would mean that an extraordinarily high number of the highpriestly terms of office (about one third of them) is preserved in the archaeological record.[6]

Therefore, Magie's position is extremely unlikely. Although he demonstrated successfully that the titles "highpriest of Asia" and "highpriest of Asia of the temple in . . ." referred to the same kind of official,[7] this does not mean there was only one such official in the province at any given time.[8] Indeed, if there was only one highpriest in Asia, there would have been no reason to mention a relationship to a specific temple.[9] Furthermore, an inscription from Magnesia on the Meander that mentions two men who had been designated as provincial highpriests—οἱ ἀποδεδιγμένοι τῆς 'Ασίας ἀρχιερεῖς—would be inexplicable if only one official was elected per year.[10]

---

[4] Some of these could be references to highpriests whose names are known from the other attestations, but the possibility of such a coincidence does not affect the argument. Also, some of the references to unnamed provincial highpriests do not mention individuals, but rather groups of relatives, all of whom held this office.

[5] Jürgen Deininger, *Die Provinziallandtage der römischen Kaiserzeit* (Vestigia 6; Munich: Beck, 1965) 182-83.

[6] The inclusion of highpriestesses in this number would be appropriate and would bring the ratio to about 45%. It must first be demonstrated, however, that "highpriestess" was not simply an honorary title without sacerdotal responsibilities (see below, p. 81-89).

[7] The inscription related to the provincial cult of Gaius in Miletus (text given above, p. 22) confirms Magie's position on this point. That inscription is dated by the service of Gaius Vergilius Capito as highpriest of the temple in Miletus, which is called his third highpriesthood of Asia. The text of the inscription assumes the equivalence of the two titles.

[8] Magie 1950, 2.1297-98 n. 59.

[9] Magie's suggestion that the official title would sometimes include the name of the town where the koinon met that year is unconvincing (1950, 2:1297-98 n. 59). The longer title does not refer to a meeting of the koinon, but rather to the location of certain provincial temples. A sole highpriest for Asia would have been in charge of all the province's temples, not just those in one city.

[10] *IvMag* 157b. Deininger 1965, 39.

Deininger assessed the situation more accurately in this respect.[11] He maintained that when provincial temples proliferated in Asia beginning in 26 CE, a provincial highpriest was appointed for each temple. Thus, every city that had a provincial cult also had an annually elected highpriest.[12] Beginning in the second century CE, some cities acquired second and third provincial cults.[13] In these cases, one highpriest served for all the provincial cults in that city,[14] for only one highpriest was necessary in a city. Finally, he argued that the highpriests of Asia were not arranged in a hierarchy but were of equal status.[15]

One assumption about provincial highpriests that has been shared by all commentators needs to be questioned at this point, namely, the idea that the highpriest of Asia's first provincial cult was always known either as ἀρχιερεὺς θεᾶς ῾Ρώμης καὶ Αὐτοκράτορος Καίσαρος θεοῦ υἱοῦ Σεβαστοῦ or as ἀρχιερεὺς ᾿Ασίας.[16] Careful examination of koinon inscriptions, honorary decrees, and coins shows that

---

[11] Jürgen Deininger (1965, 39 and n. 10) does not, however, indicate an awareness that he is in disagreement with Magie's position on the number of highpriests in a province.

[12] A provincial highpriest did not need to be a native of the city in which he served. A series of inscriptions from 4-2 BCE on one stone found in Sardis (*Sardis* 7.8 = *IGR* 4.1756) gives several examples of highpriests from the cult of Rome and Augustus in Pergamum who come from various cities.

[13] Margaret Rossner ("Asiarchen und Archiereis," *Studii clasice* 16 [1974] 111) noted that only five cities in Asia (Pergamum, Smyrna, Ephesus, Kyzikos, and Sardis) are recorded in the title "highpriest of Asia of the temples in (a given city)," even though several other cities are known to have had provincial cults. She suggested that the number of provincial highpriesthoods may have stabilized at five, one for each of these cities, by the mid-second century CE even though other provincial cults were established. It is more likely, though not demonstrable, that more than five cities had such highpriesthoods which are not attested due to the accidents of preservation and discovery. Using only the five cities known from this type of provincial highpriesthood title, we can calculate that the province had a total of approximately 1100 highpriestly terms of office during the imperial period. The extant attestations of provincial highpriests and highpriestesses would comprise less than 10% of this total, making omissions of other cities quite possible. If other cities also had highpriesthoods (as seems more likely), the total number of highpriestly terms of office for the province would go up, the extant attestations would be an even smaller percentage of this total, and omissions would be even more probable.

[14] E.g., *AvP* 8,3.30; *IvSm* 2,1.727; *IvE* 3.642.

[15] Deininger 1965, 18, 37-41.

[16] E.g., Paul Guiraud, *Les assemblées provinciales dans l'empire romain* (Paris: Imprimerie Nationale, 1887) 82, and n. 1; Magie 1950, 2.1297 n. 59; Deininger 1965, 37-41; W. G. Buckler, "Auguste, Zeus Patrôos," *RevPhil* 3d series, 9 (1935) 177. Buckler argued, however, for a more complicated chronology of the development of the Rome and Augustus title.

this was not the case. Asia's first provincial highpriesthood was not known as the "highpriest of Asia" until sometime after Augustus. The reason for the confusion in the scholarly literature is that references to this highpriest in koinon inscriptions sometimes referred simply to the ἀρχιερεύς and modern scholars have assumed that this was an abbreviated form of ἀρχιερεὺς 'Ασίας. The title ἀρχιερεὺς 'Ασίσς, however, never appears in our sources in reference to the highpriest of the provincial cult in Pergamum until the late first century or early second century CE.[17] Before this time, he was known only as the ἀρχιερεὺς θεᾶς 'Ρώμης καὶ Αὐτοκράτορος Καίσαρος θεοῦ υἱοῦ Σεβαστοῦ or the ἀρχιερεύς in contexts where the referent was understood.

In fact, the title ἀρχιερεὺς 'Ασίας seems to have come into use only in the second quarter of the first century CE. The first known usage of the term comes from the year 40 CE when it appears in the Miletus inscription related to the abortive cult for Gaius in that city.[18] In the inscription, Gaius Vergilius Capito is said to be serving as the ἀρχιερεὺς 'Ασίας for the third time, so the title was probably in use before this date for at least a few years.[19] The title appears next in 41 CE in an inscription from Hypaipa,[20] then in two other inscriptions between the years 41 and 68.[21]

The significance of this chronology lies in the observation that the title ἀρχιερεὺς 'Ασίας came into use only after the establishment of Asia's second provincial cult in Smyrna in 26 CE. Highpriest of Asia became the title of any provincial highpriest, and by the end of the first century CE it had replaced the earlier title "highpriest of Rome and Augustus" for the cult in Pergamum.[22]

---

[17] *IGR* 4.1239; see also the fragmentary inscription *IvE* 4.1393. *IvE* 7,2.3801 (perhaps Tiberian or Claudian period) might use the phrase ἀρχιερέως τῆς 'Ασίας but the title is almost completely reconstructed in a lacuna.

[18] Louis Robert, "Le culte de Caligula a Milet et la province d'Asie," *Hellenica* 7 (1949) 206-7. See above, p. 21-26.

[19] There is no reason to believe that the inscription uses the title anachronistically for the two earlier terms of office.

[20] *IvE* 7,2.3801 II.

[21] *IvMag* 157b; *MAMA* 6.104. There is also one reference in *IGR* 4.1524 to a highpriest of Asia of the temple in Smyrna that could be dated any time during the period when Smyrna had one provincial cult, i.e., 26-120 CE. "Highpriest of Asia" is attested also on coins of Eumeneia from the Domitianic period (*CollWadd* 6034; *BM Phrygia* 218, #48) and in an inscription from Phokaia (*IGR* 4.1323) in the period 85-130 CE.

[22] *IGR* 4.1239; 1639; 577.

The shift in title reflects a change in focus from the specific object of one cult (Rome and Augustus) to the growing ·institution of provincial worship in Asia. After the Rome and Augustus cult of 29 BCE,[23] no other provincial highpriesthood in Asia was named for an individual emperor without including other individuals.[24] What started as an office whose title emphasized the objects of pious activity (i.e., Rome and one particular emperor) became one of several offices entrusted with the task of expressing the province's reverence for imperial authority.[25]

In this way, the multiplication of provincial cults gradually gave rise to a category of provincial offices that could be held by an ever greater number of citizens from the wealthier stratum of inhabitants in the cities of Asia. This category began as a fairly restricted option (one highpriest of Rome and Augustus annually), but over time it included quite a few wealthy inhabitants of Asia who could serve the province as one of many highpriests of Asia in the cults of the emperors.

Provincial Highpriestesses

Appendix 1 contains 42 attestations of provincial highpriestesses of Asia from the published coins and inscriptions of western Asia Minor, including the names of 29 different women. Nearly all studies touching upon these references have concluded that some or all of the known highpriestesses from Asia received the title as an honorific designation on the basis of their husband's highpriesthood.

E. Beurlier's doctoral thesis was an early monograph on imperial cult.[26] He accepted Marquardt's interpretation of provincial highpriestesses, i.e., that the institution was inaugurated when the first

---

[23] The cult must have been for Rome and "Octavian" before 27 BCE. See above, chapter one.

[24] One possible exception is the fragmentary inscription (*IvE* 4.1404) that mentions a highpriest of Tiberius. It is not clear whether this inscription refers to a provincial cult (i.e., the one in Smyrna). In any case, a highpriesthood of Tiberius would still conform to the developments being outlined here.

[25] This post-Augustan tendency of not naming highpriesthoods for specific emperors was observed by Brandis for local imperial cults (*PW* 2 [1896] 479-81). It also fits the general pattern of developments in imperial cults in Asia Minor noted by S. R. F. Price (1984b, 57-59, 245-48).

[26] E. Beurlier, *Essai sur le culte rendu aux empereurs romains* (Paris: Ernest Thorin, 1890).

woman of the imperial house was divinized.[27] Beurlier maintained that highpriestesses held the office by virtue of being married to a provincial highpriest, and that they functioned as highpriestesses of imperial women. This explained why the highpriestess was also subject to certain purity requirements and given certain privileges because of her husband's office.[28]

One year after Beurlier's study was published, P. Paris's work on women in public office appeared. After examining a variety of different ways that women were involved in public life in Asia, Paris took Mommsen's suggestion and concluded that highpriestesses were probably wives of highpriests. The husbands did the governmental business entailed by the highpriesthood while the wives concentrated on activities considered acceptable for women, such as those of the agonothetis in the provincial games.[29]

Five years after Beurlier, Brandis took a minority position but he did not elaborate on it. In a brief statement on highpriestesses (the first half of the last sentence in his article "Archiereus") he mentioned that women could participate in all forms of highpriesthoods alone or with their husbands.[30] Chapot approved of Brandis's position, devoting a small paragraph to provincial highpriestesses.[31] Three years later, Toutain published his analysis of scholars like Beurlier who excluded women from sacerdotal functions in the provincial cults. Although he did not want to go beyond what he understood the ancient sources to say, Toutain strongly suggested that the best interpretation was that women functioned as highpriestesses in the provincial cults of the emperors.[32]

The view that provincial highpriestesses were not functioning but rather honorary officials has been accepted in the major studies that

---

[27] I. Marquardt, "De provinciarum romanarum conciliis et sacerdotibus," *Ephemeris Epigraphica* 1 (1872) 200.

[28] Beurlier 1890, 125-27, 152-53. The details of these purity requirements and privileges come from an inscription of uncertain date known as the *lex Narbonensis*; see below, p. 83).

[29] Petrus Paris, *Quatenus feminae res publicas in Asia Minore, Romanis imperantibus, attigerint* (Paris: Ernest Thorin, 1891) 112-14. Theodor Mommsen, *Römische Geschichte* (5th ed.; 1904; reprinted Munich: Deutscher Taschenbuch Verlag, 1976) 5:320.

[30] Brandis, *PW* 2 (1896) 483.

[31] Chapot 1904, 470.

[32] J. Toutain, *Les cultes païens dans l'Empire romain*, vol. 1: *Les cultes officiels; les cultes romains et gréco-romains* (Paris: Ernest Leroux, 1907) 142-48.

deal with the issue in the last half of the twentieth century.[33] Magie accepted this conclusion and even though he gathered together a list of known provincial highpriestesses in an appendix,[34] there is surprisingly little discussion of highpriestesses in his work. He was content simply to state that "the Chief Priest's [his preferred translation of ἀρχιερεύς] wife enjoyed the privilege of being called Chief Priestess."[35]

Deininger hesitated because of the nature of the sources, but came to the same conclusion as Magie. His two paragraphs on provincial highpriestesses are instructive because they illustrate that the highpriestess question has not been answered so much by an analysis of the data but by assumptions about the nature of the office. Only two important primary documents are cited in Deininger's discussion. One is the *lex Narbonensis*, which records the rules regarding contemporary and former highpriests of the province of Narbonensis.[36] It should be noted that this inscription is undated and does not come from Asia, nor even from the eastern Mediterranean. Furthermore, the text never mentions a highpriestess (*flaminica*), while the only reference to a highpriest's wife is in a restored lacuna.[37] The only way that this text can be used to support the honorary highpriestess theory is if one has already assumed that a highpriestess is the wife of a highpriest.

The second piece of primary evidence cited by Deininger is an inscription from Baetica (southern Spain) which names a certain Quintia M. f. Flaccina as a provincial priestess of the divinized imperial women (*in honorem et memoriam Quintiae M. f. Flaccinae Munig(uensi), flaminic(ae) divar(um) Aug(ustarum) splend(idissimae) provinc(iae) Baetic(ae)*).[38] Such an inscription is certainly a valuable document, but it hardly demonstrates the nature of the office of highpriestess for other provinces of the Roman Empire. On the contrary, it seems that the provincial cult of Baetica in Munigua had an eccentric

---

[33] An important exception was Robert Étienne, *Le culte impérial dans la péninsula ibérique d'Auguste a Dioclétian* (Paris: E. de Boccard, 1958) 169-71.

[34] Magie 1950, 2.1603-4.

[35] Magie 1950, 1.449.

[36] *ILS* 6964 = M. McCrum and A. G. Woodhead (eds.), *Select Documents of the Principates of the Flavian Emperors including the Year of Revolution A.D. 68-69* (Cambridge: Cambridge University Press, 1961) 52-53, #128. Deininger 1965, 154.

[37] Line 6: [- - - *uxor fla]minis veste alba aut purpurea vestita f[estis diebus - - -*], "[...the wife of the fl]amen wearing white or purple on r[eligious holidays...]"

[38] Deininger 1965, 129 n. 7, 154.

format in which the imperial cult had joined a cult of Fortuna and/or Hercules.[39]

The problem, then, is not primarily the data at our disposal but rather the questions that have been tested in the light of the data. Throughout Deininger's discussion of highpriestesses, he does not ask what the nature of the office of highpriestess was, but rather whether highpriestesses were married to highpriests.[40] Not only is this the wrong question to ask, it is a question that cannot be answered in most cases, and so he was led to introduce the peculiar argument that no highpriestess could be proven not to have been married to a highpriest.[41] Rossner repeated this argument as though it were convincing;[42] MacMullen simply accepted the conclusion.[43]

The prevailing view was challenged by Kearsley in 1986.[44] She questioned the accepted interpretative framework by pointing out that the concept of honorary priesthoods is incongruent with the practices of other Greek cults, and even with local imperial cults. She then undertook a study of 15 highpriestesses from Ephesus that allowed her to show that the honorary highpriestess theory does not conform to the data from Asia. Among the specific problems with the general consensus, she cited differences between the titles of husbands and wives, women listed with no references to husbands or fathers, and highpriestesses whose husbands were known not to have held highpriesthoods. The strength of these arguments varies from case to case,[45] but their combined force is convincing. It

---

[39] Wilhelm Grünhage, "Die Ausgrabungen des Terrassenheiligtums von Munigua," in *Neue deutsche Ausgrabungen im Mittelmeergebiet und im vorderen Orient* (Berlin: Verlag Gebr. Mann, 1959) 340-41, and 342 n. 4.

[40] Deininger 1965, 41, 154.

[41] Deininger 1965, 41, 154.

[42] Rossner 1974, 102.

[43] "It is generally agreed that incumbents held the title high-priestess not in their own right but as wives of those high-priests who happened to be married." Ramsay MacMullen, "Woman in Public in the Roman Empire," *Historia* 29 (1980) 214.

[44] Rosalinde Kearsley, "Asiarchs, *Archiereis*, and the *Archiereiai* of Asia," *GRBS* 27 (1986) 183-92.

[45] The argument based on the absence of titles for husbands or wives is particularly difficult. There are several instances where a wife's provincial highpriesthood is recorded while her husband is not called a highpriest, or where a husband is a highpriest of Asia and the wife has no titles. While the frequency of this phenomenon is suggestive, the absence of titles in a particular inscription is still tenuous support for any conclusion. For example, an inscription from Phokaia (*IGR* 4.1325)

seems that most scholars have assumed that women were not functional highpriestesses in the provincial cult of Asia without giving the evidence appropriate consideration.

The other example of this particular phenomenon can be found in the modern interpretation of Jewish women's leadership titles from antiquity, and Brooten's conclusions about so-called honorific titles of the synagogues can be appropriated for Asia's highpriestesses as well.[46] There is actually no evidence for women taking their husband's titles in the provincial imperial cult of Asia. Even if such titles had been gained by some through marriage, this would not necessarily mean that all women had received their titles in this way, nor would it mean that highpriestesses had no cultic responsibilities.[47]

It is not generally recognized that an inscription from Magnesia on the Meander provides a fairly precise date at which highpriestesses became a part of the imperial cults of the province of Asia.

```
        Ἡ βουλὴ [καὶ ὁ δῆμος ἐτείμησαν]
  2     Ἰουλιανὴ[ν Εὐσ]τρά[του τοῦ Φα-]
        νοστράτ[ου,] γυνα[ῖκα δὲ Ἀλ-]
  4     κίφρονο[ς τ]οῦ τῆς Ἀ[σίσς ἀρχιε-]
        ρέως, ἀρ[χιέ]ρειαν γε[νομένην]
  6     τῆς Ἀσία[ς πρ]ώτην τῶ[ν γυναικῶν,]
        στεφαν[ηφόρ]ον, γυμν[ασιαρχον,]
  8     ἱ(ε)[ρει]αν Ἀφ[ροδ]είτης κα[ὶ θεᾶς Ἀγριπ-]
        πείνης [μητ]ρὸς διὰ (β)[ίου], ἱ[έρει-]
 10     αν δὲ κα[ὶ ἐν Ἐ]φέσῳ Δή[μητρ]ος [διὰ]
        βίου πασ[ης ἀ]ρετῆς ἔν[εκεν.][48]
```

honored the provincial highpriestess Flavia Ammion Aristion and mentioned her husband without any of his titles, even though he is known from a different inscription (*IGR* 4.1323) to have served as highpriest of Asia of the temple in Ephesus.

[46] Bernadette J. Brooten, *Women Leaders in the Ancient Synagogue. Inscriptional Evidence and Background Issues* (Brown Judaic Studies 36; Chico, California: Scholars Press, 1982), esp. "Excursus: What is an Honorific Title?" p. 7-10.

[47] A crucial element in most arguments for honorific highpriestesses has been the equation of "provincial highpriest" with "Asiarch." Since the two titles have usually been considered to be equivalent, and since highpriestesses appeared both as wives of Asiarchs and wives of provincial highpriests, the designation "highpriestess" seemed to be simply a courtesy accorded to these women. The issue of the responsibilities of Asiarchs is discussed below, beginning on p. 92.

[48] *IvMag* 158.

> The boule and the demos honored Juliane—daughter of Eustratos (?) son of Phanostratos (?), wife of Alkiphronos the highpriest of Asia, (who) was the first among women (to serve as) highpriestess of Asia, stephanephoros, gymnasiarch, priestess for life (?) of Aphrodite and of the goddess Agrippina the mother, and priestess for life of Demeter in Ephesus—because of all (her) excellence.

The inscription, which honors the prominent benefactor and priestess Juliane, has several problems connected with it that require discussion. The first is that the marble plate upon which the inscription was made disappeared in November, 1893, so it is no longer available for inspection. Kern's publication of the text was made on the basis of a reevaluation of a squeeze of the inscription as well as the transcription that had been revised several times. The inscription was also damaged before it was found by archaeologists. The lacunae that make the text difficult to read are mostly due to two vertical grooves that were caused by a secondary reuse of the stone.[49]

Several portions of the text have been reconstructed that bear on the nature of Juliane's service as provincial highpriestess. The suggested reading for the end of line five, the participle γε[νομένην], is probably correct. The presence of γε in the middle of the phrase "highpriestess of Asia" would be difficult to understand as part of any other word, and there are good epigraphic parallels for this participle; e.g., the text from Ephesus honoring Claudia Ammion γενομένην ἀρχιέρειαν τῆς 'Ασίας ("who was highpriestess of Asia").[50]

Another lacuna is crucial to the interpretation of the inscription: the word "women" in line six is completely reconstructed. The inscriptions of Magnesia do not record any titles including the phrase "first among..." that might confirm this reading or provide alternative proposals. The phrase might have read [πρ]ώτην τῶ[ν 'Ελλήνων] ("first among the Magnesians"), though there are no parallels for this title either; or perhaps [πρ]ώτην τῶ[ν 'Ελλήνων] ("first among the Hellenes").[51] It is unlikely that the text named her first among the highpriests or highpriestesses for there is no other indication in the archaeological record of a ranking of these officials. The title "first of the city" was used in some places,[52] but

---

[49] *IvMag* 158.
[50] *IvE* 3.681.
[51] *IGR* 4.1226 (Thyatira).
[52] *IGR* 4.652 (Akmonia), 666 (Diokleia), 888 (Themisonion).

the word τῶ[ν] requires a plural noun rather than a singular. Thus, on the basis of available alternatives, "first among women" is a plausible, but not necessary, reading.

Some progress can be made if the meaning of the phrase is examined. The phrase "first among. . ." can stand alone as a title of status, but it would be quite unusual to find such a title between the offices held by an individual who was being honored. Appellations such as "first of the city" normally were placed at the end of a list of achievements,[53] and sometimes at the beginning,[54] but not in the middle of the offices. Since the phrase is found among offices in the Juliane inscription, it should be reconstructed as part of a larger unit and not as a separate title of honor.

The word πρώτην could be taken to mean temporal primacy (i.e., the first to do something), or it could simply indicate rank. Because "first" occurs in the title section and is not part of a title such as "first archon,"[55] it probably does not indicate rank. While temporal primacy can be rendered with the adverb πρώτως plus a participle as in the inscription about the cult for Gaius in Miletus,[56] the adjective πρῶτος can serve the same function. An inscription from Magnesia of the Augustan period that lists the victories of the athlete Demokrates uses this sort of construction in noting that he was the first person in the world to win the boxing competition at Olympia three times: [. . .π]υγμὴν πρῶτον τῶ[ν] ἀπὸ τῆς οἰ[κου]μένης Ὀλ[ύμ]πια τρίς.[57] The Metrobius inscription from Iasos similarly commemorates a world's record with the phrase νικήσας. . .πρῶτος ἀνθρώπων.[58]

All of this suggests that "the first among women to serve as highpriestess of Asia" is the best way to translate the Juliane inscription, but it does not prove the reconstruction beyond doubt. Confirmation of this reading comes from an independent source. The fortuitous title "priestess of Agrippina the mother" allows the inscription to be dated with a fair amount of precision, for a priesthood of Nero's mother Agrippina would only be possible between his acces-

---

[53] *IGR* 4.666 (Diokleia), 882 (Themisonion), 1226 (Thyatira).
[54] *IGR* 4.652 (Akmonia).
[55] *IGR* 4.702 (Synnada), 814 (Hierapolis).
[56] See above, p. 22 (l. 3).
[57] *IvMag* 149b l. 4.
[58] *IvI* 1.107.

sion in 54 CE and the time he had her assassinated (59 CE).[59] The
date of Juliane's provincial highpriesthood is not specified but it was
probably in the forties or fifties of the first century CE.[60] Thus,
when the forty-two attestations of provincial highpriestesses in Asia
are arranged chronologically, Juliane appears at the beginning of
the list as the first woman known to have held a provincial highpriesthood in Asia. Thus, the known dates of other highpriestesses
of Asia support the reconstructed text of the Juliane inscription.[61]

One can only speculate as to why the decision was made to include
women in the provincial highpriesthoods around the second quarter
of the first century CE, for the present state of research about
women's history in the province of Asia is not far enough advanced
to give us purchase on this problem. The existence of two provincial
cults increased the need for highpriestly candidates but this larger
need probably played little part in the decision. The archaeological
record does not indicate an abnormally high number of women in
the office in the last half of the first century CE, which is what one
would expect if the participation of women were due to a shortage
of male candidates. Another possibility is that the long-postponed
deification of Livia in 41 CE[62] occasioned the unprecedented appointment of a provincial highpriestess, since there seems to have

---

[59] The editor of the inscription in *IvMag* questioned the reading διὰ βίου in l. 9,
and the word ἱέρειαν in l. 8, but offered no alternatives. In spite of the lacunae, the
reference to Agrippina appears to be reliable.

[60] She was perhaps highpriestess of the cult in Smyrna (for Tiberius, Livia, and
the Senate). Smyrna is closer than Pergamum to the other locations known from
the geographical information about her activities: she was priestess for life of a
Demeter cult in Ephesus; and the inscription which mentions her provincial highpriesthood was found in Magnesia on the Meander (less than 20 kilometers
southeast of Ephesus). Furthermore, it is not clear whether a highpriestess of the
provincial cult of Rome and Augustus in Pergamum would have been referred to
as an *archiereia Asias* at this date.

[61] Magie (1950, 1.449) interpreted this inscription as a reference to the beginning of honorific highpriesthoods for women, even though there is no indication in
the text itself that an honorific title is involved. Kearsley took the participle as an
indication that Juliane served as highpriestess of Asia before her husband was highpriest of Asia ("Asiarchs," 190-91), rather than as a part of the phrase meaning
"who was first among women. . . ." Kearsley's interpretation, however, does not
explain the significance of the phrase [πρ]ώτην τῶ[ν γυναικῶν] in line 6, which was
replaced by κτλ. in text of the inscription given in her article.

[62] Livia, wife of Augustus, died in 29, but her son Tiberius was not anxious to
promote her deification. The emperor Claudius, her grandson (through Drusus
rather than through Tiberius), finally saw that she was enrolled among the gods.

been a larger percentage of priestesses and highpriestesses in the cults dedicated to women of the imperial house.

Whatever the reason may have been, it is clear that a significant development took place in the second quarter of the first century CE. A previously all-male provincial highpriesthood of the emperors became accessible to women, perhaps for the first time in any Roman province.

Responsibilities of the Highpriesthood

What did provincial highpriests and highpriestesses do? Deininger's study of provincial councils in the Imperial period includes the most detailed examination of the organization of the koinon of Asia and his opinion has formed the basis of much that is written about provincial highpriesthoods.[63] He wrote, "The ἀρχιερεύς appears in all official documents of the koinon during the first century [CE] as its spokesman (*Wortführer*) and chairman (*Vorsitzender*)."[64] Deininger also cited the example of all the other provincial councils as support for the leading role of the highpriest,[65] but the reader searches in vain for one clear reference to a council being led by a highpriest. No one has systematically argued this point. In place of an argument, the frequent occurrence of this official in the documents related to Asia's koinon is cited as an indication that he was obviously the koinon's leading official.

Do the koinon documents of the early Imperial period support the view that the highpriest was the highest official in the koinon? The highpriest of Rome and Augustus appears most often in the role of the one who proposed honorary decrees for individuals.[66] This nor-

---

[63] See, for example, Fergus Millar, *The Emperor and the Roman World (31 BC– AD 337)* (Ithaca, N. Y.: Cornell University Press, 1977) 387.

[64] Deininger 1965, 18: "Der ἀρχιερεύς erscheint in allen amtlichen Dokumenten des Koinon während des 1. Jahrhunderts als sein Wortführer und Vorsitzender." (My translation). Buckler's article (above, p. 79, n. 16) is listed in Deininger's n. 5 as support for this idea, but the article does not deal with this issue. In fact, Deininger assumes that all the provincial councils were organized in this way and then uses this assumption to fill in the information which is missing for so many of the councils (see his comments on Bithynia [60-61], Kappadokia [82], Kilikia [83], or Krete [84-85]). The assumption that all or most of the councils were organized in a uniform manner is itself difficult to maintain (ibid., 69-73 [Lycia]).

[65] Deininger 1965, 38.

[66] For example, *IvPr* 105; *IvE* 7,2.3825 (Hypaipa).

mally followed the formulaic opening statement that the inscription contained a decision of the Greeks in Asia.[67] The highpriest was also instructed in some cases to have these decisions inscribed in marble and displayed in certain places.[68] Other instances are known where the highpriest was the author of correspondence from the koinon to a city.[69]

These examples show that the highpriest of Rome and Augustus was normally an important member of the koinon. They do not, however, show that this highpriest was the highest official in the koinon. The prominence of the highpriest in these inscriptions could simply indicate that this λειτουργία included the responsibility of paying for inscribed documents of the koinon that were normally set up in the precincts of imperial cult temples.

The history of the provincial koinon does not require that the highest office be that of a highpriest. The koinon of Asia was functioning already in the late Republican period with no mention of a highpriest or sacerdotal office.[70] Other offices of the koinon are attested in the Imperial period. Why should the highpriest of Rome and Augustus be considered to have had the premier position in a list of other offices that included lawyers (ἔκδικος, συνδικήσας), financial overseers (ἀργυροταμίας τῆς Ἀσίας, οἰκονόμος Ἀσίας), and a secretary (γραμματεύς)?[71]

A further problem with the attempt to make the highpriest of Rome and Augustus into the head of the koinon is that such interpretations do not take into account the growing number of provincial highpriesthoods in the first and second centuries CE. When there was more than one highpriesthood in Asia, who would have been in charge of the koinon? If the highpriest of Rome and Augustus was actually the chairman of the koinon, then one would expect some distinction to be made between his office and the other highpriesthoods. We have already seen, though, that the opposite is true. As the ranks of ἀπχιερεῖς Ἀσίας swelled, the highpriesthood of Rome and Augustus came to be viewed as one of several provincial highpriesthoods, all designated simply "of Asia."

---

[67] Ἔδοξεν τοῖς ἐπὶ τῆς Ἀσίας Ἕλλησιν.

[68] See *IBM* 894 (Halikarnassos).

[69] *Sardis* 7.8 VII and VIII.

[70] Deininger 1965, 16.

[71] For bibliography, see below, p. 103, and Deininger 1965, 50-51, including notes.

Finally, the theory that the highpriest of the first provincial cult in Pergamum was also the leader of the koinon collapses under the weight of the evidence regarding provincial highpriestesses. The numerous koinon inscriptions name only men, indicating that women did not normally participate in the provincial council.[72] Yet a significant number of the individuals known to have held provincial highpriesthoods in Asia were women (about 20%), and some of them were highpriestesses of the provincial cults in Pergamum.[73] The existence of highpriestesses in this cult means that it was highly unlikely for this highpriesthood to have been the top position in the koinon.

It is to be expected that provincial highpriests also played a significant role in the koinon, but the reason for this was not the highpriesthood itself. The same families whose members could afford to serve in provincial highpriesthoods were also prominent families in the political life of the province.

It is possible that the role of the provincial highpriesthood changed with respect to the koinon, and there are three pieces of evidence that suggest this. First, the highpriest of Rome and Augustus is more prominent in the extant koinon documents dated before the provincial cult was established in Smyrna in 26 CE than in the koinon documents after 26 CE. There is too little evidence from the later period, however, to reach a firm conclusion about this.[74] Nevertheless, it is certain that after 26 CE there were two annual provincial highpriesthoods and this would have required some definition, if not a reorganization, of the highpriesthood of Rome and Augustus.

The other two pieces of evidence are the developments that occurred during the second half of the first century CE which are outlined above. During this period, the title "highpriest of Asia" appeared and women began to serve in the provincial highpriesthoods. It may be that the initiation of a second provincial cult led

---

[72] It would be unconvincing to argue that the existence of provincial highpriestesses proves that women served in the koinon. The many known documents of the koinon do not mention any women participants, and it cannot be assumed that a highpriest or highpriestess was a part of the koinon.

[73] E.g., *MAMA* 6.373; *IGR* 4.908.

[74] A decree of the koinon under Claudius from Hypaipa might include a proposal of a highpriest of Asia but the reference is partially restored (*IvE* 7,2.3801 II). One Hadrianic decree might be restored to record a proposal by the highpriest of Rome and Augustus (*IGR* 4.1410; see Buckler, "Auguste," 181).

to a reorganization within the koinon that allowed women to hold provincial highpriesthoods and that changed the relationship of the provincial highpriesthood to the koinon. While there is not enough evidence to prove that such a reorganization occurred, the convergence of these three developments—multiple provincial cults, provincial highpriestesses, and the new title "highpriest(ess) of Asia"—suggest that significant changes in the definition of Asia's highpriestly offices took place between 26 and 50 CE.

For the most part, the responsibilities of the highpriesthoods of Asia seem to have been more strictly cultic than governmental. This is born out by a difference between the provincial highpriesthoods and the highpriesthoods associated with other cults. While other cults with highpriesthoods also had priests or priestesses,[75] there are no known "priests/priestesses of Asia." Since the highpriests and highpriestesses were the only sacerdotal offices connected with the provincial cult, it is most likely that they personally performed the sacrifices of the cult.

The absence of other priestly offices in the provincial cults also suggests that cultic activity was relatively infrequent in comparison to other cults, for one official could complete the tasks. Wealthy individuals, who sometimes lived elsewhere, fulfilled their responsibilities for a year by paying certain expenses and by performing cultic acts at major festivals, perhaps only once during a term of office.

Asiarchs

According to Liddell and Scott's *Greek-English Lexicon*, an Asiarch was a "priest of the Imperial cult in the province of Asia."[76] Along with several inscriptions, three literary texts are cited—Strabo 14.1.42, Acts 19:31, and *Dig.* 27.1.6.14—that do not suggest any connection between Asiarchs and imperial cult priesthoods. LSJ cannot be faulted for its definition, though; the incorrect identification of Asiarchs with provincial highpriests permeates the secondary literature on the topic.[77] Nearly every article or book that discusses

---

[75] For the Dionysos cult, see *MAMA* 3.454 (Aphrodisias); for Aphrodite, *MAMA* 3.514 (Aphrodisias).

[76] Henry George Liddell, Robert Scott, *A Greek-English Lexicon* rev. by Henry Stuart Jones (9th ed.; Oxford: Clarendon, 1940) 256. *Dig.* 27.1.6.14 is also cited as an example of the use of ἀσιάρχης. This reference is discussed below, p. 93-97.

[77] The use of "highpriest" and male language in this section is intentional; no one has suggested that highpriestesses were called Asiarchs. See below, p. 110-11.

Asiarchs mentions the literary sources, so these three texts will provide a starting point for an examination of the nature of the Asiarchate. A review of the archaeological evidence will follow, and then scholarly interpretations of the office will be evaluated.

In his *Geography*,[78] Strabo wrote that the city of Tralles always had as many wealthy people as any other city in Asia.

> Καὶ ἀεί τινες ἐξ αὐτῆς εἰσὶν οἱ πρωτεύοντες κατὰ τὴν ἐπαρχίαν, οὓς Ἀσιάρχας καλοῦσιν.

> Always certain ones from there [i.e., from Tralles] are leaders in the province, whom they call Asiarchs.

He then went on to name one Asiarch, a certain Pythodoros, who was a prominent supporter of Pompey and whose daughter Pythodoris became the queen of Pontus.

Strabo's portrayal of Asiarchs is brief and does not go into detail. It is clear that those who held the office were wealthy. The description of Pythodoros's political activities suggests a connection with governmental affairs, both regional and international. Strabo did not clarify if the political activities of Pythodoros were directly related to the Asiarchate nor did he connect the office with any sort of priesthood.

Asiarchs are mentioned in Acts 19:31, but once again the text does not clarify the nature of the Asiarchate. The text portrays several Asiarchs in the city of Ephesus at one time who seem to be influential in city affairs, and who are friends of the apostle Paul. Again, there is no implication that Asiarchs were responsible for sacerdotal or imperial cult activities.

The third literary reference to Asiarchs—a third century text incorporated into a sixth century text—has been the most influential factor in the creation of the theory that identifies Asiarchs with provincial highpriests.[79] In *Dig.* 27.1.6.14, the subject is guardianship of minors and the third century CE author Modestinus was quoted as having said,

---

[78] *Geog.* 14.1.42.

[79] I. Marquardt ("De provinciarum romanarum conciliis et sacerdotibus," *Ephemeris Epigraphica* 1 (1872) 210-11) is just one example. Nearly every writer on the topic deals with this text.

Ἔθνους ἱερωσύνη, οἷον ᾿Ασιαρχία, Βιθυνιαρχία, Καππαδοκαρχία,
παρέχει ἀλειτουργησίαν ἀπὸ ἐπιτροπῶν, τοῦτ᾿ ἔστιν ἕως ἂν ἄρχῃ.[80]

A priesthood of an ethnic group, such as the Asiarchate, Bithyniarchate, and the Kappadokiarchate, is free of public responsibilities for
guardianships, that is, while serving in office.

Those scholars who have rejected the equation of Asiarchs and
provincial highpriests have made various suggestions about the significance of this text. Brandis argued that an inaccurate interpolation into Modestinus's text accounted for this description of
Asiarchs as priests, basing his arguments on the supposition that no
definition of an Asiarch would have been necessary in the third century, and on the geographically restricted list of examples (Asia,
Bithynia, Kappadokia).[81] Magie is one of the few scholars to accept
Brandis's interpolation theory,[82] but Deininger successfully mar-
shalled the counterarguments.[83]

Kearsley accepted Modestinus's remark as authentic, but concluded that Modestinus was referring to magistracies and not to
priesthoods. Her argument can be summarized as follows. First, she
observed that the use of οἷον and the naming of three offices from
different provinces probably was meant to include a range of officials. After noting that the same wealthy men tended to hold both
magistracies and priesthoods, she argued that Modestinus chose the
verb ἄρχω because it relates more often to magistrates than to
priests, which suggests that Modestinus thought of the Asiarchs as
magistrates. He used the term ἱερωσύνη because the same men often
held priesthoods as well.[84]

This argument falters on the fact that Modestinus was writing a
legal text. It is not convincing to suggest that a legal writer would
categorize the Asiarchate as a priesthood, but use the verb ἄρχω because he actually considered Asiarchs to be governmental officials.
In such a text, precise usage must be assumed.

---

[80] Th. Mommsen, *Digesta Iustiniani Augusti* (Berlin: Weidmann, 1870) 1.783-
84, with the widely-accepted reading of ἱερωσύνη for Mommsen's ἱεραρχία. See
Deininger 1965, 44 n. 5; Magie 1950, 2:1299 n. 61.

[81] Brandis, "Asiarches," *PW* 2 (1896) 1574-76.

[82] Magie 1950, 2.1299 n. 61.

[83] Deininger 1965, 44-46.

[84] R. A. Kearsley, "M. Ulpius Appuleius Eurykles of Aezani: Panhellene,
Asiarch and Archiereus of Asia," *Antichthon* 21 (1987) 55 n. 40.

Furthermore, Kearsley's distinction between "magisterial power" and "sacred officials" is not a helpful conceptual model for illuminating this text.[85] Municipal officials normally participated in cultic activities in the course of their "political" responsibilities, and a priesthood could be called an ἀρχή.[86] The difference between a priest and a magistrate was not that one dealt with sacred activities and the other with political matters. The duties of a priest were defined primarily in terms of sacrificial activities. A magistrate might perform sacrifices but that was not his primary duty.

The specific terminology Modestinus used in 27.1.6.14 demonstrates that the jurist did not equate the Asiarchate with the provincial highpriesthood. Rather than the technical term ἀρχιερεύς of a province, Modestinus chose the unparalleled ἔθνους ἱερωσύνη, "priesthood of an ethnic group." The absence of the term ἀρχιερωσύνη is deliberate, for Modestinus's subject was not provincial highpriesthoods. The term "province" (ἐπαρχία) was not used by the jurist either.

An examination of the larger context in *Dig.* 27.1.6 helps clarify the reference to priesthoods of ethnic groups and confirms that Modestinus did not consider the Asiarchs to be provincial highpriests of an imperial cult. The following text appears a bit earlier in the *Digest*, in which Modestinus quoted a decree of Commodus that contained material from a letter of Antoninus Pius about exemptions for certain professions.

Φιλοσόφους, ῥήτορας, γραμματικούς, ἰατροὺς ἀτελεῖς εἶναι γυμνασιαρχιῶν, ἀγορανομιῶν, ἱερωσυνῶν, ἐπισταθμιῶν, σιτωνίας, ἐλαιωνίας, καὶ μήγε κρίνειν μήτε πρεσβεύειν μήτε εἰς στρατείαν καταλέγεσθαι ἄκοντας μήτε εἰς ἄλλην αὐτοὺς ὑπηρεσίαν ἐθνικὴν ἤ τινα ἄλλην ἀναγκάζεσθαι. Ἔτι κἀκεῖνο εἰδέναι χρή, ὅτι ὁ ἐν τῇ ἰδίᾳ πατρίδι διδάσκων ἤ θεραπεύων τὴν ἀλειτουργησίαν ταύτην ἔχει· ἐὰν γὰρ Κομανεὺς ὤν ἐν Νεοκαισαρείᾳ σοφιστεύῃ ἤ θεραπεύῃ ἤ διδάσκῃ, παρὰ Κομανεῦσιν ἀλειτουργησίαν οὐκ ἔχει.[87]

Philosophers, rhetors, grammarians, (and) doctors are exempt from gymnasiarchates, offices of agoronomos, priesthoods, billeting, and governmental wheat purchases and oil purchases. (They) do not judge nor serve as presbyters, nor are they enrolled involuntarily in a military campaign nor in any other ethnic service, nor forced to any other

---

[85] Kearsley 1987a, 55 n. 40.
[86] *IGR* 4.456 (Pergamum), 470 (Pergamum), 1523 (Sardis).
[87] *Dig.* 27.1.6.8-9.

(responsibility). Moreover, it is still necessary to know that anyone teaching or healing in their native city has that *aleitourgesia*; for if someone who is a native of Komana is a sophist, heals or teaches in Neocaesarea, that person does not have *aleitourgesia* from Komana.

The adjective ἐθνικός occurs in this text in the phrase "ethnic service" as a general description of a long list of municipal *leitourgiai*. These were clearly not provincial offices. Thus, the description of the Asiarchate and similarly-titled offices in other provinces as "priesthoods of an ethnic group" in 27.1.6.14 should be understood as a general term for certain municipal offices.

The reference to Asiarchs in 27.1.6.14 came in the context of a discussion of ἀλειτουργησία, or exemption, from guardianships. The next sentence after the Asiarch reference specifies that guardianships were not a governmental matter nor were they administered by the province because citizens were to arrange and fund these guardianships.[88] The implication is that citizens were granted ἀλειτουργησία from this municipal service if they performed another municipal service like the Asiarchate.

This kind of exemption for other services rendered to a particular city was explicitly described in 27.1.6.9 (quoted above). A sophist, doctor, priest, administrator, or teacher receives *aleitourgesia* only in the city where he or she practices. Thus, *aleitourgesia* was a way of preventing a situation in which one wealthy citizen was forced to take on a number of municipal duties at the same time. In the case of Asiarchs, freedom from a citizen's duty to undertake guardianships for the good of the city was granted when the duties of the Asiarchate were carried out for the good of that city.

In its context, then, the term "priesthood of an ethnic group" for the Asiarchate, Bithyniarchate, Kappakokiarchate, and others, becomes more understandable. This title covered a range of municipal duties which lasted for a specific period and were defined primarily by the city or region in which they were found. As such, they probably varied quite a bit, not only among the cities but also among the provinces. The common element, according to Modestinus, was the priestly element. There is no suggestion in

---

[88] *Dig.* 27.1.6.15: *Tutela non est rei publicae munus nec quod ad impensam pertinet, sed civile: nec provinciale videtur tutelam administrare.* This is probably from a Latin copy of Modestinus that was incorporated in the Justinianic compilation.

the text of any connection to imperial cults, much less to those of the provinces.[89]

Such is the literary evidence for the Asiarchate. If a more precise understanding of the responsibilities associated with this title is to be found, it will come from the epigraphic and numismatic material.

There are approximately 280 references to Asiarchs in the published coins and inscriptions related to Asia, and this provides quite a bit of information about the office. The first observation to be made is that a great deal of diversity exists in the actual wording of the title "Asiarch." Appendix 1 demonstrates that 253 of the references to this office (about 90%) use the simple title Asiarch without further description. The title appears 19 times as "Asiarch of the temple(s)" or "Asiarch of the temple(s) in…",[90] and two occurrences read "Asiarch of Asia of the temples in Ephesus."[91] Since the phrase "of the temple(s) in…" is a technical designation for provincial temples,[92] at least 21 references overtly connect Asiarchs with the provincial cult of the emperors in Asia. The title "Asiarch of Asia"[93] for a member of the Vedian family from Ephesus is perhaps an abbreviation of the "Asiarch of the temples" title, which would yield 22 direct references to provincial cults (between 7 and 8% of the total Asiarch references).

"Asiarch of Asia," however, may constitute a deliberate attempt to distinguish this man's service from that of someone like Aurelius

---

[89] A scholion from the corresponding section of the *Basilica* has also been brought into the discussion of the Asiarchate; Brandis, *PW* 2 (1896) 1575. This section asserts that Asiarchs were priests of the province: οἱ ἱερεῖς τῶν ἐπαρχιῶν τοῦτ' ἔστιν ἀσιάρχαι καὶ οἱ λοιποί. (Note that the technical term ἀρχιερεῖς is not used. The office of a priest of the province is unattested for Asia, except perhaps in Aristides' *Or.* 50.101 where he recorded an offer of ἱερωσύνην κοινὴν τῆς Ἀσίας, "the common priesthood of Asia.") The *Basilica*, however, is a paraphrase of the *Dig.* and is directly dependent on the latter for its information. Furthermore, the *Basilica*, a ninth century production, is much too late to be taken at face value (Wolfgang Waldstein, *Römische Rechtsgeschichte* [7th ed. of the work begun by Gerhard Dulckeit and Fritz Schwarz; Munich: Beck, 1981] 289; Max Kaser, *Römische Rechtsgeschichte* [Göttingen: Vandenhoeck & Ruprecht, 1978] 272). Or shall we also consider the opinion of Constantine VII Porphyrogenitus (*de themat.* 3.2) from the tenth century that Asiarchs were proconsuls?

[90] It is probably correct to reconstruct the title in *IvE* 3.653 and 687 as well, yielding 23 occurences.

[91] *IvE* 3.692 (cf. IvE 4.1130) and 897.

[92] See above, p. 77-79.

[93] *IvE* 7,2.4110.

Demetrios, who was called "Asiarch of (his) native city" (ἀσιάρχης τῆς πατρίδος),[94] or someone like Julius Dionysios who was "Asiarch of the Pergamenes."[95] Two other titles—"Asiarch of the prytanis"[96] and "Asiarch of the secretariate"[97]—appear to refer to specific responsibilities that were not necessarily a part of every Asiarch's duty. Thus, it seems that the title Asiarch could encompass various sorts of functions in several different institutions.

Another activity in which Asiarchs were prominent was the staging of public spectacles. One Asiarch is known to have sponsored animal fights,[98] but they are more often linked directly to gladiatorial contests.[99] The inscriptions set up by "families" of gladiators in honor of Asiarchs may have been occasioned by support for games, or they may indicate that these Asiarchs financed such groups.[100] Since these inscriptions do not refer to other offices, but only to the Asiarchate of the individual, it is likely that in such instances their support for the gladiators was a part of their Asiarchate.

The many references to Asiarchs on municipal coins suggest that Asiarchs sometimes supplied funding for cities to mint coins,[101] for eighty-four of the Asiarch attestations (about 30% of all references) are on municipal coins.[102] The known coins are no earlier than the reign of Antoninus Pius (138-161 CE) and include no references to Asiarchs of temples. The only deviation in the numismatic evidence from the simple title "Asiarch" is the reference to Aur. Demetrios as the "Asiarch of (his) native city," and the occasional attribution of multiple terms of service to one man.[103] Since about 8% of the total Asiarch references mention provincial temples, one would expect 6 or 7 references to provincial temples on the known coins if

---

[94] *CollWadd* 6505.

[95] *IGR* 4.1247.

[96] [ἀσιάρ]χου τοῦ πρυτανέως, *IvE* 7,2.4109.

[97] ἀσιάρ[χου γραμματ]είας, *IvE* 7,1.3001 (2).

[98] Philippos of Tralles, *Mart. Poly.* 12:2.

[99] Menekles Diophantes sponsored gladiator games, *IvSm* 2,1.637.

[100] Tatianus (*IvE* 4.1182; 5.1620); Timon (*IGR* 4.1454 [Smyrna]); Pankratides (*IvE* 7,2.4346); Reginus (*IvE* 5.1621). Both the Asiarch and his wife are honored in *IGR* 4.156 (Kyzikos) and *IGR* 4.1075 (Kos).

[101] Magie 1950, 1.450.

[102] There is also one koinon coin as well as four from the Ionian League of 13 Cities that mention Asiarchs.

[103] *CollWadd* 6505. Three coins name men who were twice Asiarch, and one coin mentions a man who was three-times Asiarch.

the distribution were the same. The differential between the inscriptional and numismatic references probably reflects different responsibilities for the Asiarchs attested epigraphically and those attested on coins.

The Modestinus text in *Dig.* 27.1.6.14 stated that the Asiarchate entailed responsibilities for a fixed amount of time. This is confirmed by the archaeological evidence, for some inscriptions and coins use the office as a way to record the date of the respective object,[104] and many individuals are known to have been Asiarchs more than one time. The length of the term is not known, though. In view of the wide range of functions an Asiarch might play, it is probably best to assume that there was no single, fixed amount of time that applied to all terms of office. Thus, a coin dated by the office of an Asiarch may indicate a longer term of service, while an inscription like *IvSm* 2,1.638 implies that Julius Menokles Diophantes was an Asiarch for five days while he sponsored gladiatorial battles.[105]

Nearly all recent scholarly discussions of the office of Asiarch have agreed with the conclusion that "Asiarch" was simply a different title for the office of the provincial highpriest.[106] The following review of their arguments demonstrates that the identification of the two titles is an incorrect scholarly tradition that pays too little heed to the extant data, and minimizes the distinctions between the provinces of the empire.[107]

---

[104] This is clearly indicated in some inscriptions. For example, *IvE* 4.1130 l.7 dates the inscription to the time when M. Fl. Rufus was serving as Asiarch (ἐπὶ M. Φλ. Ῥούφ[ου] ἀσιάρχου).

[105] *IvE* 7,1.3070 is a similar inscription in which an Asiarch is honored for staging thirteen days of fights with "Libyan animals." It is not certain whether these spectacles were staged as the responsibility of the Asiarchate, or whether the man who held the games happened to have been an Asiarch at some time.

[106] One of the most important early works to identify the two offices was I. Marquardt, "De provinciarum romanarum conciliis et sacerdotibus," *Ephemeris Epigraphica* 1 (1872) 208-14. Ramsay agreed ("The Province of Asia," *ClRev* 3 [1889] 175), as did Beurlier (*Essai sur le culte rend aux empereurs romains* [Paris: Ernest Thorin, 1890] 131-34), Mommsen (*ÖJh* 3 [1900] 8), Deininger, (1965, 41-50), Bowersock (*Augustus and the Greek World* [Oxford: Clarendon, 1965] 117), Rossner ("Asiarchen," 102-7), Millar (*The Emperor and the Roman World* [Ithaca, N. Y.: Cornell University Press, 1977), and R. Merkelbach ("Der Rangstreit der Städte Asiens und die Rede des Aelius Aristides über die Eintracht," *ZPE* 32 [1978] 287-96).

[107] See J. A. O. Larsen , *Representative Government in Greek and Roman History* (Berkeley and Los Angeles: University of California Press, 1955) 118-19, for an

The arguments of the scholars who identify the Asiarchs and the provincial highpriests can be summarized under six headings. The first argument is that several men are known to have held both titles, Asiarch and provincial highpriest. The actual number of men in this category is approximately 15, but the fact that they held both titles indicates only that they were from the small wealthy sector of society in Asia that could afford such offices.[108]

Of the men who held both titles, there are only three individuals whose titles have had a significant effect on the argument. In particular, the discussion has focused on Tiberius Julius Reginus[109] because he was called both ἀρχιερεύς β ναῶν τῶν ἐν Ἐφέσῳ[110] and ἀσιάρχης β ναῶν τῶν ἐν Ἐφέσῳ[111] in the last half of the second century CE. This example was crucial evidence for Taylor and Deininger, for it seemed impossible to them that one man would happen to hold both offices with such similar titles twice.[112] Such reasoning is hardly convincing, though. There are other examples in the archaeological record of individuals holding different offices the same number of times.[113]

The comments of Taylor and Deininger exemplify the sort of superficial observation which has hampered the debate for so long.

---

example of these tendencies. There is less evidence for these types of offices in other provinces than in Asia, and so they are not of much help in understanding the nature of the Asiarchate. Furthermore, the extant evidence suggests that each area with such an office defined it in its own way. Even Deininger (1965, 69-73) recognized that the Lycian koinon had its own historical development that resulted in particular organizational structures and offices, and warns against facile comparisons with other areas. Another indication of province-specific peculiarities is the fact that Asia had a male dominated Asiarchate, while both Macedonia and Lycia had special terms for the Μακεδονιάρχισσα and the Λυκιάρχισσα (Deininger 1965, 76).

[108] Magie (1950, 2:1300-1301 n. 61) pointed out that the small number of men known by both titles can be used as an argument against the identification of the two offices. If the titles had been interchangeable, one would expect a larger number of men known to have held both titles.

[109] E.g., Beurlier 1890, 131.

[110] "Twice highpriest of the temples in Ephesus;" IvE 5.1605; 1611.

[111] "Twice Asiarch of the temples in Ephesus," IvE 4.1130. See also IvE 4.1105a (β ἀαιάρχου ναῶν τῶν ἐν Ἐφέσῳ); and IvE 3.692 (δὶς ἀσιάρχην τῆς Ἀσίας ναῶν τῶν ἐν Ἐφέσῳ).

[112] Lily Ross Taylor, "The Asiarchs," in F. J. Foakes Jackson and Kirsopp Lake, eds., The Beginnings of Christianity, part 1: The Acts of the Apostles (London: Macmillan, 1933) 258; Deininger 1965, 44.

[113] In IGR 4.907 (text below in n. 177, p. 112), Tiberius Claudius Hiero is shown to have served twice as Asiarch and twice as a municipal highpriest.

If a title is viewed as part of a text, rather than detached from its context, a different picture emerges. One of the inscriptions that calls Reginus "twice Asiarch" makes a clear distinction between the two offices, for Reginus is listed as δὶς ἀσιάρχην in l. 10 while his father, Tiberius Claudius Melito, is called ἀρχιερέως τῆς 'Ασίας in line 9.[114] If the two titles referred to the same office, there would be no reason to use different appellations for a son and his father in successive lines of the same honorary inscription. The example of Reginus supports a distinction between the two offices.

The second alleged example in the identification argument is Gaius Julius Philippos.[115] He is known as a provincial highpriest[116] and Asiarch[117] from inscriptions, and is perhaps to be identified with the Philip of Tralles who is called an Asiarch in the *Martyrdom of Polycarp* 12 and a highpriest (not necessarily provincial) in chapter 21.[118] If these all refer to the same person, they still do not indicate an identity of office. In fact, at least one of the inscriptions again makes a distinction by naming him as an Asiarch but mentioning his father as a highpriest of Asia.[119] The literary references to Philip further distinguish the offices. In the *Mart. Poly.* 12:2, Philip the Asiarch is mentioned because, as Asiarch, he was responsible for games involving animal fights. In chap. 21, a highpriesthood is mentioned because an eponymous official was needed for dating the martyrdom. The functions are quite different and there is no reason to equate them. Furthermore, chap. 21 cannot be assumed to contain reliable historical information about the second century CE because it is a later, hagiographical interpolation into the text of *Mart. Poly.*, introduced into the text in order to date the martyrdom for the church calendar.[120]

---

114 *IvE* 3.692. *IGR* 4.12, (Thyatira) provides a similar example. In this inscription, the local breadbakers honored the Asiarch and local highpriest Gaius Julius Julianos Tatianos (l. 2-6) and mentioned that his mother and father had served in highpriesthoods of Asia. (l. 12-14).

115 E.g., Marquardt 1872, 211, whom Guiraud (1887, 98) followed.

116 *AthMitt* 26 (1901) 239 #3; Sterrett 1883-84, 100 #6; *BCH* 29 (1905) 361.

117 Sterrett 1883-84, 325 #375; *OGIS* #498 (Olympia).

118 Note, however, Louis Robert's opposition to the identification in "Étude d'epigraphie grecque," *RevPhil* 56 (1930) 34 n. 4.

119 Sterrett 1883-84, 325 #375.

120 Hans Frhr. von Campenhausen, "Bearbeitungen und Interpolationen des Polykarpmartyriums," *Sitzungsberichte der Heidelberger Akademie der Wissenschaften. Philosophisch-Historische Klasse* 1957, no. 3:31.

Quass, among others, cited a third individual, Tiberius Claudius Aristio of Ephesus, as another example of a man whose "similarity of titles" suggests that "provincial highpriest" and "Asiarch" designated the same office.[121] At least three inscriptions indicate that Aristio was an Asiarch three times,[122] but the references to three provincial highpriesthoods comes from the restoration of a very fragmentary inscription.[123] The restoration may be correct, but it is meager support for a theory identifying Asiarchs and provincial highpriests. None of the 19 Ephesian inscriptions that mention Aristio call him twice highpriest of Asia, and both references to a third highpriesthood are in restored lacunae.[124] All we know for certain about Aristio is that he served three times as an Asiarch and at least one term as a provincial highpriest.[125]

A second kind of argument used to identify "Asiarch" with "highpriest of Asia" is related to the first. Rossner[126] and others claimed that since both Asiarchs and provincial highpriests sometimes have the phrase τῆς ᾽Ασίας ("of Asia") and/or ναῶν τῶν ἐν κτλ. ("of the temples in . . ."), they most likely refer to the same

---

[121] F. Quass, "Zur politischen Tätigkeit der munizipalen Aristokratie des griechischen Ostens," *Historia* 31 (1982) 193 n. 56.

[122] *IvE* 2.424; 7,2.5101; 5113 l. 23.

[123] [Τι. Κλ. ᾽Αρ]ιστίω[να]
       [τὸν τ]ρὶ[ς] ἀρχ[ι]ερέα [τῆς ᾽Ασίας]
       [. . . .]ελ[   ]
       ρ[   ]
       [. .]ου [. .]ο[   ]
       [πρύτ]ανι[ν κ]αὶ νε[ωκόρον] κτλ.

IvE 2.425 l. 1-6 (*Addenda et corrigenda*). The title has been completely restored in a larger lacuna in *IvE* 2.425a, l. 4: [ ]Κλ. ᾽Αριστίω[ν τρὶς ἀρχιερεὺς ᾽Α]σίας[ ].

[124] Rosalinde Kearsley ("14. Some asiarchs from Ephesos," in G. H. R. Horsley [ed.], *New Documents Illustrating Early Christianity* [Macquarie University: Ancient History Documentary Research Centre, 1987] 53-54) argued that the traditional conclusion (Asiarch = provincial highpriest) is contradicted by the example of Aristio. For if the two titles had referred to the same kind of office, the extant inscriptions would record four terms of office (two dated Asiarch references and two separate highpriesthoods) by the time of Trajanic inscriptions calling Aristio "three-times Asiarch." Therefore, she concluded that the two titles must refer to two kinds of service. This would be a convincing argument, except that Kearsley counted one highpriesthood twice. The two references (*IvE* 2.234 and 235) name two different proconsuls and so Kearsley separated them as two highpriesthoods. However, the two references come from Aristio's one datable highpriesthood that overlapped the tenure of two proconsuls (see above, p. 44; and the chart on p. 46-47). Thus, the Asiarch and highpriesthood references in her hypothetical scenario could total three in Trajan's reign.

[125] *IvE* 2.234, 235, 239.

[126] Rossner 1974, 102-3.

office. Such reasoning, however, is without foundation unless one assumes beforehand that the offices are identical. There are other offices in the province of Asia with these phrases in them, such as γραμματεὺς τῆς ᾽Ασίας ναῶν τῶν ἐν ᾽Εφέσῳ ("secretary of Asia of the temples in Ephesus"),[127] ἀργυροταμίας τῆς ᾽Ασίας ("treasurer of Asia"),[128] or οἰκονόμος ᾽Ασίας ("financial administrator of Asia").[129] No one has ever argued that these offices are identical with the highpriesthood of Asia because the meanings of the terms γραμματεύς, ἀργυροταμίας, and οἰκονόμος are better understood than that of ἀσιάρχης. These examples show, however, that the designations "of Asia" or "of the temples in. . ." were present in several titles and cannot be used to establish equivalence of separate titles.[130]

Rossner employed a third line of argument used to identify the two titles when she maintained that the functions associated with the two titles are too similar to designate different offices.[131] Specifically, the association of these titles with animal fights and gladiator contests was cited. The actual evidence, however, reveals little similarity of function. Robert has documented the important role that Asiarchs, priests and highpriests played in the staging of such contests, but his view that Asiarchs were provincial highpriests prevented him from examining the differences.[132] One highpriest of Asia is mentioned as having sponsored animal fights[133] and only two more are recorded as the benefactors of gladiatorial spectacles.[134] It was observed above, however, that Asiarchs are much more often associated with gladiators;[135] in this they are distinguishable from provincial highpriests.

---

[127] *IvE* 7,1.3080. 7,1.3040 mentions a secretary of Asia without reference to temples, and *IGR* 4.821 and 822 (Hierapolis) refer to a secretary of the temples in Asia.

[128] *CIG* 2782.

[129] *IGR* 4.1474 (Smyrna).

[130] Brandis (1896b, 1577-78) was correct in so far as he distinguished Asiarchs of the temples and highpriests of the temples, but his view that Asiarchs were representatives to the koinon detracted from this argument.

[131] E.g., Rossner 1974, 103-5.

[132] Louis Robert, *Les gladiateurs dans l'Orient grec* (Paris: Edouard Champion, 1940) 270-75.

[133] M. Aurelius Mindius Mattidianus Pollio: *IvE* 3.627, on the basis of which the lacunae of *IvE* 7,1.3056 are restored.

[134] Tiberius Flavius Montanus: *IvE* 6.2061 (II); and, Marcus Aurelius Diadochos: *IGR* 4.1230 (if Robert's interpretation of τοῖς ὄξεσιν in l. 10-11 is correct [1940, 219 and n. 1]).

[135] See above, p. 98.

Deininger gathered evidence for another similarity of function between Asiarchs and provincial highpriests. He argued that both had a sacerdotal function (i.e., in the imperial cult).[136] While this was clearly the case for highpriests of Asia, there is little evidence beyond Modestinus's general label that Asiarchs exercised any priestly function. Deininger's main argument that Asiarchs could have officiated in sacrificial rituals is the title "Asiarch of the temple" and its variants.[137] We have seen above, however, that the inclusion of a temple in a title does not necessarily indicate a sacerdotal office.[138]

In his attempt to show that Asiarchs were priestly officials, Deininger cited the "fact" that the wives of Asiarchs were sometimes called highpriestesses to prove that their Asiarch husbands were highpriests.[139] This takes us to the fourth kind of argument used to prove that Asiarchs were provincial highpriests. The reasoning is as follows. Since provincial highpriestesses were honorary officials married to highpriests, and since highpriestesses were in some cases named as wives of Asiarchs and in other cases as wives of highpriests, "Asiarch" and "provincial highpriest" must be different titles for the same office.

It was already observed above that there is no ancient evidence to suggest that provincial highpriestesses were anything but functioning officials. Another problem with this argument, as Kearsley has noted,[140] is that it is circular. One of the main rationales for the honorary highpriestess interpretation is that various highpriestesses were married to functionally equivalent officials: Asiarchs and highpriests.[141] But the honorary highpriestess interpretation is also taken as proof that Asiarchs and provincial highpriests were functionally equivalent.[142]

Rossner used a fifth kind of argument to show that Asiarch must have been another title for provincial highpriests. She pointed to the absence of any single piece of evidence in which someone is called both Asiarch and provincial highpriest as proof that the terms were

---

[136] Deininger 1965, 47.

[137] The other piece of evidence is *Dig.* 27.1.6.14, which is discussed above, p. 93-97.

[138] See p. 103.

[139] Deininger 1965, 47.

[140] Kearsley 1986, 183.

[141] E.g., Rossner 1974, 102.

[142] Taylor 1933, 259; Deininger 1965, 47.

redundant. There are about 15 men to whom both, titles are attributed, but the two titles never appear in the same coin or inscription. If the titles indicated distinct offices, according to this interpretation, surely some inscription or coin would have recorded someone as holding both offices.[143]

This fifth argument does not correctly understand the nature of Greek honorific inscriptions. Rossner refers to them as "inscriptions with an enumeration of all offices similar to a *cursus honorum*."[144] The structured nature of Roman equestrian and senatorial careers led to the kind of Latin inscription that listed an ascending series of offices known as a *cursus honorum*. The careers of the Greek provincial elite did not follow such a pattern. Rather, members of the provincial elite served a variety of offices that appear in different combinations in Greek honorific inscriptions.[145] The absence of a single inscription or coin that calls someone Asiarch and highpriest of Asia is simply a gap that is consistent with Greek municipal and provincial service in the Roman imperial provinces, and in accord with common practice in Greek inscriptions. It does not prove that the unrecorded titles are equivalent to those recorded.[146]

The final argument used to identify Asiarchs with provincial highpriests is a fourth century CE inscription (372-78 CE). This imperial rescript to the proconsul Festus that mentions Asiarchs was found in Latin and Greek copies in Ephesus.[147] The rescript pro-

---

[143] Rossner 1974, 104.

[144] "...Inschriften mit cursus-honorum-ähnlicher Aufzählung aller Ämter ..." Rossner 1974, 104.

[145] The difference between Greek provincial and imperial careers can be observed in a Greek "*cursus honorum*" like *IGR* 4.1213 (Thyatira; early third century CE). After an enumeration of his many positions in the imperial service, T. Ant. Cl. Alfenus Arignotus was listed as the son and descendent of highpriests of Asia, a provincial office. He held one municipal office in Kyzikos, but his own accomplishments do not include the provincial highpriesthood because he had moved beyond the provincial sphere of activity to a career in the service of the empire.

[146] The Library of Celsus in Ephesus provides a rare example of a *cursus honorum* in Asia in two copies, Latin and Greek; *IvE* 7,2.5102-03. The Asian mason was unfamiliar with the standard Latin pattern and used the accusative case (the Greek pattern) rather than the dative for the offices listed in Latin. The fact that the Greek translation is not slavish also contradicts Rossner's view of Greek honorific practice. Allusions to service during Domitian's reign are somewhat more elaborated, and one office in the Latin cursus—*XV viro s(acris) f(aciundis)*—is omitted in Greek. See Steven Friesen, "Ephesus A," *ARNTS* 2 (Philadelphia: Trinity, forthcoming).

[147] *IvE* 1a.43.

vides the imperial response to several proposals for revivifying the province's festivals. The main concern of the rescript is that the four large cities of fourth century Asia be able to sponsor provincial festivals. To this end, they are permitted to recruit from other cities Asiarchs or alytarchs, who are referred to earlier in the inscription as those wearing the crown of Asia.[148] Special mention is made in the inscription that such officials should not be allowed to abandon their responsibilities to their cities of origin if they gain renown in the *metropoleis*.

Rossner and the translator of the inscription for *IvE* interpret the "crown of Asia" reference to mean provincial highpriests.[149] This is not the conclusion to which this inscription leads, though. Crowns were not only a sacerdotal symbol. They were also votive offerings to deities, prizes for competitions, or honors for benefactors.[150] Moreover, no one who equates Asiarchs with imperial priests has addressed the question of the status of cults of the emperors in the last half of the fourth century CE. There is nothing about this text that would suggest a sacerdotal function for Asiarchs. Rather, the text indicates that Asiarchs sponsored festivals, and that cities were dependent on their gifts and services.

The attempt to equate Asiarchs and provincial highpriests creates a scenario otherwise unknown in the Graeco-Roman world: two distinct and unrelated titles for the same prominent, provincial office. In order to explain this anomaly, scholars like Deininger have resorted to a historical reconstruction that is both implausible and inaccurate.[151] His explanation for the existence of the two titles is that the koinon of Asia was led by an Asiarch in the Republican period, even though this assumption is not supported by any evidence from antiquity. It is then supposed that when the province of Asia established its first provincial cult in 29 BCE, the Asiarch who led the koinon became the provincial highpriest[152] and was given this title as well as that of Asiarch. Both titles remained in use but, for some unknown reason, the title Asiarch disappeared from public documents in the early principate only to come back into vogue in

---

[148] *IvE* 1a.43 l. 7, 22 (titles); l. 5, 18-19 (crowns).

[149] Rossner 1974, 102; *IvE* 1a, p. 277.

[150] *Kl.P.* 3.324-25.

[151] Deininger 1965, 50. Millar (1977, 387) accepts Deininger's reconstruction.

[152] Arguments against this definition of the highpriesthood are given above, p. 89-91.

the second and third centuries CE, at which time Asiarch almost completely replaced the title highpriest of Asia.[153]

The "almost exclusive" (*fast ausschliesslich*) use of the title Asiarch in the inscriptions and coins of the second and third centuries that is asserted by Deininger is not correct. There are about 40 known references to provincial highpriests of Asia that can be securely dated to the period 27 BCE – 100 CE (127 yrs.). The number of known references between 100 – 268 CE (168 yrs.) approximately doubles to about 85. Since the number of cities with provincial cults in Asia increased after the first century CE, and since the total number of available inscriptions and coins from the later period is greater, it appears that the usage of the highpriest title remained relatively stable throughout both periods. The title highpriest of Asia did not fall into disuse after the first century CE, as Deininger would have us believe.

The question of the temporal distribution of references to Asiarchs, however, requires closer scrutiny. It has often been noted that Strabo, a literary source from the early principate, provides the earliest preserved occurrence of the word Asiarch and that we hear nothing of the office for most of the first century CE. After this lone literary source from the Augustan period, a surprising pattern emerges in the references to Asiarchs. Once the attestations are ordered chronologically, it becomes clear that there are no known references to Asiarchs in coins or inscriptions before the late first century CE.[154] The first reference appears in the year 89/90 under the proconsul M. Fulvius Gillo, after which Asiarchs proliferate rapidly in the public record. At least 16 references to Asiarchs are attested from the years 90 to 120 CE. By the year 300 CE (210 years after Gillo's proconsulship), there are a total of about 280 references to Asiarchs.

The large number of total attestations involved and the sudden emergence of the title in the archaeological record make it impossible to conclude that the absence of Asiarchs from inscriptions and coins before 89 CE is an accident of preservation or discovery. The

---

[153] Deininger 1965, 48.

[154] Kearsley argued ("A Leading Family of Cibyra and some Asiarchs of the First Century," *AnSt* 38 [1988] 43-51) that the lineage of one family with several Asiarchs in it could be traced back so that at least one Asiarch could be dated to the late first century BCE. The problems with her reconstruction are discussed in Appendix 2.

contrast with the attestations of provincial highpriests and highpriestesses is instructive, for at least 24 out of about 185 references
to the highpriesthood are known from coins or inscriptions that can
be dated with certainty before the year 89 CE. These data lead to
the conclusion that the institution of the Asiarchate, an inheritance
from the Republican era in Asia, was either redefined or reinvigo-
rated in the eighties of the first century CE. The exact nature of this
change is not clear from the sources, but something happened in that
decade which caused the Asiarchate to begin to enter the archaeological record. The significance of this shift will be addressed in chapter
six, after an examination of the games associated with the Cult of
the Sebastoi in Ephesus.

A few interpreters have rejected the identification of the Asiarchate with the provincial highpriesthood of Asia. Writing in the
third quarter of the nineteenth century, Waddington argued that
Asiarchs were distinct from provincial highpriests. The highpriests
were responsible for provincial imperial cult, he maintained, while
the Asiarchs were in charge of the provincial festivals.[155] His view
has attracted some adherents; however, he was working with much
less data than was available later on, and could do little more than
suggest his conclusion.

The connection of Asiarchs with gladiators and games, discussed
above (p. 98, 103), is evident, and so a variant of Waddington's
theory was developed. After examining the evidence, Monceaux
concluded that the provincial festivals were pentaeteric and that the
Asiarchs were provincial highpriests who served in the year when a
provincial festival was held.[156] It later became clear that provincial
festivals occurred more often than every four years in Asia, but the
argument for Asiarchs as provincial highpriests who also served as
the agonothete of a provincial festival has survived *mutatis mutan-
dis*.[157]

Brandis reached a different conclusion in his interpretation of the
Asiarchate. After attempting to disprove the arguments for an iden-

---

[155] Philippe Le Bas, and William H. Waddington, *Voyage Archéologique en Grece
et en Asie Mineure* (Paris: Firmin Didot, 1870) 3.245-46.

[156] Paulus Monceaux, *De communi Asiae provinciae* (ΚΟΙΝΟΝ ΑΣΙΑΣ) (Paris:
Ernestum Thorin, 1885) 55-67. Monceaux was not the first to associate Asiarchs
with the provincial games; he is credited with developing this particular refinement
of the general position.

[157] Dieter Knibbe, "Ephesos vom Beginn der römischen Herrschaft in Kleinasien bis zum Ende der Principatszeit (Historischer Teil)", *ANRW* 2.7.2 (1980)
773.

tification of Asiarchs with provincial highpriests, he went on to assert his confidence that Asiarch was the title of the men who represented the cities of Asia in the koinon.[158] His position, though, was hampered by a complete lack of evidence. As proof for his conclusion, he compared the fact that there were several Asiarchs in a large city with Aristides' indication that there were several koinon representatives in a large city.[159] Aristides' use of the term σύνεδροι for the koinon representatives perplexed Brandis, though.

The interpretation that is most congruent with the extant evidence regarding the Asiarchate is Magie's conclusion that the title of Asiarch was used for a special category of *leitourgia* in Asia that could encompass a variety of responsibilities. It is not known how the title was accorded, but it clearly corresponded to municipal and not provincial duties.[160]

Magie's conclusion can be strengthened by another line of argument. There is a dramatic difference in the number of numismatic attestations for the offices discussed in this chapter.[161] While eighty-nine of the references to Asiarchs (about 32% of the total) are found on coins, only ten out of over 140 references to provincial highpriests, and no references to provincial highpriestesses, come from coins. Two of the ten numismatic attestations of highpriests are on coins of the koinon minted in Ephesus during the Augustan period that name the highpriest Alexander, son of Kleon.[162] The other eight attestations are from Eumeneia and name either Julius Kleon[163] or M. Cl. Valerianus.[164]

This numismatic evidence provides strong support for a distinction between the Asiarchate and the provincial highpriesthood, for the differences in the media of the attestations are expressions of the fact that the two offices had distinct responsibilities. The relative

---

[158] Brandis 1986b, esp. 1577-78.

[159] Aristides *Or.* 50.103.

[160] Magie 1950, 1.449-50; 2.1298-1301.

[161] There is a peculiarity about Ephesian attestations of Asiarchs that should not be forgotten in evaluating the data. Ephesus is the largest source of references to Asiarchs, but all 107 of these are in inscriptions and none on coins. The reason for this is unclear, for other large cities like Pergamum, Smyrna, Sardis, and Kyzikos all have epigraphic and numismatic attestations of Asiarchs. Apart from Ephesus, then, there are still 153 references to Asiarchs, of which 76 (nearly 50%) are known from coins.

[162] *BM Lydia* 251 #104-5.

[163] Imhoof-Blumer *Kleinasiatische Münzen* (Vienna: A. Hölder, 1901-02) 1:211 #683; *BM Phrygia* 217 #41-42; *SNGvA* 3591; Neronian.

[164] *BM Phrygia* 218 #47-48; *CollWadd* 6033-34, Domitianic.

paucity of references to provincial highpriests on the coins confirms the conclusion that the province's highpriesthoods were distinct from the Asiarchate, and that they were focused less on the cities than on the region and its festivities.

Kearsley accepted Magie's conclusion that the Asiarchate was related primarily to the cities of Asia, but she disagreed with the characterization of Asiarchs as benefactors. Kearsley pointed out the frequency with which the title Asiarch occurs with other titles of high civic offices. Her conclusion was that the Asiarchate was a municipal magistracy in which men served for a fixed period of time.[165]

There are other signs of the involvement of Asiarchs in the administration of city life in Asia as well. Kearsley's interpretation of various inscriptions, and especially of two proconsular letters, one from Ephesus and one from Sardis, led to the conclusion that "[t]he most likely interpretation of the asiarch's role in these two letters is that he was the foremost member of the cities' boards of magistrates."[166]

Kearsley noted the gender differential in attested Asiarchates as support for her interpretation that the office was magisterial.[167] In the approximately 280 known references to Asiarchs, only one woman has entered the historical record, and in this case only in conjunction with a man, who was probably her husband.[168] This virtual absence of female Asiarchs has been observed by others,[169] but Kearsley is the only scholar to use this as a clue to the nature of the office. She cited Van Bremen's observation that while women often held priesthoods or acted as benefactors in the Imperial period, they tended to be excluded from activities which included travel,

---

[165] Kearsley has written on several aspects of this issue in various articles. A succinct summary of her interpretation of the responsibilities of Asiarchs is found in 1987a, 49-56, a copy of which she was kind enough to send to me. On the length of office, see esp. 52-56.

[166] Kearsley 1987a, 55; see also 54-56.

[167] Kearsley 1987a, 54, and n. 35.

[168] M. Cl. Juliana and M. Aur. Zeno are called Ἀσιάρχαι τὸ δεύτερον in an inscription from Bournabat; IGR 4.1481. Kearsley says the two may or may not have been married (1987a, 54 n. 34), but the fact that the inscription is a gravestone for the two suggests that they were man and wife.

[169] Brandis used this as an argument for distinguishing between the Asiarchate and the provincial highpriesthood; 1896b, 1566-67. Magie 1950, 2.1299-1300 n. 61.

deliberation, or voting.[170] While I agree with Kearsley that the overwhelming number of male Asiarchs is significant, the extant evidence regarding the nature of the Asiarchate is not specific enough to allow us to conclude exactly why it is significant. In the case of an office with high status such as the Asiarchate, women might have been excluded for ideological reasons that were not related to governance of the cities.

The crux of Kearsley's argument that Asiarchs were officials in municipal governments, however, is in the "inscriptions which show asiarchs in action."[171] Such inscriptions often name the Asiarch as a *grammateus* or as holding some other high office.

> This connection is so consistent that it suggests the asiarchy involved some executive power in the city allied to that of the *grammateus*.[172]

The problem with this argument is in the criteria by which certain inscriptions are deemed to show Asiarchs in action. Kearsley cited several factors such as overt reference, participial constructions, or "the application of two titles to the same person" in which case "it is the context which determines the interpretation."[173] The bulk of her supporting data, however, consists of those inscriptions in which the title Asiarch is one of two or more that are attributed to an individual, and this criterion is not a reliable one for showing Asiarchs in action.

As mentioned above, Asiarch was clearly the title of an office with a fixed term. It was also a title that could be mentioned later in honoring that same person. For example, Ti. Cl. Aristio was called "three-times Asiarch" in an architrave inscription from the Trajan fountain in Ephesus that can be dated to 102-114 CE by the imperial nomenclature.[174] He was later called "three-times Asiarch" on the endowment inscription from the Celsus library that is dated sometime later than 114.[175] Kearsley's criteria do not help us distinguish

---

[170] Kearsley 1987a, 54 n. 35. Riet Van Bremen, "Women and Wealth," in Averil Cameron and Amelie Kuhrt (eds.), *Images of Women in Antiquity* (Detroit: Wayne State University Press, 1983) 223-42, esp. 235-37.

[171] Kearsley 1987a, 54.

[172] Kearsley 1987b, 53.

[173] Kearsley 1987b, 53 n. 32.

[174] *IvE* 2.424. See Kearsley 1987a, 54.

[175] The endowment inscription (*IvE* 7,2.5153) names Aristio along with the heirs of Aquila, a man who was still alive when mentioned in an inscription from the years 114-117 (*IGR* 3.173; Ankara).

whether both of these references or only the second came after Aristio's third Asiarchate.

Another example of an Asiarch in action cited by Kearsley demonstrates the uncertainty introduced into the discussion by concluding that most multiple titles indicate offices held at the same time.[176] In *IGR* 4.907, Tiberius Claudius Polemo is named as an Asiarch.[177] Kearsley's criteria, however, would require us to suppose that many of the relatives named in the same inscription also held their offices at that same time for there is no grammatical distinction between Polemo's title of Asiarch, his father Tiberius Claudius Hiero's titles of Asiarch for the second time and municipal highpriest for the second time, and the Asiarch title of his brother Tiberius Claudius Deioterianus. It is conceivable that they all held these positions at the same time, but the further references to his forefather Marcius Deioterianus as Lyciarch and his forefather Flavius Krateros as Asiarch for the second time as well as municipal highpriest indicate that the title Asiarch may occur long after a person's Asiarchate.

In fact, many (and perhaps most) of our references to Asiarchs come after the term of service. It cannot be assumed that a particular inscription or coin comes from that man's term of office unless there is a clear reference to this fact from the use of the preposition ἐπί, the appearance of a present participle of the verb ἀσιαρχέω, some other overt contextual indication, or knowledge from external evidence. For this reason, many crucial pieces of evidence from Kearsley's argument for Asiarchs as foremost municipal magistrates must be disallowed.[178]

Summary

This analysis of the ancient and more recent sources related to the provincial highpriesthoods and the Asiarchate has produced the following reconstruction. During the period when Asia had only one

---

[176] Kearsley 1987a, 54, and n. 38.

[177] In this inscription from Cibyra, a guild of leatherworkers honored Τιβέριον Κλαύδιον Πολέμωνα, Ἀσιάρχην, ἱππικὸν, Τιβερίου Κλαυδίου Ἱέρωνος, Ἀσιάρχου δὶς καὶ ἀρχιερέως δὶς ὑὸν, Τιβερίου Κλαυδίου Δηιοτηριανοῦ Ἀσιάρχου ἀδελφὸν, Μαρκίου Δηιοτηριανοῦ Λυκιάρχου καὶ Φλαβίου κρατεροῦ Ἀσιάρχου δὶς καὶ ἀρχιερέως ἔκγονον.

[178] This involves especially the inscriptions cited in her footnotes 31-32, 36-38, and 41 in 1987a, 53-55.

provincial cult (29 BCE – 26 CE), the highpriest of that cult was known as the highpriest of Rome and Augustus but never as the highpriest of Asia. He was often active in the provincial koinon but there is no reason to suppose that he was the chairman of that council.

The establishment of a second provincial cult in Smyrna in 26 CE created a new situation: there were now two provincial highpriest-hoods in a given year. Not long after this, two significant develop-ments are attested. By 40 CE, the title "highpriest of Asia" was in use in the province; by the end of the first century CE it had become the title for the highpriestly official in the cult of Rome and Augustus in Pergamum as well. The second development was that women were admitted to the provincial highpriesthood beginning in the forties or fifties of the first century CE. These were not simply honorary officials but rather women involved in sacrificial activities. The coincidence of these two developments in the second quarter of the first century CE might indicate that the role of the provincial highpriesthood underwent revision because of the initiation of a second provincial cult, but the evidence only allows us to suggest this in a tentative fashion.

Finally, Asiarch was not another name for a provincial highpriest, nor was the Asiarchate directly related to the provincial cults of the emperors. Certain prominent men were called Asiarchs already in the late Republican period but the exact nature of their service is unclear. In the eighties of the first century CE, the Asiarchate underwent revision and quickly became a vital part of public life in Asia. In the second and third centuries CE, Asiarchs performed a variety of public services that were especially related to municipal life in Asia. Their duties were sometimes priestly and sometimes involved provincial temples, but imperial cults were not a necessary component of the Asiarchate.

CHAPTER FIVE

GAMES AND FESTIVALS OF THE CULT

Provincial Games

A large number of athletic festivals were celebrated in the province of Asia on a regular basis during the Roman period, many of which are attested in the epigraphic record. One particular kind of festival—the κοινὰ ᾿Ασίας—was sponsored by the whole province under the auspices of the koinon. These provincial games are known to have been celebrated in eight cities: Pergamum, Smyrna, Ephesus, Kyzikos, Philadelphia, Laodikeia, Sardis, Tralles.[1]

The view that the provincial games were associated with the provincial cults of the emperors is affirmed by nearly all scholars who deal with the topic. Deininger is one of the most explicit in this. He wrote that the provincial games, one of the major cultic activities of the koinon, were inaugurated in Pergamum with Asia's first provincial cult as pentaeteric games for Rome and Augustus. The growing number of provincial cult centers in Asia resulted in a growing number of corresponding provincial games that became known as κοινὰ ᾿Ασίας.[2] Price agreed with this scenario, although he held that there was a change in the frequency with which the games were celebrated.

> At the beginning, the Pergamene games of Rome and Augustus, the only provincial games for over fifty years, were probably annual, but the gradual addition of seven more cities changed the system.[3]

Moretti has shown, however, that this supposed connection between provincial games and provincial cult does not conform to the extant evidence.[4] He demonstrated convincingly that there was no connection between they κοινὰ ᾿Ασίας and the provincial cults. His first argument was that inscriptions commemorating victories of particu-

---

[1] Deininger 1965, 55.
[2] Deininger 1965, 54-55.
[3] Price 1984b, 104.
[4] Luigi Moretti, "ΚΟΙΝΑ ΑΣΙΑΣ," *Rivista di Filologia* NS 32 (1954) 276-89.

lar athletes show that several cities had provincial games before they
had provincial imperial cults.[5] For example, an inscription found
near Rome lists victories in the provincial games at Laodikeia. The
inscription can be dated to approximately 60 CE, when only
Pergamum and Smyrna had provincial cults in Asia.[6] Similarly, an
inscription from Iasos informs us that a harp player by the name of
Phanias was involved in provincial contests in Ephesus in the mid-
first century CE.[7]

Secondly, Moretti pointed out that the city of Smyrna advertised
itself as the first city to have established κοινὰ Ἀσίας.[8] This would
not have been possible if the games had been a part of the provincial
cults, since Pergamum's provincial cult preceded that of Smyrna by
over half a century.[9]

It seems, therefore, that the only games known to have been established by the koinon of Asia in conjunction with a provincial cult
are those from the cult of Rome and Augustus in Pergamum. These
games were probably not later than the cult, for an inscription dated
to about the year 5 CE refers to the victory of a pentathlete from Kos
in the "Romaia Sebasta (games) established by the koinon of Asia
in Pergamum".[10] The provincial highpriest of Rome and Augustus
sometimes served as the "agonothete for life" of these games.[11]

The eight cities known to have held κοινὰ Ἀσίας each had their
own pentaeteric cycle, yielding an average of two provincial athletic
competitions in Asia every year.[12] The frequency of the games of
Rome and Augustus in Pergamum is more controversial. The more
widely held view is that these were also pentaeteric games, but an

---

[5] Morretti 1954, 279-80.

[6] Luigi Moretti, *Iscrizioni Agonistiche Greche* (Rome: Angelo Signorelli, 1953)
174-79 #65.

[7] *IvI* 1.110.

[8] *IvSm* 2,1.635: τῶν πρώτων κοινῶν τῆς Ἀσίας ἀγώνων ἐν Σμύρνῃ (mid-third
century CE); *IGR* 4.824: πρῶτα κοινὰ Ἀσίας (Hierapolis, first half of third century). The title appears also on coins: e.g., *BM Ionia* 283 #368-71; 294 #440; 295
#,3; 299 #473.

[9] Moretti 1954, 289.

[10] [Ῥ]ωμαῖα Σεβαστὰ τὰ τιθέμενα ὑπὸ τοῦ κοινοῦ τῆς Ἀσίας ἐν Περγάμωι;
Moretti 1953, 156-59, #60 (= *IGR* 4.1064).

[11] See *IvE* 7,2.3825. Even though the games are not explicitly called the κοινὰ
Ἀσίας these are most likely provincial and not local games, for the official is the
provincial highpriest and the reference is found in the formulaic opening of a
koinon decree.

[12] Moretti 1954, 283-88.

inscription from Pergamum creates difficulties for this interpretation.

Οἱ νέοι ἐτίμησαν

2 Γαῖον Ἰούλιον Σακέρδωτα, τὸν
νεωκόρον θεᾶς Ῥώμης καὶ θεοῦ

4 Σεβαστοῦ Καίσαρος καὶ ἱερέα
Τιβερίου Κλαυδίου Νέρωνος καὶ

6 γυμνασίαρχον τῶν δωδεκάτων
Σεβαστῶν Ῥωμαίων τῶν πέντε

8 γυμνασίων, ἀλείφοντα ἐγ λουτήρων
δι' ὅλης ἡμέρας ἐκ τῶν ἰδίων,

10 προνοήσαντα τῆς τε αὐτῶν καὶ τῶν
[ἐφ]ήβων ἀγωγῆς, νόμους τε πατρίους

12 [καὶ ἤ]θη κατὰ τὸ κάλλιστον
[ἀν]ανεωσάμενον.[13]

The *neoi* honored Gaius Julius Sakerdos, the neokoros of the goddess Rome and of the god Augustus Caesar, priest of Tiberius Claudius Nero, gymnasiarch of the five gymnasia for the twelfth Sebasta Romaia, who supplied oil in all the bathing basins throughout the day with (his) own (money), who cared for these and for the guidance of the ephebes, who revived the ancestral laws and custom regarding (what is) best.

If the Rome and Augustus games were pentaeteric and they began in 29 BCE, then the twelfth celebration would have occurred around the year 16 CE. In 16 CE, however, a priest of Tiberius Caesar Augustus would not have used the name that Tiberius had abandoned when he was adopted by Augustus in 4 CE. Magie pointed out that a biennial cycle would yield a date of 7/6 BCE for the twelfth competition; if the games were an annual event, the date would be 18/17 BCE.[14] The later two dates are more plausible, but there is not enough evidence to decide the matter.

This leads to the conclusion that the κοινὰ Ἀσίας ἐν Ἐφέσῳ were not connected with the Cult of the Sebastoi in Ephesus. The games probably predated the cult. There is evidence, however, that other games were established in connection with the Cult of the Sebastoi.

---

[13] *IGR* 4.454.

[14] Magie, *Roman Rule in Asia Minor to the End of the Third Century After Christ* (Princeton: Princeton University Press, 1950) 2:1297 n. 57. The epithet θεός for Augustus need not imply a date after his death, for this is a local document where the use of divine terminology is not restricted by Roman practice. See above, p. 22-23.

The Ephesian Olympics

An athlete from Iasos by the name of Titus Flavius Quirina Metrobius enumerated some of his victories in inscriptions set up in his native city. They are of interest to us because they give the earliest reference to Olympic games held in Ephesus. Near the beginning of a list of his accomplishments that is dedicated to Herakles, Metrobius mentioned winning once in the Olympics in Ephesus and twice in the provincial games of Asia in Ephesus.[15] The inscription does not provide an accurate date, but another victory list set up by Metrobius helps remedy that problem.

An inscription with a dedication to Zeus Olympios by the same athlete in the 217th Olympiad informs us that he was the first inhabitant of Iasos to win the men's long distance race in all four of the major Panhellenic festivals,[16] and that he was also the first person ever to win a competition in the Capitoline Games in Rome.[17] The Capitoline Games were first celebrated in 86 CE by Domitian in honor of the rebuilding of the temple of Jupiter on the Capitoline Hill after it had been destroyed by fire. One of the prizes in the games was Roman citizenship, which means that Metrobius probably received the emperor's *gens* (Flavius) and tribe (Quirina) as a result of this victory. The date of the 217th Olympiad is also known: the games took place in Olympia in late August or early September in the year 89 CE.[18] For these reasons, Moretti dated the first inscription with the reference to the Ephesian Olympics to about 90 CE.[19]

After the Metrobius inscription, there are no more attestations of Ephesian Olympics until well into the reign of Hadrian, but after about 125 CE, a great number of references to the festival accumulate.[20] This nearly forty-year gap in attestations is highly unusual, especially because it covers a period for which there is a great deal of extant documentation regarding civic affairs in Ephesus. The gap

---

[15] *IvI* 1.108; νικήσας. . . καὶ Ὀλύμπια τὰ ἐν Ἐφέσῳ καὶ κοινὰ Ἀσίας ἐν Ἐφέσῳ δίς.

[16] Nemian, Pythian (Delphi), Isthmian, and Olympic games.

[17] *IvI* 1.107.

[18] *IvI* 1.109, n. 1, 3.

[19] Moretti 1953, 181-83 #66. L. Robert (*Opera minora selecta* 3 [Amsterdam: Adolf M. Hakkert, 1969] 366 n. 1) mentioned a third, unpublished inscription of Metrobius but provided no new information.

[20] Over 30 references.

and the subsequent rapid flourishing of the games have led scholars
to the conclusion that the Ephesian Olympics were begun as a festival for Domitian that had to be discontinued. The games were later
revived for Hadrian and were celebrated at least into the third
century.[21]

Domitian's connection to these early Ephesian Olympics is
certain. Lammer pointed out that the Olympics were unusual for
Ephesus because the city never had a strong cult for Olympian
Zeus.[22] Lammer exaggerated the dominance of Artemis over the
cultic life of Ephesus, but it is true that Ephesian piety, and that of
western Asia Minor in general, focussed much more on Zeus's twin
children Artemis and Apollo than upon Zeus himself. In fact, the
name of Zeus Olympios appears in only seven Ephesian inscriptions, six from the mid-second century CE, and one fragment that
is too damaged to interpret.[23] In general, then, Zeus Olympios was
not the recipient of major cultic honors in Ephesus.

The six well-preserved inscriptions which mention Zeus Olympios
give an idea of the character of his veneration in Ephesus. All five
are short dedications that read (with slight variations), Αὐτοκράτορι
Καίσαρι Ἀδριανῷ Διὶ Ὀλυνπίῳ, "to Emperor Caesar Hadrian Zeus
Olympios."[24] This seems to have been an Ephesian adoption of the
Hadrian/Zeus connection manifested in Athens at the completion of
the Athenian Olympieion.[25] When Hadrian arrived in Ephesus in
129 CE for his second visit to the city, he was acclaimed there also
as Ζεὺς Ὀλύμπιος.[26] Thus, a strong imperial component was involved in the reintroduction of Olympic games in Ephesus under
Hadrian, which is in accordance with what is known of other Olympic games of the Roman period established outside of Olympia.[27]

This imperial aspect of the Ephesian Olympics was present also
in the false start under Domitian. The fact that the games were dis-

---

[21] Manfred Lammer, *Olympien und Hadrianeen im antiken Ephesos* (Ph.D. diss.,
Cologne, 1967) 3-11; Knibbe, "Ephesos" *ANRW* 2.7.2 (1980) 775, 785.

[22] Lammer 1967, 4-6.

[23] *IvE* 2.267-71; 5.1556 (fragmentary); *ÖJh* 53 (1981-82) 135 #31.

[24] *IvE* 2.270.

[25] Anna S. Benjamin, "The Altars of Hadrian in Athens and Hadrian's
Panhellenic Program," *Hesperia* 32 (1968) 57-86; Daniel N. Schowalter, et al.,
"Athens B," 55-60 *ARNTS* 1.

[26] Lammer 1967, 11-12; Knibbe 1980, 785.

[27] Lammer 1967, 2. Lammer provided a list of Olympic festivals in the
Mediterranean world on p. 1, n. 1.

continued is an indication of their close connection to the emperor Domitian who suffered the *damnatio memoriae*. The provincial cult in Ephesus survived this crisis because it could be redirected toward other figures: Domitian dropped out, but Vespasian, Titus and perhaps Domitia remained viable recipients of cultic honors. The games honoring Domitian as Zeus Olympios, however, were doomed.

The numismatic evidence from Ephesus provides a significant image of the association of Domitian and Zeus Olympios. During his reign, the Ephesian mint produced a coin with the head of Domitian and the title Δομιτιανὸς Καῖσαρ Σεβαστὸς Γερμανικός on the obverse.[28] On the reverse is an image of Olympian Zeus, an unprecedented symbol in Ephesian coinage.[29] Zeus is seated left on a throne in the style of the world-renowned, chryselephantine statue from Olympia, with a scepter in his left hand.[30] The outstretched right hand, however, does not hold a Nike but the temple statue of the Ephesian Artemis. Around the image of Zeus is the inscription Ζεὺς Ὀλύμπιος Ἐφεσίων, "Zeus Olympios of the Ephesians."

The imagery of the coin goes beyond that which was evident on the "twice neokoros" coins examined earlier in chapter three.[31] The "twice neokoros" coins elevated the relationship between Ephesus and the emperors to the status of the city's relationship to Artemis. The Zeus Olympios coin, however, made two new statements. It assimilated the emperor to Zeus,[32] and it placed the emperor in a direct relationship to Ephesian Artemis. This represents a major reorganization of the city's divine hierarchy, but it is not unexpected, for this is essentially the same message designed into the terrace of the Temple of the Sebastoi where the emperors, housed above the ranks of the deities, presided supreme over the world. The coin differs from the imagery present in the temple terrace in that

---

[28] *SNGvA* 1879; *BM Ionia* 75 #215.

[29] See Giesela M. A. Richter, "The Pheidian Zeus at Olympia," *Hesperia* 35 (1966) 166-70, pl. 53-54; Steven Friesen, "Olympia," 15-16, 55-58, *ARNTS* 1.

[30] The scepter in the left hand was also a feature of the statue of Titus from the temple of the Sebastoi that was discussed above, p. 60-63.

[31] See above, p. 56-59.

[32] The placement of two images on either side of a coin does not necessarily imply an assimilation of the two images. In this case, though, the specific context in Ephesus of Olympic games honoring Domitian and the obvious symbolic potential of the emperor as supreme ruler lead to the conclusion that the head of Domitian and the classic figure of Olympian Zeus are not coincidentally on the same coin.

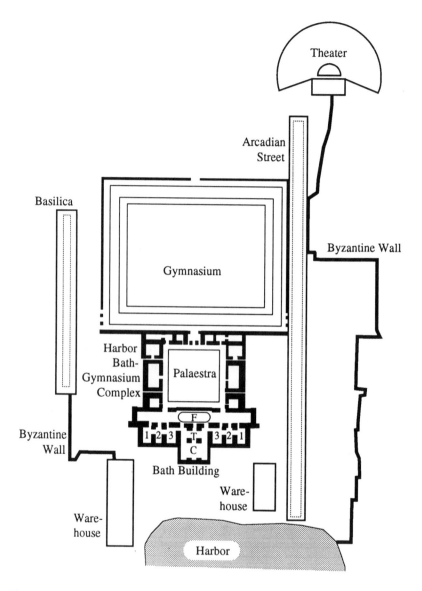

Fig. 5. The Ephesian Harbor Bath-Gymnasium and Environs. (after PWSup 12 [1970]).

the terrace precincts were related to several emperors, while the coin focussed solely on Domitian. This coin type occurred once under Domitian, and was not used again until late in the reign of Hadrian, this time with the heir apparent Lucius Aelius Caesar on the obverse.[33]

The Harbor Bath-Gymnasium

The largest building complex in the ancient city of Ephesus was the one now known as the Harbor Bath-Gymnasium (Fig. 5). European visitors in the eighteenth and early nineteenth centuries observed the tops of the baths' massive piers protruding through the topsoil and assumed this was the site of the Temple of Artemis.[34] J. T. Wood's excavations during the mid-nineteenth century located the actual site of the temple, leaving these remains unidentified.[35] Austrian excavators who began excavating the site of the Bath-Gymnasium complex during the closing years of the nineteenth century at first gave credence to the hypothesis that the area was the site of the Roman agora.[36] It soon became apparent that their excavations revealed a much more complicated set of buildings.

The complex consisted of three distinct but connected units. For the sake of analysis, I refer to them as the bath building, the palaestra, and the gymnasium.[37] Although the three units were of different sizes and heights, they shared a central axis and were joined at their eastern and western walls. The central axis of the entire complex was 360 m. long; the widest part of the complex, the gymnasium, measured 240 m. in width.[38]

Disputes about the date when the complex was built have been mostly resolved. While Keil argued for a late second century CE

---

[33] *SNG Cop Ionia* 391.

[34] Otto Benndorf, "V. Erzstatue eines griechischen Athleten," *FiE* 1 (Vienna: Alfred Hölder, 1906) 181.

[35] J. Keil, "XVII. Vorläufiger Bericht über die Ausgrabungen von Ephesos," *ÖJh* 28 (1933) Beib. 14. J. T. Wood, *Discoveries at Ephesus, Including the Sites and the Remains of the Great Temple of Diana* (London: Longmans, Green, & Co., 1877) esp. 128-43.

[36] Otto Benndorf, "Vorläufiger Bericht über die Ausgrabungen in Ephesos I." *ÖJh* 1 (1898) Beib. 64-65; idem, "Erzstatue," 183; Rudolf Heberdey, "Vorläufiger Bericht über die Ausgrabungen in Ephesos II." *ÖJh* 1 (1898) Beib. 71-77; idem, "Vorläufiger Bericht über die Ausgrabungen in Ephesos V." *ÖJh* 5 (1902) Beib. 59-61; idem, "Vorläufiger Bericht über die Grabungen in Ephesos 1902/3," *ÖJh* 7 (1904) 38-43.

[37] Later in this chapter I suggest that the inscriptional evidence indicates that the bath building and the palaestra were called the "baths" and the gymnasium was called the "xystos." See below, p. 135-37.

[38] A summary description of the complex can be found in W. Alzinger, "Ephesos. B. Archäologischer Teil," *PWSup* 12 (1970) 1608-11.

date on the basis of the forms of architectural fragments in the baths, he allowed that this date could be a little late, or might be based on pieces that came from later remodelings of the earlier building.[39] Miltner dated the baths to the late first century CE on the basis of epigraphic evidence.[40] While Alzinger agreed with this date, he extended it to the entire complex because the bath building was such an integral part of the complex that all three parts must have been planned, and probably built, as a single project.[41]

Three inscriptions are crucial to the dating argument. *IvE* 2.508 reproduces the text that was found on a statue base in the large hall of the bath building. The inscription named the proconsul, giving the precise date of 92/93 CE for the statue and base. Since the statue would have been part of the final ornamentation, the bath building must have been complete, or nearly complete, by that time.

A second inscription was found in one of the halls of the gymnasium.[42] The modern name "Verulanus Halls" has been given to the gymnasium because this inscription names Gaius Claudius Verulanus Marcellus as the benefactor who provided the marble revetment for the halls. Since the inscription can be dated to 130/31 by the naming of the proconsul, some scholars have questioned the Domitianic date for the gymnasium. The excavation reports show, however, that the marble revetment was part of a later remodeling for it assumed a higher floor level than that of the original floor.[43]

The third inscription confirms a Domitianic date for the complex. *IvE* 2.518 was also found in the halls of the gymnasium, but further north than the previous inscription, located at the monumental doorway connecting the gymnasium with the palaestra. The inscription, naming the donor of a statue group, included the name of the emperor Domitian that was later erased.

These arguments have resulted in a scholarly consensus that the Harbor Bath-Gymnasium is to be dated to the Domitianic period,

---

[39] J. Keil, "XVII. Vorläufiger Bericht über die Ausgrabungen von Ephesos," *ÖJh* 28 (1933) Beib. 14-20.

[40] Franz Miltner, "XXIV. Vorläufiger Bericht über die Ausgrabungen in Ephesos," *ÖJh* 45 (1960) Beib. 35.

[41] Alzinger, *PWSup* 12 (1970) 1611.

[42] *IvE* 2.430.

[43] The floor of the original building may have sunk because of the high water table in the area near the harbor. R. Heberdey, "Vorläufiger Bericht über die Grabungen in Ephesos 1902/3," *ÖJh* 7 (1904) Beib. 42-43.

although certain parts of the complex may have taken longer to complete.[44] It has not been previously noticed, however, that the Harbor Bath-Gymnasium complex—the only Domitianic building project in Ephesus larger than the precincts of the Temple of the Sebastoi—must have been related to the Cult of the Sebastoi.

No satisfactory explanation has ever been proffered as to why such a large bath-gymnasium was built in Ephesus at this time. Although literary sources do not address this question, the architecture suggests the answer, and the epigraphic evidence confirms this conclusion. The reason for the construction of these immense facilities was to provide the buildings necessary for conducting the Ephesian Olympics instituted in honor of Domitian.

Yegül's study of the bath-gymnasium complexes of Asia Minor is an invaluable resource for understanding the development of this type of building in the Roman period.[45] He demonstrated that the bath-gymnasium complexes joined two forms—a modified form of the Hellenistic Greek gymnasium and the Roman bath building—into a creative, though ambivalent, union. Although the known examples of this architectural genre display a variety of solutions to the challenge of combining the two forms, they all have a "family resemblance." Each consisted of a public bath building with strong western influences, directly accessible from a palaestra that developed the Hellenistic gymnasium tradition.

The details of his exposition and typology need not be elaborated here, for the main concern of this section is not the similarity of the Harbor Bath-Gymnasium of Ephesus with other bath-gymnasia but rather its distinctive nature. While Yegül occasionally alluded to this

---

[44] Alzinger, PWSup 12 (1970) 1610-11; Fikret Yegül, "The Bath-Gymnasium Complex in Asia Minor during the Imperial Roman Age," (Ph.D. diss., Harvard University, 1975) 88. Fasolo's criticisms of the generally accepted Domitianic dating are unconvincing; Furio Fasolo, L'Architettura Romana di Efeso (Bullettino del Centro di studi per la storia dell' architettura 18; Rome: Casa dei Crescenzi, 1962) 34-38. He does not indicate an awareness of the two inscriptions from the Domitianic period found in the complex (IvE 2.508, 518), but cites only the Hadrianic inscription that names Verulanus (IvE 2.430). His alternative proposal—a five-phase development of the Harbor Bath-Gymnasium complex—cannot be sustained by the extant evidence. Further excavations would be necessary to provide enough data to document five distinguishable phases of construction. Such a large complex would certainly take several years to finish, but the Domitianic inscriptions found in different areas show that the Harbor Bath-Gymnasium was usable before 96 CE.

[45] Yegül 1975, esp. 181-200, 218-22.

subject, he could not address the question systematically for his study was essentially synthetic.[46] It is still necessary to describe and explain the peculiarities of this particular complex within the framework of the typology he proposed.

The bath building at the far western end of the Harbor Bath-Gymnasium complex is noteworthy for its particularly clear arrangement of rooms. Entry to the large rectangular *frigidarium* (F) with *piscina* (cold water pool) was through the flanking halls. From here traffic could circulate clockwise or counterclockwise through rooms 1-3 and through the *tepidarium* (T) toward the *caldarium* (C) protruding from the middle of the second row of rooms. Thus, movement was clearly defined and given a limited number of options within a traditional set of bathing rooms.[47]

The demand for public hot-water bathing facilities that spread throughout the Mediterranean world in the Roman period had its origins in Italian cultural patterns; this bath building is an example of the widespread use of the Italian building form in Asia Minor. It is unique among the known Asia Minor bath buildings in that the caldarium protrudes abruptly from the building's exterior in the style of Roman *thermae*.[48] Yegül summarized Western influence on this bath building in the following way.

> The organization and the construction of the caldarium and the flanking halls of the Thermae of Titus [in Rome] show remarkable similarities of design and structure to the corresponding elements of the Domitianic (?) Harbor Baths in Ephesus . . .[49]

While the bath building of the Harbor Bath-Gymnasium is not unusual for this kind of complex in Asia Minor, the palaestra component (P) must be distinguished from other palaestrae of the time, whether in the east or the west, for no attempt was made to incorporate the Ephesian baths and the gymnasium into a rectangular architectural unit. Both components were aligned to the same central axis and direct access from one to the other was provided by

---

[46] Yegül 1975, 144-47.

[47] Yegül (1975, 145) described this arrangement as so orderly as to be overly literal and lacking in dynamism or drama.

[48] Yegül 1975, 298 n. 289. The second century CE baths in Aizanoi may be similar, but the complex is only partially excavated and the caldarium protrudes only slightly from the external facade. Fig. 7.

[49] Yegül 1975, 193. For the Baths of Titus, see Fig. 11.

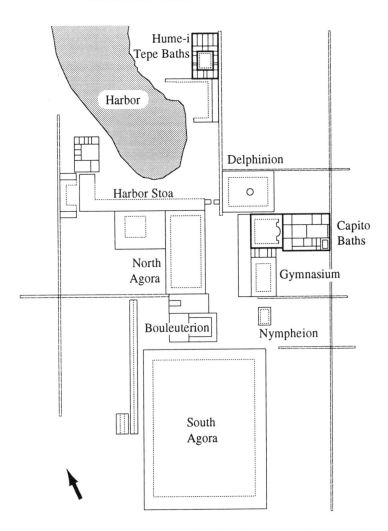

Fig. 6. Plan of Miletus Highlighting Bath Buildings. (after Akurgal, 214).

doors between them, but the Harbor palaestra was intentionally portrayed as a distinct, although related, unit. Rather than designing a single linear facade for the two units, the architects planned a bath building with two variations in its own width that are both different from the width of the palaestra. This was a deliberate deviation from Asia Minor practice (Fig. 6: the Capito Baths built 47-52 CE, and Hume-i Tepe Baths of the late first century CE, both at

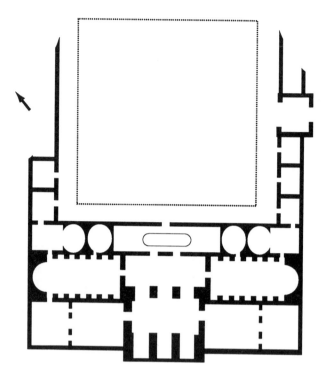

Fig. 7. Reconstructed Plan of the Bath-Gymnasium at Aizanoi. (after
Broedner, 78).

Miletus; and Fig. 7: Bath-Gymnasium at Aizanoi) and from
western models (Fig. 8-12).

The large gymnasium of the Harbor Bath-Gymnasium complex
also deviated from standard practices in several respects. First, the
inclusion in the complex of a third building—the gymnasium—is
unparalleled. The only example which has any resemblance to this
arrangement is the Capito Baths of Miletus which were built next
to a gymnasium, but no evidence of direct access between the estab-
lishments has been found.[50] Secondly, the size of the gymnasium

---

[50] This calls Yëgul's terminology into question. His category "bath-
gymnasium" actually deals with complexes that correspond to the bath building
and the palaestra of the Harbor Bath-Gymnasium, and were simply called "baths"
in inscriptions (see p. 135-37). The term may be influenced by his work on the later
"bath-gymnasium" at Sardis, which has a very large courtyard next to the bath
building. The use of the term, however, draws attention away from the unique,
three-fold design of the Harbor Bath-Gymnasium.

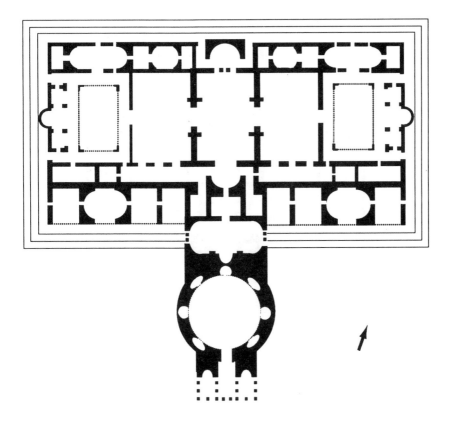

Fig. 8. The Baths of Agrippa at Rome. (after Heinz, 62).

(200 × 240 m.) required that this related building also be distinguished from the other two components of the complex, for its width was almost double that of the adjoining palaestra. Finally, the interior arrangement is that of a "pure gymnasium." There were no rooms incorporated into any part of this component. It consisted solely of colonnaded halls, or ξυστοί,[51] arranged around an open courtyard. No comparable building has been found in Ephesus or elsewhere in Asia Minor, or in Italy. Not even the Hellenistic

---

[51] Technically, ξυστός indicated a covered, indoor exercise area or running track, often long enough for a one-stade sprint to be run (approximately 200 m. long). In general usage, it could also signify an entire gymnasium.

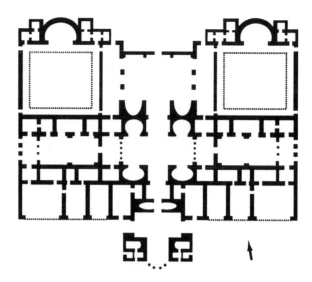

Fig. 9. The Baths of Nero at Rome. (after Broedner, 49).

gymnasia of Miletus (Fig. 6) or Priene (Fig. 13) are designed in this manner.

Only one explanation accounts for the particular character of the Harbor Bath-Gymnasium. This complex was designed as a conscious development of the athletic facilities in Olympia (Fig. 14), so that the home of the original Olympic games would provide the architectural model for the Ephesian Olympics.[52]

The palaestrae at the two sites are so similar that the first excavator of the Ephesian site commented on this.[53] Both palaestrae are almost exactly square buildings around a colonnaded courtyard with rooms behind the colonnades, and both provide access to their respective gymnasia through a door in the middle of one side. The Harbor palaestra in Ephesus is not a strict imitation, though, for it is much larger[54] and its predecessor's long room opposite the gym-

---

[52] For a description of the palaestra and gymnasium in Olympia, see Alfred Mallwitz, *Olympia und seine Bauten* (Athens: S. Kasas, 1981) 278-89; Steven Friesen, "Olympia," 21-29, *ARNTS* 1 (Philadelphia: Fortress, 1987).

[53] Otto Benndorf, "Erzstatue," 183-84; Josef Keil ("XVII. Vorläufiger Bericht über die Ausgrabungen von Ephesos," *ÖJh* 28 [1933] Beib. 20) noted Benndorf's observation, but it has been mostly ignored elsewhere in the literature.

[54] Olympia: approx. 54 m. square; Ephesus: approx. 119 m. square.

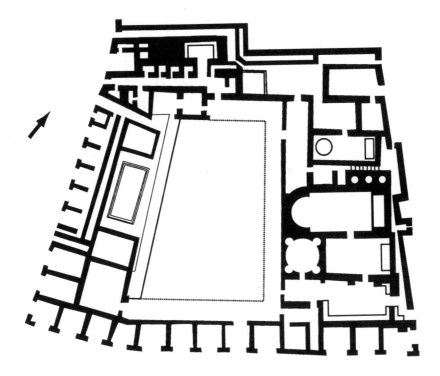

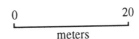

Fig. 10. The Stabian Baths at Pompeii. (after Heinz, 56).

nasium side has been replaced by the long wall of the Harbor bath building. The Harbor palaestra has also regularized the room arrangement behind its colonnade, most noticeably with two "Marble Halls"[55] on the north and south sides, and has enlarged the entry

---

[55] For a summary of the evidence for the Marble Hall, or "*Kaisersaal*," as an imperial cult room, see Fikret Yegül, "A Study in Architectural Iconography: *Kaisersaal* and the Imperial Cult," *Art Bulletin* 64 (1982) 7-31. Price (1984b, 144, esp. n. 34) is more reserved in his assessment of the evidence. The interest of this chapter is not whether a certain room was used for imperial cult activities, but whether the entire complex was associated with the Cult of the Sebastoi.

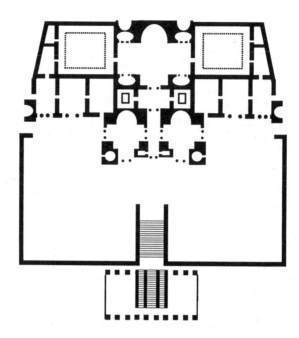

Fig. 11. The Baths of Titus at Rome. (after Heinz, 76).

to the gymnasium.[56] These changes do not alter the essential character of the building but rather modify details of the late Hellenistic model to meet early Imperial tastes.

By the first century CE, the gymnasium area at Olympia had developed into an enclosed area of considerable dimensions. Although changes in the course of the Kladeos River have destroyed the remains of the western side, the excavated South and East Halls provide information about the ancient world's most important Greek gymnasium. The East Hall was a two-aisled ξυστός where indoor sprinting could take place. It measured 220 m. in length which would have been long enough to practice a sprint the length of the Olympic stade.[57] The South Hall was built as a standard stoa,

---

[56] The Olympia palaestra was built in the third century BCE. The door that gave access to the gymnasium was a pragmatic renovation after the construction of the gymnasium's South Hall in the early second century BCE. This sequence of construction, however, would have been neither obvious nor relevant to a first century CE architect.

[57] An Olympic stade, the distance between the starting and finishing lines in the stadium at Olympia, was 198.28 m.

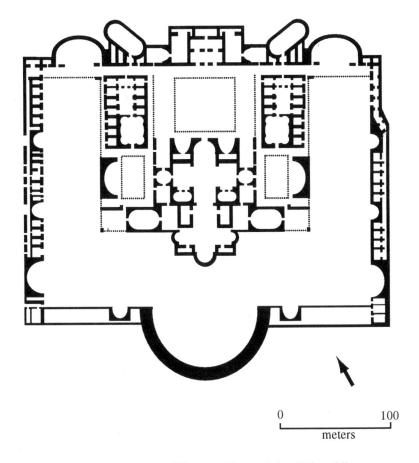

0   100
meters

Fig. 12. The Baths of Trajan at Rome. (after Heinz, 86).

whose back wall was punctuated by occasional doors to allow access
to the south.

The Harbor gymnasium in Ephesus was built to accommodate
the same functions with a few more contemporary details.[58] The
strong connection of palaestra and gymnasium was retained and

---

[58] Rosanna Maccanico commented on the canonical Hellenistic design of the
Harbor gymnasium in Ephesus, and mentioned in passing its similarity with the
gymnasium at Olympia; "Ginnasi Romani ad Efeso," *Archeologica Classica* 15
(1963) 50. The Harbor gymnasium might have replaced a Hellenistic gymnasium
on the same site, but the high water table in the area has prevented extensive excavation.

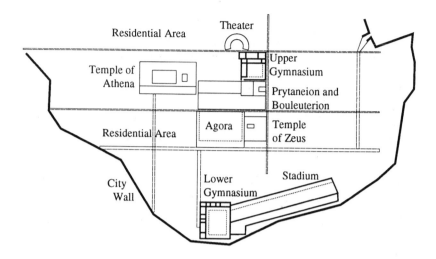

Fig. 13. Plan of Priene, with Gymnasia Highlighted. (after Akurgal, 186).

emphasized with a large entryway, and the two buildings were adjusted to an axial arrangement in keeping with the Hellenistic urban planning tradition of western Asia Minor. The dimensions of the gymnasium and its placement in the city, however, indicate its importance for the city as a whole. According to Yegül,

> [The Harbor gymnasium's] size and position leave no doubt that it was primarily conceived to serve the city as a major and autonomous gymnasium establishment although it was combined in a grand planning gesture of urban environmental control..."[59]

The north and south halls of the Ephesian gymnasium served as ξυστοί, measuring 200 m. which was in accord with the shorter Ephesian stadium. Four gates directed pedestrian traffic to the middle of the east and west halls and to the northeast and southeast corners, presumably to avoid crossing the running areas in the north and south halls. The most significant innovation was the use of the three-aisled hall that was recommended by Vitruvius.[60]

---

[59] Yegül 1975, 175.

[60] Vitruvius, *de arch.* 5.11.3. He advised that the middle aisle in such a hall be at a lower level so that it could be used as a practice track where no one would accidentally walk into the path of a runner. There is no evidence, though, that the Ephesian gymnasium had lower middle aisles.

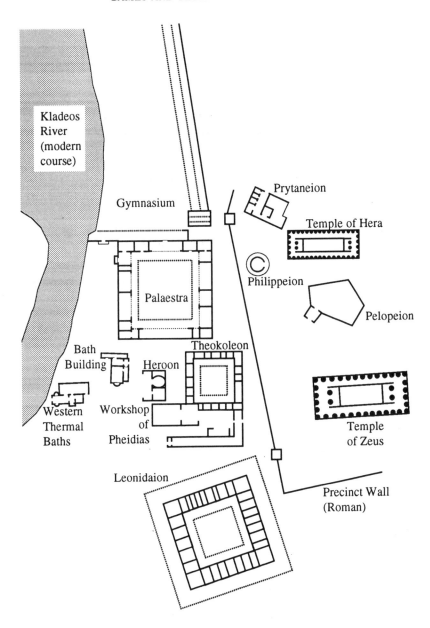

Fig. 14. The Palaestra, Gymnasium, and Western End of Precincts at Olympia. (after Mallwitz).

In Olympia, there was no bathing facility directly accessible from the palaestra, except for the palaestra rooms designated for washing. Although there were Greek and Roman period baths near the palaestra's southwest corner, these were not contiguous with the complex. Thus, the Ephesian bath building was the Harbor Bath-Gymnasium's most important departure from the Olympian model. The bathing facilities do not dominate the design as they did in other Asian complexes, though. The palaestra court occupies a larger area relative to the bath building than is the case at most other bath-gymnasia in Asia Minor. Once the gymnasium area is taken into consideration, it becomes clear that the athletic area of the Harbor Bath-Gymnasium was its most prominent feature.[61]

The distinctive features of the Harbor Bath-Gymnasium, can be explained, therefore, as the result of an early Imperial adaptation of a Classical model. Although the actual buildings at Olympia are Hellenistic by our periodization,[62] for first-century Ephesians they represented an ancient, Panhellenic institution. The Ephesians chose the facilities of the most venerable athletic festival in the Greek world rather than the more immediately available models, such as those at Miletus or Priene, as a basis for the city's largest building complex. They used the Olympic model, however, in such a way as to meet contemporary expectations of axiality and symmetry, and the growing demand for public hot-water bathing facilities.

Properly understood, the epigraphic evidence confirms the identification of the Harbor Baths with the Olympic games for Domitian. Several Ephesian inscriptions mention baths by name without any other clues about the building to which they refer.[63] One of these is the name βαλανεῖα Σεβαστῶν/Σεβαστοῦ ("baths of the Sebastoi/Sebastos") that occurs in three inscriptions. This has been interpreted as a possible reference to the mid-second century Vedius Baths[64] situated to the north of the Ephesian stadium, because the

---

[61] Later Ephesian bath-gymnasia have a progressively smaller proportion of space devoted to sports and an increasingly large amount of space for bathing; Maccanico "Ginnasi," 47. While this is a valid observation (Fig. 15), the immense size of the Harbor Bath-Gymnasium complex has skewed the data. Furthermore, once the Harbor gymnasium was planned and built, the city had no need for another large gymnasium. Thus, later complexes did not need to provide so much space.

[62] Erika Brödner, Die römischen Thermen und das antike Badewesen (Darmstadt: Wissenschaftliche Buchgesellschaft, 1983) 56.

[63] These are summarized in Alzinger 1970, 1620-21.

[64] Alzinger 1970, 1620-21. No. 21 in the Plan of Ephesus, p. XVI above; and, Fig. 15.

sixth-century chronicler Malalas recorded that Antoninus Pius founded a bath (λουτρόν) in Ephesus which was named after him, and Pius's name was found on an architrave fragment from the Vedius Baths.[65] The name "Baths of the Sebastoi" does not specify Antoninus Pius, but the identification is possible. A different interpretation has more to commend it, however.

All three references to the Baths of the Sebastoi occur in reference to an official: "the highpriest of the whole Xystos (who is) also over the Baths of the Sebastoi."[66] In addition, two of the inscriptions call the official a "xystarch."[67] Two aspects of these titles suggest that they refer to the Harbor Bath-Gymnasium rather than to the Vedian Baths built during Antoninus's reign. The phrase "the whole Xystos" only makes sense in relation to a large enclosure like the Harbor gymnasium. None of the other known baths or gymnasia in Ephesus have halls suited to such a description. Secondly, the title makes a distinction between the baths and the *xystos*, a situation which fits the Harbor complex, with its distinctive components, better than any other (Fig. 15: Bath Designs at Ephesus).

The crucial evidence, however, is not in the texts of the inscriptions but in their findspots. Two of the three were discovered far from the Vedius Baths in the area of the Harbor complex: *IvE* 4.1125 was found built into the Byzantine wall that is on the opposite side of the Arkadian St. from the site of the Harbor Bath-Gymnasium, and 4.1155 was found in debris on the Arkadian St.[68] Furthermore, another fragmentary inscription that again names the individual from 1155 as highpriest of the whole xystos was found inside the Harbor gymnasium.[69]

---

65 Alzinger 1970, 1620-21; and Malalas 11.25.

66 *IvE* 4.1104 l. 3-6: ἀρχιερέως τοῦ σύνπαντος ξυστοῦ καὶ ἐπὶ βαλανείων τῶν Σεβ(στῶν). *IvE* 4.1125 l. 3-5: [ἀρχιε]ρεὺς τοῦ σύμπαντος [ξυστο]ῦ διὰ βίου, ξυστάρχης [καὶ] ἐπὶ βαλανείων τῶν Σεβ(αστῶν). *IvE* 4.1155 l. 3-8: [ἐπιμεληθέντο]ς Μ. Οὐλ[πίου Δομεστί]κου παρα[δόξου ξυστά]ρχου, [ἀρχιερέως] τοῦ σύν[παντος ξυστο]ῦ καὶ ἐπὶ [βαλανείων Σεβ]αστοῦ.

67 In *IvE* 4.1125 and 1155, the official is also a xystarch; the latter inscription has "Sebastos" in the singular. *IvE* 4.1104 has no reference to a xystarch but uses the plural "Sebastoi."

68 The third inscription was found in a fig orchard outside of Ephesus.

69 [Μᾶρκος] Οὔλλπιος
[Δομεστικὸς] ὁ ἀρχιερεὺς
[τοῦ σύμπαντος ξ]υστοῦ
[ ]ν ἅπασι...
IvE 4.1089, l. 3-7

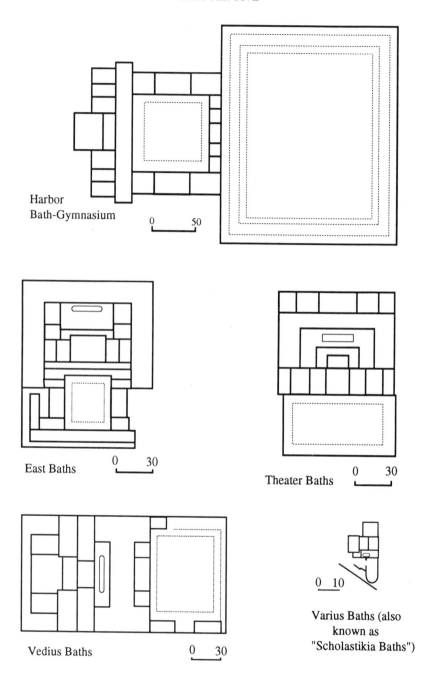

Harbor
Bath-Gymnasium

0 ____ 50

East Baths 0 ___ 30

Theater Baths 0 ___ 30

Vedius Baths 0 ___ 30

0 _ 10

Varius Baths (also
known as
"Scholastikia Baths")

Fig. 15. Bath Designs at Ephesus. (after PWSup [1970] 1608-18).

Thus, the Harbor Baths (i.e., what is referred to in this chapter as the bath-building and the palaestra) must have been known as τὰ βαλανεῖα τῶν Σεβαστῶν: "the Baths of the Sebastoi." The gymnasium portion of the complex was called the "Xystos" and was closely related to the "Baths" in terms of architecture, athletic activity, and cultic institutions.[70]

The complex was named for the Sebastoi because it was built for the Olympic games established in conjunction with the provincial Cult of the Sebastoi in Ephesus. The appearance of the singular in *IvE* 4.1155 may come from Domitian's lifetime when the baths may have been named for him alone. Since no reference is made to the koinon in relation to the the Ephesian Olympics or the buildings, both the games and the related facilities were municipal projects sponsored by the city of Ephesus.

The Date of the Ephesian Olympics

We must now return to the inscriptions related to the inauguration of the Temple of the Sebastoi, for they contain vital evidence for the date of the Olympic games in Ephesus near the end of the first century CE.

An often overlooked feature of the inscriptions from the Temple of the Sebastoi is the existence of an erasure from 3 1/2 to 4 lines long on four of the inscriptions (those dedicated by Aphrodisias, Silandos, and both copies from Aizanoi).[71] The erasures occur at a highly significant point, the end of the inscriptions, after the high-priest's name. While at first glance it may seem that the original text is no longer recoverable, a consideration of the possibilities can give us a good idea of what the erasures were meant to conceal.

The key to reconstructing the lost text is the intentionality of the erasures. Someone carefully chiseled away not more than about 110 characters from a specific point in certain inscriptions. This must have taken place at the same time as the Domitian erasures, i.e., 96 CE, for there is no other known reason for such a thoroughgoing erasure of inscriptions in Ephesus at that time.

---

[70] There are also two inscriptions that refer to a gymnasium of Sebastos: *IvE* 3.633 (γυμνασίαρχον τοῦ Σεβαστοῦ γυμνασίου) and 661 (ἐν τῷ Σεβαστῷ γυμνασίῳ). While this title might refer to the Harbor gymnasium, there is no evidence in the text or the context that directly supports such an interpretation.

[71] There are also two inscriptions whose endings are no longer extant, one from Synaos (*IvE* 6.2048) and an inscription of unknown provenance (*IvE* 2.242).

The examination in chapter two of the elements of the pattern of the inscriptions suggests that the erasure was made in a part of the text that contained the names and positions of wealthy citizens from the cities of Asia. The office would have been related in some way to the Cult of the Sebastoi for it was placed after the name of the provincial highpriest as a closing for the inscription. Was the erasure due to the listing of a person, or an office, or both?

The question of whether the erasure eliminated a reference to a person who was too closely linked to Domitian is intriguing. The evidence from Ephesus, however, shows that this hypothesis is untenable. First of all, every member of the provincial elite mentioned in these inscriptions was thereby connected to Domitian. Why should any one of them have been singled out? Tiberius Claudius Aristio appears to have played an especially prominent role in organizing and funding the new cult, yet he suffered no censure and continued to play a prominent role in the city's administration for at least another 30 years.

After the death of Domitian, there was no stigma attached to activities connected with the emperor Domitian. The provincial elite continued to function without apparent disturbance or interruption. Public offices held under the Flavians, including Domitian, were publicly commemorated in the inscriptions like those from the Celsus Library (built ca. 125 CE) in Greek and in Latin. Although Domitian's personal name was not recorded, his generic titles were used in such a way that the identity of the emperor was clear.[72] Strong political loyalties to the Flavians did not cause problems for the elite of the province of Asia.

If the erasure was not designed to eliminate references to an individual, was it intended to remove the name of an office? It has been suggested that the erasure may have mentioned a neokoros of the temple.[73] The office of neokoros, however, was never a problem. Two other references to a neokoros were not excised from the inscriptions dedicated by Stratonikeia and Tmolos. If the person who held the office of neokoros had been suspect, only that individual's name would have been removed. Thus, we can be certain that the erasures did not mention a neokoros of the Temple of the Sebastoi.

---

[72] See Steven Friesen, "Ephesus A," *ARNTS* 2 (forthcoming).
[73] *IvE* 2.232 commentary.

The contents of the original text were related to a different office. The chronological chart of the inscriptions (above, p. 46-47) demonstrates that the erasures, like the references to the neokoros of this temple, are not found in inscriptions from various dates. The erasures all come from one short period, the months when Gillo was proconsul and Ti. Cl. Pheseinos was highpriest, i.e., September 23, 89 CE through mid-summer, 90 CE. The last two inscriptions, dated later than this, did not contain the offending phrases, for they were not edited by the stonemasons. The phrases that were erased in 96 CE related to something that lasted for less than a year in 89/90.

The obvious solution is that these erasures related to the short-lived Olympic games established in Ephesus in honor of Domitian. The original inscriptions must have named the agonothete who sponsored these games in honor of Domitian. If correct, this allows us to date the games accurately to 89/90 CE.[74] We can even suggest a precise day on which the festivities began, for the province of Asia tended to celebrate provincial imperial festivals on the birthday of the emperor involved.[75] The most likely date for the festival to start, then, would have been Domitian's birthday—October 24 of the year 89 CE.[76] Since the original Olympic games in Olympia ran for five days during the early Imperial period, the Ephesian games may have lasted through October 28.[77]

---

[74] I am inclined to think that this was the first celebration of the Ephesian Olympics because it seems to have coincided with the opening of the temple, because there are so few extant references to the games, and because construction of the bath-gymnasium complex would have taken several years. Since the games were technically separate from the provincial cult of the Sebastoi, however, it is possible that the games began four years earlier in 85/86. The games were probably held a second (or perhaps third) time in 93/94. Another inscription with no apparent connection to the Cult of the Sebastoi (*IvE* 7,1.3005) has the same type of erasure found in the temple inscriptions. It comes from the Domitianic period and deals with the benefactions of an Alexandrian family living in Ephesus. This inscription should also be dated in the autumn either of 89 or of 93 CE.

[75] For Augustus, *IvPr* 105; for Tiberius, *IvE* 7,2.3801 II (Hypaipa).

[76] The inscriptions from Iasos mentioned above (p. 146) record that T. Fl. Metrobius won a long distance running event in the original Olympics in 89 CE. This date in late October would have allowed Metrobius enough time to return from the 217th Olympiad in order to participate in the Ephesian Olympics.

[77] Lammer (1967, 20) also thought that Domitian's birthday was a likely date to begin the festival, and that it could have lasted five days because of the Olympic model, but he was not certain of the exact year.

It may also be possible to name the agonothete in our proposed reconstruction of the original text. On the basis of his service both as highpriest and neokoros in the other inscriptions from the Temple of the Sebastoi, Ti. Cl. Aristio is the most likely candidate. Inspection of the inscriptions shows that his alleged service as agonothete occurs precisely between Aristio's other two offices. If this is the case, it means that Aristio is the first known highpriest and temple neokoros in the Ephesian provincial cult as well as the first agonothete of the Ephesian Olympics, and that his name appeared at the end of all of the temple inscriptions in one function or another.

Since there is a high probability that the erasure removed references to the Ephesian Olympic games, and a possibility that the officeholder was none other than Aristio, the following reconstruction can be proposed for the original text that was removed. The original text may have read: καὶ ἀγωνοθετοῦντος τῶν μεγάλων Ὀλυμπίων Δομιτιανείων τῶν ἐν Ἐφέσῳ Τιβερίου Κλαυδίου Ἀριστίωνος, "and when Tiberius Claudius Aristio was agonothete of the Great Olympic Domitianeia in Ephesus."

Summary

In this chapter evidence has been presented to show that the provincial Cult of the Sebastoi in Ephesus was accompanied by an athletic festival which was modeled on the Panhellenic Olympic games. The games were not a provincial institution, but a municipal initiative. They were not established for a group of emperors; rather, the games focussed only on Domitian and identified him with Zeus Olympios. The games were held for the first (or possibly second) time between September of 89 and June of 90, perhaps on October 24-28, 89 CE.

In order to provide appropriate facilities for the city's new Olympic games, Ephesus constructed the largest known bath and athletic complex in western Asia Minor. While the buildings included certain contemporary features such as the Roman bath building and the Marble Halls, in its overall design the complex was an adaptation of the palaestra-gymnasium arrangement at Olympia.

After the assassination of Domitian in 96 CE, the games were discontinued, but the bath-gymnasium complex, known as the Baths of the Sebastoi (or Sebastos), remained a prominent municipal institution. It was apparently in this gymnasium that Apollonios of Tyana is reported to have had a vision of the death of Domitian at the time the emperor was assassinated.[78] Philostratos does not seem to be aware that the vision took place in a building constructed in honor of Domitian, but the irony would certainly not have been lost on Ephesians hearing the story in the late first or early second century CE.

---

[78] Philostratos, *Vit. Apol.* 8.26. The comment that Apollonios was discoursing in the groves of the *xystoi* (διαλεγόμενος γὰρ περὶ τὰ τῶν ξυστῶν ἄλση) probably refers to the Harbor gymnasium. Since there were no rooms in the gymnasium, lectures or discussions would have taken place in the stoas or in the landscaped courtyard.

CHAPTER SIX

CULT, CITY, PROVINCE, EMPIRE

The Cult of the Sebastoi had implications for many spheres of life both in the province of Asia and beyond. The institutions, values, and activities which it included touched the lives of many communities and individuals. The primary interest of this study is the question of what the Cult of the Sebastoi did to and for the inhabitants of Ephesus and of Asia. In pursuing this question, it is important to remember that the task of analysis is not to simplify such phenomena, but rather to elucidate their complexity.

The task is made more difficult by gaps in the evidence. Many pieces of the puzzle are missing and are, perhaps, lost forever. We have no descriptions of the details of the normal ritual activities and there are no eyewitnesses to listen to nor informants to question. But we do have some indication of how mythology was used in the cult. In addition, we possess a significant body of data that can be reassembled and assessed through the work of the disciplined imagination in order to present a coherent reconstruction of the significance of the provincial Cult of the Sebastoi for Ephesus and for the province of Asia as a whole. But first of all, two methodological questions should be addressed.

Imperial Cult

What sort of phenomenon is "imperial cult?" Most studies on this topic have discussed the evidence as if all examples of cultic honors for emperors can be used as data to explain a more or less uniform phenomenon. This approach has allowed a certain amount of progress to be made in our understanding of the topic but has proven itself to be unsatisfactory as a hermeneutical framework. The diverse nature of the evidence for imperial cults will prevent any study from obtaining detailed conclusions if that study is predicated on the assumption that "imperial cult" was a static phenomenon, rather than a modern reification of a group of ancient cults, each of which had its own historical and cultural context.

This is an important methodological problem in Simon Price's landmark study *Rituals and Power: The Roman imperial cult in Asia Minor*. Price's book has been rightly acclaimed as a major advance in the study of imperial cults. It is exceptionally informative, methodologically sophisticated, nuanced, and full of insight. In my research I have consulted it repeatedly and benefited greatly. On the issue of historical development, however, Price chose to emphasize continuity above change. His argument for the choice was twofold: the gaps in the surviving data require a wide-ranging search for evidence, and the fundamentally static urban institutions allow for generalized conclusions. He summarized his orientation in this way.

> The evidence, though plentiful, is very scattered in both time and place...In order to handle this dual diversity of place and time [this] book generally offers a synchronic analysis which assumes that the archetypal Greek city, whose institutions were relatively uniform, provides an adequate framework in which to slot evidence from different places.[1]

It would not be fair to say that Price ignores historical developments in his analysis. In fact, he makes several important observations about such processes.[2] The problem lies in the fact that the conceptual framework defines these developments as secondary shifts within a relatively unchanging phenomenon.[3] As a result, it is difficult to describe the changes precisely and even more difficult to relate them to the evolution of social structures during the period in question.

These weaknesses become evident in three ways. The first problem is that this theoretical orientation cannot adequately account for changes in cult that occur over time within a particular region. The evolving nature of provincial cults in Asia from those devoted to the emperor and another person or institution, to cults

---

[1] Price 1984b, 4-5. The quote goes on, "It does, however, also analyse historical developments, the range of the imperial cult in towns large and small, and the diversity of cultures in the area."

[2] See for example his chapter 3 (p. 53-77). Price also mentions the "changing nature of the Greek city" in relation to changes in hero cults during the Hellenistic period (p. 36) but he does not explain how this is to be reconciled to his assumption of an unchanging municipal system.

[3] Note the undefined relationship between the singular "cult" and the plural "cults" in the following quote. "The imperial cult was far from being a static, monolithic structure, erected once and for all. Cults were constantly being invented and revised." (p. 61) What is "the imperial cult" and what part do individual "cults" play in it?

devoted solely to an emperor or emperors cannot be explained if the archetypal Greek city is assumed to be ever present. The Greek cities underwent fundamental changes between the times of Alexander and Constantine, and even within the Roman imperial period.[4] This is what we would expect in an area like western Asia Minor where multicultural influences and established international trade routes were facts of life.

More importantly, the use of the Greek city as a framework for organizing diverse data cannot account for the invention of "provincial imperial cults" in the early Augustan period. Municipal and individual cults of rulers were known before this time but no Greek or Roman cults, either for rulers or for others, had been organized on a regional basis. The unprecedented spread of such institutions in the second century indicates that new social relationships were in formation.

A second problem for Price's orientation is that contemporaneous religious groups and institutions from the Graeco-Roman world could vary greatly, even when devoted to the veneration of the same deity. Two analogies illustrate this problem. What degree of precision could be gained about the worship of Demeter if Demeter cults were treated as a single phenomenon? Data would be gathered from throughout the Mediterranean world, with evidence from Andania in Messenia[5] being given approximately equal value to the evidence from a cult like the one on the Pergamene Acropolis.[6] Such an approach would result in certain generalizations about "Demeter cult," but dramatic differences would be overlooked among cults such as the Athenian women's rites known as the Thesmophoria,[7] the mysteries celebrated with international participation at Eleusis,[8] and the rites practiced in the sanctuary on the

---

[4] A.H.M. Jones, *The Cities of the Eastern Roman Provinces* (2d ed.; Oxford: Clarendon, 1971) esp. 91-94.

[5] See Marvin W. Meyers, *The Ancient Mysteries. A Sourcebook* (N.Y.: Harper & Row, 1987) 47-59.

[6] C.H. Bohtz, *Das Demeter-Heiligtum* (AvP 13; Berlin: Deutsches Archäologisches Institut, 1981).

[7] Walter Burkert, *Greek Religion* (Cambridge, Mass.: Harvard University Press, 1985) 242-46.

[8] Alderink, L.G. "The Eleusinian Mysteries in Roman Imperial Times," *ANRW* 2.18.2 (1989) 1457-98; K. Clinton, "The Eleusinian Mysteries: Roman Initiates and Benefactors, Second Century B.C. to A.D. 267," *ANRW* 2.18.2 (1989) 1499-1539.

slopes of Acrocorinth.[9] While the analogy between Demeter cults and imperial cults has its limits, it nevertheless illustrates the methodological problem of treating imperial cults as a supralocal phenomenon.

Christian groups[10] of first century Asia provide a second analogy. The day is long past when early Christianity could be considered a homogenous phenomenon;[11] even regional distinctions have limited descriptive value for our understanding of the character of these groups. For example, Koester characterized the situation in Ephesus at the end of the first century CE in this way.

> Several rival Christian groups (whether they were organized as separate institutions is difficult to know) must have existed simultaneously [in Ephesus]: the originally Pauline church, supported by the Qumran-influenced Paulinist who wrote Ephesians, but also represented by the author of Luke-Acts who in his own way accommodated the tradition of the great apostle to the expediencies of the church; a Jewish-Christian "school" engaging in a daring interpretation of the Old Testament (an early gnostic like Cerinthus would fit this description rather well); a heretical sect, called the Nicolaitans by the Apocalypse of John (Rev. 2:6); and finally, a Jewish-Christian conventicle which was led by the prophet John, and which produced the book of apocalyptic revelations which has been preserved under his name.[12]

A third problem is that imperial cults may have been even more diverse than other cults because they honored many different individuals and several families. Although these all offered cultic honors to political leaders, we should not assume that they necessarily had to share the same features. Imperial cults did not comprise a static phenomenon; they were a series of historically-contextualized, culturally-conditioned institutions. The analyst must discover and explain not only their commonalities but also their distinctive features.

---

[9] Nancy Bookidis and Ronald S. Stroud, *Demeter and Persephone in Ancient Corinth* (Corinth Notes 2; Princeton, N.J.: American School of Classical Studies at Athens, 1987).

[10] "Cult," defined in this study as an institution devoted to sacrificial activity (see above, "Introduction"), would not be completely appropriate here as a designation for early Christian communities.

[11] Walter Bauer, *Orthodoxy and Heresy in Earliest Christianity* (Philadelphia: Fortress, 1971).

[12] H. Koester, "GNOMAI DIAPHOROI: The Origin and Nature of Diversification in the History of Early Christianity," in idem and James M. Robinson, *Trajectories through Early Christianity* (Philadelphia: Fortress, 1971) 154-55.

Human or Divine?

A second question of method in the interpretation of imperial cults
has been the agenda of the interpreters. One prominent concern of
the interpreters has been the ascribed ontological status of the emperors. This concern manifests itself in the scholarly debate about
whether the ancients actually thought the emperor was divine. It has
been hard for modern western scholars to answer this question in the
affirmative, since the recipient of imperial cult was manifestly (to us,
at least) human and not divine. The result has been some rather
cynical interpretations, like that of Kenneth Scott,[13] as well as more
refined positions. Price has outlined this problematic history of interpretation and pointed out many of the difficulties.[14] Of immediate interest here is his own synthesis of the evidence.

Price eschewed the traditional way of framing the question in
terms of "politics vs. religion." Rather than accepting this dicho-
tomy, Price tried to explain a tension he observed in the extant
evidence for imperial cult. On the one hand, the evidence ac-
knowledges that the emperors belong in the divine category.

> Some parts [of the ritual system] treated the emperor like a god. The
> ceremonial of the imperial cult was closely modelled on divine
> ceremonial. Imperial temples and their images were called by the
> same names. . . as those of the traditional gods. They also looked iden-
> tical. . . The image of the emperor, despite being partially controlled
> by Rome, was largely comprehensible within divine categories.
> Sacrifices were sometimes offered to the emperor as to a god. So too
> the emperor was called *theos* (god) and the main aim of the cult was
> to display piety (*eusebeia*) towards him.[15]

On the other hand, Price detected certain aspects of imperial ritual
that were more restrained in attributing divinity to the emperors.
He found support for this primarily in four phenomena: the placement of imperial statues in precincts of traditional gods; details of
sacrificial practice; the use of the term *eusebeia*; and, double prayers

---

[13] In the preface to *The Imperial Cult under the Flavians* ([Stuttgart-Berlin:
Kohlhammer, 1936; reprinted N.Y.: Arno, 1975] no page number), Scott wrote,
"It appears that much of the cult of the Flavian family was the result of shameless
flattery or was dictated by political motives."

[14] Price 1984b, 7-19.

[15] Price 1984b, 231-32.

directed both *to* the emperors and to the gods *on behalf of* the emperors.[16]

Price explained the tension between the ascription of deity to the emperors and the reluctance to deify them completely with the following conclusion. By placing the emperors in the divine category, and yet distinguishing them from the gods, the Greeks put the emperors in an intermediate position between divine and human. This did not break down the old categories of divine and human. Rather, the experience of imperial power was very similar to divine power and actually functioned to reinforce the cults of the traditional gods. In this way the emperors became the focal point between the divine and the human.[17]

The first observation by Price—that the emperors were represented in the divine category—is in agreement with the evidence from the Cult of the Sebastoi at Ephesus. The buildings were religious—a temenos with temple and altar. In the temenos there were statue bases referring to εὐσέβεια toward the Sebastoi. The fragments of the temple statue depict Titus with the iconography of divinity. Religious functionaries were appointed; religious games were established. The only distinction between emperor and deity in any extant evidence is a reticence to use the word θεός in reference to Domitian, which should be understood as a concession to the requirements of the Roman Senate for approval of provincial cults. For those who established the cult, the use of religious traditions in the imperial cult was quite appropriate.

The second observation—the alleged distinctions between emperors and gods—produces the tension that generates Price's conclusion. It is supported primarily by Price's arguments regarding the relative status of emperors and traditional gods in a given precinct,[18] and his reading of the evidence for imperial sacrifices.[19] Earlier in this study I showed that the subordination of emperors to traditional deities in the temples of the gods was a symbolic repre-

---

[16] For a concise summary, see Price 1984b, p. 232-33.

[17] Price 1984b, 233. Price rightly rejected hero cults as the background for imperial cults. The power of heroes was limited, and was manifest only after their death (p. 32-36, 233). Emperors, on the other hand, were most deserving of worship while alive. Cults for emperors were established during their lifetimes and only rarely after their death.

[18] Page 146-56.

[19] Page 207-27.

sentation of the place of that emperor in that precinct, and not a general statement about the divinity of the emperors. In imperial temples like the Temple of the Sebastoi, statues, architecture, and dedications focused on the emperors with the gods in a subordinate position.[20] This means that the issue of sacrifical ritual is the crucial argument for Price's conclusion that a distinction was made between the emperors and the traditional deities. A detailed examination of this issue is necessary.

Simon Price is one of the few modern writers on imperial cult to take sacrifice seriously. His thesis was that imperial sacrifices were nearly always made to a deity *on behalf of* the emperor, and only seldom *to* the emperor.[21] The sacrifices on behalf of the emperors conveniently left the relationship of the emperors to the gods unexplained, according to Price.[22] The sacrifices to the emperors were not petitionary, but were restricted to offerings of honor and gratitude, which left the relationship of emperors to humans ambiguous.[23]

> In the Greek world, however, the offering of such sacrifices [directly to the emperors] remained a troublesome activity because of the failure to create a clear intermediate category for the emperor between human and divine. In Greece, as also in Rome, where no clear relationship was established between the categories of *deus* and *divus*, the institution of the imperial cult produced a system whose relationship to both gods and men was ambiguous.[24]

My examination of the evidence from Asia leads me to conclude that Price has created the alleged distinction between the emperors and the gods by organizing selected data about sacrifice in a particular threefold manner: sacrifices on behalf of the emperors, "possible" sacrifices to the emperors, and "ambiguous" evidence. Price assumed that sacrifices on behalf of the emperors were normative and that they suggested some sort of hesitation in divinizing the rulers and their families.[25] In the section on sacrifices directly to the imperial family, his discussion did not explore the clear import of the texts, but rather asked how they might possibly be considered

---

[20] Above, chapter 3.
[21] Price 1984b, 233.
[22] Price 1984b, 215.
[23] Price 1984b, 219-20.
[24] Price 1984b, 220.
[25] Price 1984b, 210-214.

"ambiguous." For sources on sacrifices directly to the emperors, Price cited imperial altars as a group, a first century inscription from Naples, a second century Athenian inscription, and a disputed *hapax legomenon* in a fragmentary text from Mytilene.[26] References to "sacrifices of the emperors" were then taken to be ambiguous, and assumed to constitute an intentional obfuscation of the relationship between emperors and deities.[27]

It is important to note first of all that there is quite a bit of evidence from Asia and not cited by Price that equates the gods and the emperors in a sacrificial context. In fact, the vast majority of the evidence does not distinguish gods from emperors. For example, an inscription from Ephesus from the year 88/89 CE records an official letter to L. Mestrius Florus, the Roman proconsul of the province, stating that mysteries and sacrifices "were made to Demeter Karpophoros and Thesmophoros, and to the gods Sebastoi by the initiates in Ephesus every year."[28] Another inscription, dated 102-114 CE, that honors Trajan's doctor L. Statilius Crito was set up in Ephesus by "the doctors who sacrifice to forefather Asklepios and to the Sebastoi."[29] An example from Eresos is even more explicit. The inscription honors a man who was "priest and highpriest for life of the Sebastoi and of all the other gods and goddesses."[30] These and many other examples show no hesitation in assimilating the emperors to the gods.

The fundamental problem in Price's analysis of ritual is that sacrifices to the emperor and those on behalf of the emperor were not in tension with each other. They are only in conflict if we presume that imperial sacrifices functioned as a unified system whereby gods and emperors were placed on a single spectrum that defined who was human and who was divine in ontological terms. This question of human nature and divine nature propelled Price's examination of sacrifice, just as it has dominated the deliberations of most modern

---

[26] Price 1984b, 216-20.

[27] Price 1984b, 214-15.

[28] Μυστήρια καὶ θυσίαι, κύριε, καθ' ἕκαστον ἐνιαυτὸν ἐπιτελοῦνται ἐν Ἐφέσῳ Δήμητρι Καρποφόρῳ καὶ Θεσμοφόρῳ καὶ θεοῖς Σεβαστοῖς ὑπὸ μυστῶν; *IvE* 2.213 l. 3-6.

[29] [οἱ] θύοντες τῷ προπάτροι Ἀσκληπιῷ καὶ τοῖς Σεβαστοῖς ἰατροί; *IvE* 3.719.

[30] Τὸν εἴρεα καὶ ἀρχείρεα τῶν Σεβάστων καὶ τῶν ἄλλων θέων πάντων καὶ παίσαν διὰ βίω; *IGR* 4.18.

interpreters of imperial cult.[31] He concluded that the system left the question of the divine nature of the emperor ambiguous, and that it did so for reasons that are understandable in terms of social function. The ambiguity of the system, according to Price, allowed the Greek cities to reconcile themselves to an overwhelming foreign power by describing the power in terms of their own religious traditions.[32]

My proposal is that ancient imperial sacrifices should not be understood as a way of indicating who was divine and who was human. Particular kinds of sacrifice were appropriate in the context of particular relationships. It was appropriate for the inhabitants to sacrifice to the emperors because the emperors functioned like gods in relationship to them. It was also correct for inhabitants of the empire to sacrifice to the gods on behalf of the emperors because the emperors were not independent of the gods. Put succinctly, sacrifice was not so much a means for expressing divinity as a way of demonstrating and maintaining a variety of relationships. Sacrificing to the emperors and sacrificing to the gods on behalf of the emperors were not contradictory actions. They were two complementary aspects of the larger sacrificial system.

This relational framework for understanding imperial sacrifices is actually supported by Price's last two arguments regarding ambiguity in the imperial cult sacrificial system. The use of εὐσέβεια in relation to the emperors is considered by Price to be a sign of ambiguity since ''reverence'' could be shown to gods or to humans.[33] By contrast, I have tried to show that reverence for the emperors did not imply a blurring of categories nor the creation of an intermediate status. It described the relationship of Asians to emperors in the language of benefaction that was well-known to the inhabitants of Asia.[34] In the context of benefaction, reverence was normally shown to a deity. If reverence was shown toward humans in exceptional circumstances, this only underlines the fact that the decisive question was not divine nature, but rather godlike authority in the context of a specific hierarchical relationship.

---

[31] For a recent example, see the persistence of W. Liebeschuetz in his review of *Rituals and Power*, *JRS* 75 (1985) 262-64.

[32] Price 1984b, 1, 247-48.

[33] Price 1984b, 232.

[34] See above, chapter 2.

The final "ambiguity" mentioned by Price is a reference by Aristides to "a double prayer, one to the gods on the emperor's behalf, the other concerning his personal affairs to the emperor himself."[35]

> The idea of a twofold prayer, to the gods on behalf of the emperor and to the emperor himself, well expresses the ambivalence of the imperial cult.[36]

The reference to the double prayer, however, comes from an encomium to Roman rule, delivered before the imperial court in Rome, probably in 155 CE.[37] It is highly unlikely that Aristides would bring up ambivalent features of imperial cults in this context. On the contrary, this double prayer reveals the reason that the emperors were worshipped, when the prayer is examined in its literary and historical context.

Imperial cults were appropriate because the emperors accomplished the work of the gods in an unparalleled manner. Aristides expressed it in this way.

> Indeed, the poets say that before the rule of Zeus everything was filled with faction, uproar, and disorder, but that when Zeus came to rule, everything was put in order and the Titans were banished to the deepest corners of the earth, driven there by him and the gods who aided him. So too, in view of the situation before you [i.e., before Antoninus Pius] and under you, one would suppose that before your empire everything was in confusion, topsy-turvy, and completetly disorganized, but that when you took charge, the confusion and faction ceased and there entered in universal order and a glorious light in life and government and the laws came to the fore and the altars of the gods were believed in.[38]

Aristides then went on to specify how the emperors accomplished the purposes of various deities.

> And it seems that the gods, watching from above, in their benevolence join with you in making your empire successful and that they confirm your possession of it. Zeus, because you well care for the inhabited world. . . Hera, because of the marriages which take place under law.

---

[35] Aristides, *Or.* 26.32. Translation from Charles A. Behr, *P. Aelius Aristides: The Complete Works* (Leiden: Brill, 1981) 2:80.

[36] Price 1984b, 232.

[37] Behr 1981, 2:373 n. 1.

[38] *Or.* 26.103, in Behr 1981, 2:96.

Athena and Hephaestus, since the arts are honored. Dionysus and
Demeter, because their fruits are not injured. Poseidon, since his sea
is cleansed of fighting and he has exchanged merchant vessels for
warships."[39]

Having said this, it is important to note that Aristides clearly indicated that the emperors were humans. In the same oration, he
praised Antoninus Pius for excelling all previous human rulers by
as much as he surpasses other men.[40] But this was not a problem in
Aristides's perspective because the cults of the emperors were not a
question of divine ontology. Rather, they were a sign that the emperors functioned like gods in the organization of social life.

Thus, the double prayer—*to* the emperor and to the gods *on behalf
of* the emperor—does not reveal a deep-seated ambivalence at the
heart of imperial cults. Rather, the twofold prayer accurately reflected imperial theology: the gods looked after the emperors, who
in turn looked after the concerns of the gods on earth to the benefit
of humanity. Imperial authority ordered human society, and divine
authority protected the emperors. This is why the prayer to the emperors was a petition regarding various personal affairs, and the
prayer to the gods was simply for the continued well-being of the
emperors.

If we ask whether imperial cults envisioned a divine or human
emperor, we have already framed the question inappropriately.
Questions of ontological status were not unknown in the Roman
world,[41] but they were relatively unimportant in imperial cultic
contexts. The crucial issue was the role of imperial authority in
creating the kind of society which pleased the gods.

Neokoros

The concern for establishing society in accord with the will of the
gods was the fundamental similarity between cults for rulers and
Olympian cults, and it is evident long before the Roman imperial
period. The distinctive feature of cults for rulers in western Asia

---

[39] *Or.* 26.104-05 in Behr 1981, 2:96. Aristides went on to mention also Apollo,
Artemis, the Muses, Hermes, Aphrodite, Asklepios, the Egyptian gods, Ares, and
Helios.

[40] *Or.* 26.107

[41] See for example Cicero's discussion of the relative status of various super-
natural beings in *de Natura Deorum*.

Minor during the Hellenistic and Roman periods was the particular kind of grace which the cities and region received, or hoped to receive, from a θεός. In the cult established by the cities of western Asia Minor for Antiochos I and his family in the mid-third century BCE, a direct connection was made between the province's cult and the ruler's role as protector of the rights of the cities.

[παρακαλείτω]σαν δὲ οἱ πρέσβεις τὸμ βασι-
[λεία 'Αντίοχον πᾶσαν ἐπιμ]έλειαν ποιεῖσθαι τῶμ πόλε-
[ων τῶν 'Ιάδων ὅπως ἂν τὸ λοιπὸ]ν ἐλεύθεραι οὖσαι καὶ δημο-
[κρατούμεναι βεβαίως ἤδα πολι]τεύωνται κατὰ τοὺς πατρί-
[ους νόμους...] κτλ.[42]

The emissaries will request of King Antiochos that all care be taken for the cities of Iados[43] so that henceforth they, being free and firmly democratic, will now be constituted in accordance with ancestral laws...

In the late Republican period and some 200 years after the cult for Antiochos I, Publius Servilius Isauricus was given cultic honors as a result of his two years as proconsul of Asia (46-44 BCE) in almost exactly the same terms.

Ὁ δῆμος ἐτίμησεν
Πόπλιον Σεροίλιον Ποπλίου υἱὸν 'Ισαυρι-
κὸν τὸν ἀνθύπατον γεγονότα σωτῆρα καὶ
εὐεργέτην τῆς πόλεως καὶ ἀποδεδωκότα τῆι
πόλει τοὺς πατρίους νόμους καὶ τὴν δημοκ[ρα-]
τίαν ἀδούλωτον.[44]

The demos honored Publius Servilius Isauricus, son of Publius, who was proconsul, saviour, benefactor of the city, and the one who gave back to the city the ancestral laws and unrestricted democracy.

At the inauguration of the Temple of the Sebastoi approximately 130 years after Isauricus's proconsulship, Aphrodisias and Stratonikeia called themselves "free and autonomous from the beginning by the grace of the Sebastoi" (ἐλεύθερος ὢν καὶ αὐτόνομος ἀπ' ἀρχῆς τῆι τῶν Σεβαστῶν χάριτι).[45] While developments in cults for

---

[42] *OGIS* 222 l. 14-18 (268-62 BCE).

[43] According to Dittenberger, an ancient league of Ionian cities, dissolved by the Persians but restored by Alexander. *OGIS* 222, p. 349 n. 7.

[44] *IGR* 4.433 (Pergamum). *IGR* 4.434 is an inscription that honors his daughter Servilia in similar, although less expansive, terms.

[45] *IvE* 2.233; 237.

rulers certainly occurred during the course of over three centuries, one theme persisted in the public rhetoric of ruler cult: the preservation of the cities' ancient rights and traditions.[46]

This conclusion is similar to Price's argument that imperial cult was a means by which the Greek cities integrated foreign Roman power into their traditions of independence. Because Price assumes that the structures of the Greek cities remained relatively uniform throughout this period, he sees imperial cult as a continuous attempt to reconcile traditions of autonomy with foreign power. The inscriptions above suggest, however, that the reconciliation of the Greek cities to foreign authority occurred fairly early in the Hellenistic period. Ruler cults quickly became an established facet of Greek urban life. The changes in ruler cults over the succeeding centuries were not new negotiations between authority and autonomy, but rather modifications of an established institution resulting from developments in the exercise of authority. The Cult of the Sebastoi is therefore an important witness to the changing nature of imperial authority in the late first century, and not a sign of a new struggle to explain the loss of independence.

Some of the developments in the pattern of social relationships in late first century Asia can be observed in the special features of the Cult of the Sebastoi. First of all, the cult signals the growing importance of the province as the fundamental unit of the empire. Even though the rhetoric of the free city was employed in the Cult of the Sebastoi, the cities of western Asia Minor were becoming increasingly interdependent through transportation and commerce. Social networks were becoming regional, and cultic life needed to reflect this situation.

By the time Aristides delivered his encomium to Rome in the mid-second century CE, he could describe the shift from urban institutions to regional ones as the signal achievement of the Romans. They had not simply gained a large empire for themselves, but had also surpassed all former democracies by including the whole world in their government, either as citizens or as those who are governed.[47] Rome had brought the nations together; the inhabited

---

[46] This same theme is suggested in the fragmentary text of *IvE* 2.449. This municipal decree is probably from the Domitianic period, and it draws a logical connection between the restoration of ancient buildings in the city and the greatness of the new Sebasteion.

[47] *Or.* 26.58-61.

world had become like one city.[48] The empire is thus represented by the metaphor of the "city."

The Cult of the Sebastoi did not simply respond to this process of regionalization, but also contributed to it and shaped it. As a result of the establishment of the cult, the koinon's responsibilities were increased, the number of people involved in provincial highpriesthoods grew, and interurban networks of personal contact and of official responsibility extended beyond their former boundaries.

The appearance of Asiarchs in the archaeological record at the end of the first century CE was probably a separate manifestation of these same processes. The Asiarchate was not directly connected to the provincial imperial cult, but the reinvigoration, or even redefinition, of the office in the eighties of the first century CE gave provincial status to those who undertook certain municipal *leitourgiai*. In this way, the tradition of voluntary municipal service became a part of the growth of provincial institutions. This creation of provincial institutions did not replace the cities; rather, the Greek cities were being subsumed into new, larger social networks. Municipal service was placed in a provincial context.

Even though regional institutions were expanding, the Cult of the Sebastoi was still an exceptional innovation involving multiple provincial cults within a single province. Tiberius's grant to Asia of a second provincial cult in 23 CE became a problem for him. After three years of intercity dissension and an appeal to the Senate, Smyrna was awarded the honor of providing the location for the province's temple. Certain senatorial factions thought that Tiberius's grant had been inappropriate and their opposition to such cults was sufficient for the emperor to make it a policy not to grant further provincial cults for himself. The provincial cult of Caligula in Miletus from around the year 40 CE was started but soon abandoned when the emperor was assassinated. Outside of Asia, there is no known example of a second provincial cult before the second century CE, and some provinces do not seem to have had any provincial cults at all. The third provincial cult of Asia under Domitian was an unprecedented attempt to build a network, rather than a center, of provincial worship.

One reason that a third provincial cult was needed in Asia was the

---

[48] *Or.* 26.36.

change that had occurred in the relationship of the province with Rome. A new dynasty had consolidated its power since the turmoil of the year 68/69 CE. Since both of the earlier provincial cults were for emperors of the Julio-Claudian line, the advent of Domitian to power as the third Flavian to rule the empire emphasized a weakness in the cultic life of Asia. The new cult thus functioned at one level to provide the reverence that was appropriate for the new ruling family.

Another innovative aspect of the Cult of the Sebastoi was the use of the concept "neokoros." In municipal imperial cults, emperors and their families could be referred to as divine or as specific deities, but in the provincial cults such identifications were much less frequent, being reserved mostly for deified emperors. The neokoros imagery hinted at such an identification, but to understand it merely as a veiled reference to deity is to miss the salient point. The appellation "neokoros" for the city was not so much concerned with an emperor's alleged divine status; rather, it addressed the question of the relationship between emperor, province, and city. Through the neokoros imagery that was adopted from the cult of Ephesian Artemis for the Cult of the Sebastoi, Ephesus proclaimed its unique status within the province as the caretaker of the cult that was offered by all the cities of the province. Here again, the metaphors of empire are drawn from municipal life.

There is evidence that other cities in Asia were not pleased with the Ephesian initiative in this particular instance. Thus, the free cities made an official response to Ephesus in the formula for the temple inscriptions displayed on statue bases in the Temple of the Sebastoi precincts.[49] The free cities emphasized that their own status was a direct benefit to them by the grace of the emperor, and then, while affirming the neokorate status of Ephesus, portrayed themselves as the benefactors of Ephesus through the use of the εὐσέβεια/εὔνοια vocabulary. In this way, the other free cities of Asia tried to use the imagery of the neokoros to define their status as higher than that of their capital, by virtue of the fact that they had bestowed the province's cult on the city of Ephesus.

Cities that were not free and autonomous would have assessed the situation in other ways, and at least one testimony to a different

---

[49] *IvE* 2.233; 237. See above, p. 32-33, for text and translation of the former.

viewpoint has been preserved. An inscription set up in Ephesus by the city of Philadelphia used the neokorate symbol for its own purposes.

	[τ]ὸν νεω[κό]ρον
2	καί φιλοσέβαστον
	καὶ κοσμοῦντα τὴν Ἀσίαν
4	Ἐφεσίων δῆμον ἐτείμησεν
	ὁ Φλαουίων Φιλαδελφέων
6	δῆμος διά τε τὴν εἰς τοὺς
	Σεβαστοὺς εὐσέβειαν καὶ
8	τὴν πρὸς αὐτοὺς συγγένειαν
	καὶ ἐκ προγόνων φιλίαν
	[vacat]
10	ποιησαμένου τὴν ἐπιμέ-
	λειαν Τ. Φλ. Ἑρμογένους
12	υἱοῦ. Κυρίνα. Πραξέου
	τοῦ πρώτου. ἄρχοντος.[50]

The demos of the Flavian Philadelphians honored the neokorate demos of the Ephesians that is devoted to Sebastos and adorns Asia, because of piety toward the Sebastoi, and (because of) kinship to them and ancestral affection. Supervised by the first archon T(itus) Fl(avius) Quirina Praxeos, son of Hermogenes.

In this inscription, found on a base that once held a statue of Ephesus personified, the Philadelphians could not claim free status by the grace of the emperors. They adopted instead the epithet "Flavian"[51] and mentioned their reverence for the emperor, using the same phrase found in the temple inscriptions.[52] They did not, however, cast themselves as benefactors of Ephesus but rather emphasized their mythological kinship with the Ephesians. Thus, the inscription was used to raise Philadelphia above the other cities in its class, although not quite up to the level of Ephesus or the other free cities. This was accomplished by adopting the pattern of the ter-

---

[50] *IvE* 2.236.

[51] Under Caligula, the Philadelphians called themselves "Neocaesareia" on their coins; *OCD* 813.

[52] It could be argued that the inscription refers to the reverence of Ephesus in l. 5-6 rather than to the reverence of the Philadelphians, but this would not be the most likely reading. The demos of the Philadelphians is both the subject of the sentence and closer in proximity to the prepositional phrase in l. 5-6. All three nouns dependent on the preposition διά refer to the Philadelphians and serve as a stylistic counterweight to the three phrases in l. 1-3 that describe the demos of the Ephesians.

minology in the free city inscriptions to the extent that this was permissible, and by describing the Philadelphians as relatives of the Ephesians. The position of Ephesus was not lowered in any way, but rather praised through text and sculpture.

After these initial disagreements between the cities about the precise meaning of the neokoros image, it soon became a standard symbol for the relationships of the cities of the province to each other as well as to the emperor. In fact, this innovation—the use of "neokoros" in a provincial imperial cult context—was the most enduring and influential facet of the Cult of the Sebastoi. It proved to be a very successful experiment.

Grace

In the province of Asia, the economic and cultural position of Ephesus had changed in significant ways, and the establishment of the Cult of the Sebastoi reflected some of these changes. The most important of these was the fact that Ephesus over time had come to function as the *de facto* capital of the province of Asia. Pergamene primacy in western Anatolia had continued after the Romans inherited the area in 133 BCE, for the establishment of the Roman province of Asia (126 BCE) left Pergamum as the leading city of the area. It was not until Augustus reorganized the province in 29 BCE that Ephesus became its administrative center. Augustus, however, authorized the establishment of the empire's first provincial cult in Pergamum as a way of claiming continuity with the past. Pergamum had been the center of Attalid rule and of Roman rule during the Republican period. A provincial cult founded anywhere else except Pergamum in 29 BCE would not have helped consolidate the authority of Augustus in Asia.

Over the next century, Ephesus's leading position became evident as economic, governmental, and cultural activity increasingly gravitated toward that city rather than toward the other large cities of the province.[53] There was, however, an important facet of Ephesus's status as the capital of Asia that was still missing: her position in the province and the empire had not been sanctified by a provincial cult. Prior to about 85 CE, the chances for establishing such a cult in the city seemed slight, for Asia already was unique

---

[53] D. Knibbe 1980, 750-52, 759.

among the provinces in possessing two provincial cults. Around 85 CE, however, the Cult of the Sebastoi in Ephesus was approved as a confirmation and enhancement of the relationship that existed between the city and the imperial center. It provided the appropriate ritual context by which Ephesus could express reverence for the emperor, and affirmed the city's preeminence in the province through powerful symbolic language.

The emperor's favor was not directed just toward Ephesus, though. Domitian's general policies toward the provinces made it especially fitting that he be honored with this new provincial cult. Even a hostile witness like Suetonius commented on Domitian's concern for honesty and justice in the administration of the provinces.[54] Domitian opposed certain corrupt Roman governors and began to reform Asia's tax system, slowly replacing the *publicani* with equestrians to oversee collections.[55] When he needed more revenue in the early nineties, Domitian seems to have refused to raise the extra money through increased provincial taxation.[56] In the city of Rome, wealthy citizens from the eastern provinces were entering the upper echelons of the senatorial class, with the Asian Tiberius Julius Celsus Polemaianos becoming the first citizen from an eastern province and not of Italian descent to serve as consul (92 CE).[57]

It seems, then, that the province of Asia fared better under the Flavians, and especially under Domitian, than it had under their predecessors. Pleket argued that several of Domitian's decisions benefitted not just the provincial elite of Asia and the nearby provinces, but also the general populace. According to Pleket, this was not caused by Domitian's desire to help the lower classes but proceeded from his concern for the welfare of the provinces in general.[58]

---

[54] Suetonius, *Dom.* 8. See H.W. Pleket, "Domitian, the Senate and the Provinces," *Mnemosyne* 4th series, 14 (1961) esp. 301-10.

[55] H.G. Pflaum, *Essai sur les procurateurs équestres sous le haut-empire romain* (Paris: Adrien Maisonneuve, 1950) 50-54; Knibbe 1980, 772.

[56] Perry M. Rogers, "Domitian and the Finances of State," *Historia* 33 (1984) 78.

[57] Mason Hammond, "Composition of the Senate, A.D. 68-235," *JRS* 47 (1957) 78-9. Steven Friesen, "Ephesus A," (on the Celsus Library) *ARNTS* 2 (Philadelphia: Trinity, forthcoming).

[58] Pleket 1961, 301-9.

It is not sufficient, however, to attribute one opinion to all the inhabitants of Asia, for some would have been helped and others hurt by the developments during the reign of Domitian. Domitian's attempts to reduce the number of abusive Roman officials in the provinces probably appealed to the general populace of the provinces, but the longterm benefit would have been for other competing groups within the provincial elite. For when Domitian moved against corrupt Roman officials, it also affected their provincial allies. Thus, one would expect that this was a time when some of the leaders within the province were discredited and some others were ascendant.

In this context, then, the establishment of the new Cult of the Sebastoi was a mixed blessing for the provincial elite. It offered many advantages for them, such as new opportunities for involvement in sacred activities and a more comprehensive cultic system. There was also increased political influence, as well as control of new financial operations. The new cult occasioned certain problems for some of them, though, for the new activities created new economic demands. Furthermore, the expansion of civic and provincial offices presented new avenues for competition that made the position of some individuals within the social hierarchy more vulnerable than before. Finally, there was the possibility that the recipient of cultic honors might be dethroned, creating difficulties for those most closely connected to the cult. This problem affected Miletus in 41 CE, and threatened Ephesus in 96 CE.

Reverence

One significant expression of reverence for the emperors was the remodeling of the city of Ephesus. The changes in the city's physical image affected both the lower area by the harbor as well as the region near the upper agora. The harbor area became the site for a large Hellenistic complex that combined Roman baths with the quintessential feature of the Greek city, the gymnasium. While gymnasia were by no means a rarity in the first century CE, the Harbor gymnasium stands out in two ways: its size and its design. The amount of land occupied by the Harbor gymnasium was such that it dwarfed all other buildings in the area. The design of the Harbor gymnasium was even more dramatic than its size. Gymnasia of the late Republican and early Imperial period tended to include rooms and assume the character of what might technically be called a "palaestra," i.e., a porticoed courtyard for exercise with adjacent rooms for various purposes (lectures, bathing, sacrifice, etc.). The Harbor gymnasium, however, did not follow current fashions. It harkened back to a model in which there was only a courtyard surrounded by porticoes. The distinctiveness of the building was emphasized by placing it right next to a palaestra that reflected more recent architectural trends.

Why a gymnasium? The Harbor gymnasium involved the city with an older urban ideal in which such a building, where physical and philosophical training were inseparable, functioned as a center of municipal cultural life. The decreased size of other gymnasia of the first century CE and their proximity to bath buildings show that the Harbor gymnasium was an anachronism when it was built, for Roman fashion deemphasized physical exercise but encouraged bathing. Roman baths were one facet of urban life, not the municipal center for physical and aesthetic education.[59] By means of its architectural design, the Harbor gymnasium embodied its builders' vision for the future of Ephesus. The capital of Asia was to be a Greek city in the Hellenistic tradition that was also loyal to the Roman emperors.

The remaking of the visual image of Ephesus was not confined to the harbor area. The Temple of the Sebastoi, with its terraced precincts and pseudodipteral floorplan, appealed to the same Hellenistic fashions that inspired the design of the Harbor Bath-Gymnasium complex. Together, the designs of the two building projects related to the Cult of the Sebastoi tried to remodel Ephesus not in the image of Rome or Italy, but in accordance with Greek traditions of western Asia Minor. Roman elements, such as hot water bathing, were incorporated into the plan, for both cultures had already assimilated many features from the institutions of the other. The overall effect of these building projects, however, was an affirmation of the local Hellenistic heritage and an optimistic assessment of the possibilities for maintaining this heritage in a world ruled by Rome.

Some information has been preserved about the individuals involved in these projects. While the nature of our sources does not

---

[59] Fikret Kutlu Yegül, "The Bath-Gymnasium Complex in Asia Minor during the Imperial Roman Age," (Ph.D. diss., Harvard University, 1975) 218-21.

allow a systematic analysis of the developments among the elite of
the province of Asia in the late first century CE, there are suggestions in the epigraphic record that some individuals were indeed becoming more influential at the time of, and perhaps because of, their
involvement in the provincial Cult of the Sebastoi.

Three men of the province who appear in the temple inscriptions
as early highpriests of the Cult of the Sebastoi are illustrative of the
developments that were taking place. One of the three, Tiberius
Julius Dama Claudianus, is impossible to trace because his name
does not appear in any other extant source. His name reveals that
he was a Roman citizen, and it is probable that he or earlier members of his family became citizens during the Julio-Claudian period.

Another of the three, Tiberius Claudius Aristio, appears in most
of the temple inscriptions, and is known from many other Ephesian
inscriptions. His first datable appearances in the epigraphic record,
however, are in these temple inscriptions. After this, his name is
associated with nearly every major civic office in Ephesus. His wife
Julia Lydia Laterane was also active in civic life and she probably
held a prominent municipal highpriesthood at some time before
114 CE.[60]

Aristio's numerous benefactions and services to the region made
him well-known, both to friends and opponents, throughout the
province and beyond. Thus, it is no wonder that Pliny the Younger
called Aristio the leading citizen of Ephesus, nor is it surprising that
Pliny's reference to him was occasioned by Aristio's appearance as
a defendant on trial before Trajan, accused by fellow Asians of an
unspecified crime.[61] Aristio was acquitted and continued to play a
major role in Ephesian municipal affairs into the second quarter of
the second century CE.

The third highpriest from the inscriptions associated with the
Temple of the Sebastoi was Tiberius Claudius Pheseinos. Pheseinos
appears in five of the inscriptions from the Temple of the Sebastoi
but nowhere else in the Ephesian inscriptions. The reason for this
is that he seems to have been from Teos, where inscriptions have
been found that mention him and his father.[62] Another inscription

---

[60] *IvE* 2.424, 424a.
[61] Pliny, *Ep.* 6.31.
[62] *IvE* 2.232 notes.

from Teos informs us that his daughter Claudia Tryphaina and his wife Stratonike both served as provincial highpriestesses of Asia.[63] Even though Pheseinos was not a native of Ephesus, he was influential enough to be appointed by the koinon to serve as the provincial highpriest for the dedication of the Temple of the Sebastoi.

These three men demonstrate some of the social developments in Asia at the time of the new provincial cult established in Ephesus. All three were wealthy members of the provincial elite whose Roman citizenship was probably attained in the early Imperial period. All three are known to us as holding provincial offices for the first time in the inscriptions of the Temple of the Sebastoi. They were members of families that were active in public life, for two of the three are known to have been married to women who held important highpriesthoods, and to have had other relatives who were prominent in public life.[64]

The highpriest who is the best known to us of the three, the Ephesian Aristio, was also the most actively involved in the inauguration of the Cult of the Sebastoi. Members of the elite from outside of Ephesus were not excluded from important responsibilities, though, since appointment to the highpriesthood was within the jurisdiction of the provincial koinon and did not depend upon Ephesian institutions. The determining factor in such an appointment was one's standing within the social network of the provincial elite.

There were also occasions for meritorious service in the Cult of the Sebastoi that depended primarily upon an individual's municipal standing. Ephesus had the most to offer in this respect, for the city could appoint an agonothete to sponsor the Ephesian Olympics and probably determined the neokoros of the temple. Cities outside of Ephesus could offer positions in the koinon, commission embassies to provincial cult festivals, and provide opportunities to underwrite dedications, such as the temple inscriptions set up in Ephesus by other cities.[65]

---

[63] *IGR* 4.1571 (Teos).

[64] For Aristio the younger, see *FiE* 5,1.65-66

[65] Ten of the thirteen known inscriptions for the inauguration of the Temple of the Sebastoi mentioned prominent citizens of the respective donor cities who facilitated these dedications. The inscription from Philadelphia honoring Ephesus that was discussed above (p. 209-211) also recorded such a benefactor. Among all these men, only the Philadelphian is known from other sources (see R. Münsterberg, *Die*

It should be noted that all of the people clearly associated with the inauguration of the Cult of the Sebastoi are men. Vedia Marcia, daughter of Publius Vedius, was a provincial highpriestess (probably in Ephesus because of her family's prominence there) before the end of the first century. Flavia Ammion Aristio was certainly a provincial highpriestess in Ephesus, but her office cannot be dated more precisely than before 130 CE. The resulting pattern of participation according to gender is that men held most of the offices connected with the cult; women also held some offices after the initial phase but their numbers never matched those of the male officials.

What of the rest of the society? How did the Cult of the Sebastoi affect those inhabitants of Asia who did not have the wealth or prestige to hold significant offices in the cult? We have little evidence that speaks to this issue. Only the elite had their names and careers inscribed in stone, or their tastes enshrined in public monuments that can be excavated for examination some 2000 years later. We can be certain that the opinions of the general populace of Ephesus and of Asia were no more uniform than were those of the provincial elite. The voices silenced by historical circumstance certainly articulated a variety of religious, ethnic, political, and economic perspectives.

If there is little direct evidence for the affect of the Cult of the Sebastoi on the general populace, a few broad inferences can nevertheless be drawn. There were many aspects of the cult that would have appealed to many inhabitants of the region. The cult symbolized significant facets of life in Roman Asia in the late first century CE: the benefits of imperial authority, gratitude toward and dependence upon the emperors, the ordering of the cities of the province, and the role of the elite in the mediation of imperial influence. The Cult of the Sebastoi likewise provided regular opportunities for entertainment, travel, social intercourse, and extra economic activity. Finally, this particular provincial cult affirmed local religious traditions and the larger heritage of the Greek world as a mode of life in the period of Roman supremacy.

Which members of the general populace might have objected to the Cult of the Sebastoi? There are few, if any, signs of opposition to Roman rule in Asia by the late first century CE. By the beginning

---

Beamtennamen auf den griechischen Münzen [Subsidia Epigraphica 3; Hildesheim: Georg Olms Verlag, 1973] 145).

of Domitian's reign, Rome had controlled the area for over 150 years and the disturbances noted by Roman writers appear to be nothing more than the kinds of local disputes one would expect in a complex urban setting.[66] In any event, there was no need to station Roman legions in the area.[67]

The construction of the Temple of the Sebastoi and of the Harbor Bath-Gymnasium would have involved the displacement of some Ephesians and could have aroused some opposition. Also, certain individuals with significant commitments to the cult of Ephesian Artemis may have suspected that reverence toward her would be eclipsed by the new imperial neokorate responsibilities of Ephesus. Neither of these factors appears in any of our sources, though.

At least some Christians in Ephesus, and in Asia in general, would have had reasons to object and several scholars have suggested that imperial cult in general or even the Cult of the Sebastoi in particular was the catalyst for the production of the Book of Revelation.[68] There is often a tendency to make Domitian the focus of this opposition. For this reason, one theme from the literature on Revelation and the Cult of the Sebastoi should be discussed by way of conclusion, namely, the role of Domitian and other emperors.

Domitian, the Emperors, and the Cult of the Sebastoi

The unfavorable portrait of Domitian that we have inherited from the ancient Roman historians has often influenced the interpretation both of Rev and of the Cult of the Sebastoi. But the attempt to see in this cult the delusions of a mad emperor does not conform to the available data. This analysis of the Cult of the Sebastoi that was established in Ephesus in the mid-eighties of the first century CE has

---

66 For a summary discussion, see Leonard L. Thompson, *The Book of Revelation: Apocalypse and Empire* (New York: Oxford University Press, 1990) 154-56.

67 There is only evidence for one cohort in Asia at any given time. M. Speidel, *Roman Army Studies* (Amsterdam: J.C. Gieben, 1984) 1:278-79.

68 E.g., Elisabeth Schüssler Fiorenza, *The Book of Revelation: Justice and Judgment* (Philadelphia: Fortress, 1985) 192-99; Price 1984, 197-98; Helmut Koester, *Introduction to the New Testament* (Philadelphia: Fortress, 1982) 2.250-51; G.R. Beasley-Murray, *The Book of Revelation* (London: Oliphants, 1974) 217; Ethelbert Stauffer, *Christ and the Caesars. Historical Sketches* (London: SCM, 1955) 147-91; R.H. Charles, *A Critical and Exegetical Commentary on the Revelation of St. John* (International Critical Commentary; Edinburgh: T. & T. Clark, 1920) 1:351. The issue of the relationship of imperial cults to Rev is too complicated to be addressed in this context. It is a question to which I hope to return in a separate study.

uncovered little evidence for the conclusion that the cult was initiated by the emperor or even greatly influenced by him in a direct
fashion. Aspects of the provincial cult which were subject to Roman
supervision, such as the exact name of the temple that avoided the
use of θεός for the emperor, were actually the most reserved. Conversely, the aspects of the cult that were the responsibility of the city,
such as coin design, architecture, and athletic games, were the most
daring. It cannot be argued that the Cult of the Sebastoi was a foreign import, foisted upon the province of Asia by a tyrant seeking
divine glory. The Cult of the Sebastoi depended very little upon an
individual emperor for its vitality. Rather, the cult was an integral
part of developments in Ephesus and in the province of Asia.

The remains of the Cult of the Sebastoi indicate that the cult
belonged specifically to the category of the worship of Olympian
deities.[69] The games and their mythology, the buildings, the sculpture, and even the coin images all point in this direction. Olympian
"religion" was not primarily concerned with emotional sincer-
ity, assent to doctrines, or divine essence;[70] rather, it dealt with
temples, sacrifice, priesthoods, games, χάρις ("grace"), and εὐσέβεια ("reverence"). The issue of whether a given figure was divine
mattered little; at issue was the establishment of proper hierarchies,
the maintenance of relationships, the preservation of ancestral ways.

Olympian religion provided a useful, perhaps even necessary,
model for the imperial cult. The Olympian pantheon expressed the
supremacy of the emperor (Zeus) and provided an analogy for the
importance of the imperial family. It also underlined the fundamental social function shared by the Olympians and the emperors.

As highpriests and highpriestesses in this system, the provincial
elite of Asia affirmed and promoted its role as the mediators between
the province and the imperial center. Grace flowed to the province,
and reverence was given to the emperor. The democratic ideals of
the Greek cities were affirmed even as those cities were being incorporated into the growing imperial system. In this way, contemporary developments in the ordering of social life of Asia were integrated with Greek civic traditions.

---

[69] Price 1984b, 233.

[70] For an example of such a definition of ancient religion, see Ramsay
MacMullen, *Paganism in the Roman Empire* (New Haven: Yale University Press,
1981) esp. 65-66, 131-37.

Augustus was ambivalent toward the use of the Olympian model for the living emperor, preferring to link his cult to that of Rome for the Greeks and to maintain the cult of Divus Julius for Romans. Tiberius seems to have avoided Olympian honors as much as possible. Gaius, on the other hand, accepted such worship with a fervor that was unacceptable to his contemporaries.

The Cult of the Sebastoi in Ephesus represented a step back from the radical position of Gaius. But in contrast to the cult of Rome and Augustus in Pergamum or the Cult of Tiberius, Livia, and the Senate in Smyrna, the imperial family appeared alone as the object of the province's worship without reference to other centers of Roman power. As such, the cult served as a prototype for the fully developed cults of Hadrian Zeus Olympios in Greece and Asia that sprang up in the second quarter of the second century CE.

When the Senate voted to have Domitian's name removed from the public record, the Cult of the Sebastoi established for his family survived and flourished without him. The cult was too firmly anchored in the life of the province to fall with Domitian. In fact, it seems that the Cult of the Sebastoi set a precedent for other provincial imperial cults. The unparalleled proliferation of provincial imperial cults that took place in Asia under the Antonines included these three aspects found in the Cult of the Sebastoi—the use of Olympian religious traditions, multiple provincial cults, and neokoros imagery—and extended their influence throughout the province and beyond.

The popularity of the Ephesian model was no coincidence. The Cult of the Sebastoi was an accurate assessment of crucial developments in late first century Asian life. The earlier provincial cults that expressed reverence for the emperor and Rome, or for the emperor and the Senate, no longer served as viable models. Henceforth, the emperors would be the primary source of divine grace for the cities. In the provincial Cult of the Sebastoi, the new metaphor for this relationship emerged. It was based on neokoros imagery drawn from the city's relationship with its primary deity, Ephesian Artemis. But the city quickly shifted its focus from the status of being twice neokoros (of Artemis and of the Sebastoi) to the honor of being neokoros of the emperors. The recontextualized municipal religious tradition took on a life of its own in the provincial cults of the emperors. The mediators in this new relationship were the members of the elite who moved from their municipal base into the arena of provincial service. This became the mechanism by which the Ephesians, and others, fulfilled their responsibilities to the Sebastoi and to the other gods and goddesses.[71]

---

[71] See *IGR* 4.18 (Eresos).

PROVINCIAL HIGHPRIESTS, PROVINCIAL
HIGHPRIESTESSES, AND ASIARCHS

The goal of this collection is to provide greater access to the archaeological evidence for provincial highpriests, provincial highpriestesses, and Asiarchs. Since the tables summarize a great deal of information they should be used as a guide to, rather than as a substitute for, consultation of the relevant publications.

I have organized the materials into six columns which are described below. The arrangement of the data reflects my interests and facilitates certain kinds of inquiry. The primary organizing principle is a threefold division: references to highpriests, highpriestesses, and Asiarchs. Each group of attestations is given in a separate section of this appendix so that each kind of title can be examined independently. Within each of the three sections, the overall arrangement is in rough (not exact) chronological order. The principles of arrangement in the description of the Date column (below) should be read carefully. Along with dates of attestations, the columns also allow easy reference to exact titles, names of officials, origins of data, media, and publication.

In order to render the information as succinctly as possible, I have used the following conventions.

[ ]   a lacuna in the text, calculated to reflect the amount lost in the original language.
?   probable but not certain.
???   missing information.
*   estimated date of office assuming 30-year generations in a family.
In.   inscription.
Cn.   coin.
k   koinon (provincial assembly).

Date. This column is organized primarily according to the date of attestation, i.e., the date of the coin or inscription, and not strictly according to the date of office. Sometimes the data clearly comes from the period of service and in most cases one can assume that the date of office was not much earlier than the attestation. Occasionally, reference is made to ancestors who held a particular office

much earlier. When possible, I have estimated the date of service for
these people assuming that an average generation lasted 30 years.
These cases are listed according to the estimated date of office and
marked with an asterisk. The date of attestation is then listed in
parentheses in the column giving publication information.

Some of the materials on the three kinds of titles can be dated with
precision, many can be dated within a period of several years, and
others cannot be dated with any useful specification. Dates which
are rounded off to decades (e.g., 120) are normally accurate within
about 5 years. Mid-century is indicated by 40-60, 140-160, etc.
100-150 or 50-100 is my way of noting a half-century. A blank after
a dash (130-) signals that the terminus ad quem is unknown.

Using this system, I have arranged each attestation by its earliest
possible date as one means of illuminating patterns in historical developments. It is important to remember that an element of uncertainty remains. The ranges of possible dates means that a given
attestation may actually have been earlier than one listed earlier in
this appendix, and this fact should be noted in any attempt to make
judgments of chronology based on this collection. Moreover, attestations whose date is completely uncertain are listed at the end of
each section since their vocabulary and style usually suggest a later
rather than earlier date.

Title of office. I have translated the titles into English as accurately as
possible, occasionally sacrificing good style to reflect the original
word order. The goal is to inform the discussions of the various
specific titles.

Name of official. Full names of officials are included in this column.
Some abbreviations of names have been introduced in the appendix
to compress the data. These do not necessarily reflect the abbreviations in the inscriptions or coins. I have also tried to include information about relatives in order to clarify family relationships. The
relatives are sometimes, but not always, listed in a given inscription
or coin. In the few case where unnamed ancestors are described as
holding highpriesthoods, I have assumed that these might be male
or female ancestors. These unnamed officials are included both in
the sections on highpriests and those on highpriestesses.

I have found no perfect system for rendering names in English.
In general, Greek names are transliterated from Greek and Latin
names from Latin. Many exceptions were made, however, in cases
where modern academic tradition uses some other form of the name.

Findspot of data. This column indicates where the materials were found, not where the official served.

Medium. The materials in this appendix come from inscriptions and coins. Coins or inscriptions of the koinon are marked with the letter k, since this sometimes affects the conclusion of whether an office was provincial or local. The scattered references to the three offices in literary sources have not been included because they are discussed in chapter 4.

Publication. When an inscription or coin has been published in more than one place, I have only included the latest publication or the one which appears to me to be most accurate. When evidence is arranged according to date of office rather than to date of attestation, the date of attestation is given in this column in parentheses after the publication information (see above "Date"). Occasional cross-references and comments are also included in this column.

I have made every effort to insure the accurate and exhaustive nature of this collection. It includes materials available in publications until about 1990. I welcome any corrections, or any suggestions on additional material that might have been overlooked or that came to light at a later time.

ATTESTATIONS OF PROVINCIAL HIGHPRIESTS

Date	Title of office	Name of official	Findspot of data	Medium	Publication
27 BCE–14 CE	highpriest (of Rome and Augustus)	Alexandros, son of Kleon	Sardis	kCn	BM Lydia 251 #104
27 BCE–14 CE	highpriest (of Rome and Augustus)	Alexandros, son of Kleon	Sardis	kCn	BM Lydia 251 #105
27 BCE–14 CE	highpriest (of Rome and Augustus)	Gaius Julius M[...]	Halikarnassos	In.	IBM 4.894
9 BCE	highpriest (of Rome and Augustus)	Apollonios, son of Menophilos	Priene	kIn.	IvPr 105 l. 31
9 BCE	highpriest (of Rome and Augustus)	Apollonios, son of Menophilos	Priene	In.	IvPr 105 l. 78-79
4 BCE	highpriest of Rome and Augustus	Charinos, son of Charinos	Sardis	kIn.	Sardis 7.8 VII
3 BCE	highpriest of Rome and Augustus	Demetrios, son of Heraklides	Sardis	kIn.	Sardis 7.8 VIII
3/2 BCE	highpriest of Rome and Augustus	Philistes, son of Apollodoros	Sardis	kIn.	Sardis 7.8 IX
2 BCE	highpriest of Rome and Augustus	M. Ant. Lepidus	Sardis	kIn.	Sardis 7.8 X
2 BCE–14 CE	highpriest (of Rome and Augustus, Pergamum)	G. Ju. Pardala	Hypaipa	kIn.	IvE 7,2.3825
14-114 CE	highpriests (provincial?)	???	Ephesus	In.	IvE 4.1393 (fragmentary)

Cont.

Date	Title of office	Name of official	Findspot of data	Medium	Publication
14-114 CE	[...high]priest of the temple in Per[gamum...]	???	Ephesus	In.	IvE 4.1393 (fragmentary)
26-120	highpriest of Asia of the temple in Smyrna	Ti. Cl. Meidias	Sardis	In.	IGR 4.1524
40	highpriest of the temple in Miletus of Gaius Caesar the first time; highpriest of Asia for the third time	Corn. Vergilius Capito	Miletus	In.	Hellenica 7 (1949) 206-7
41	[highpriest of Asi]a (Pergamum)	Anaxagoras	Hypaipa	kIn.	IvE 7,2.3801 II
41-68	highpriest of Asia	[Lu]cius Anto[nius] Zeno, son of [Pole]mon	Herakleia Salbake	In.	MAMA 6.104
44?	highpriest (provincial?)	???	Ephesus	kIn.	IvE 1.17 l. 68 (fragmentary)
44?	highpriests of Asia	???	Ephesus	kIn.	IvE 1.17 l. 70-71 (very fragmentary)
50-54	designated highpriest of Asia	Ti. Cl. Demokrates	Magnesia	In.	IvMag 157b
50-54	highpriest of Asia	Ti. Cl. Timon	Magnesia	In.	IvMag 157b
54-59	highpriest of Asia	Alkiphron, husband of Juliane	Magnesia	In.	IvMag 158

Cont.

Date	Title of office	Name of official	Findspot of data	Medium	Publication
54-68	highpriest of Asia	(G.) Ju. Kleon	Eumeneia	Cn.	Imhoof-Blumer, (1972) 211 #683
54-68?	highpriest of Asia	G. Ju. Kleon	Ephesus	In.	IvE 3.688
54-68	highpriest of Asia	(G.) Ju. Kleon	Eumeneia	Cn.	BM Phrygia 217 #41
54-68	highpriest of Asia	(G.) Ju. Kleon	Eumeneia	Cn.	BM Phrygia 217 #42
54-68	highpriest of Asia	(G.) Ju. Kleon	Eumeneia	Cn.	SNGvA 3591
80-114	highpriest of Asia (Pergamum)	Ti. Cl. Sokrates, husband of Antonia Caecilia	Thyatira	In.	IGR 4.1238
80-114	highpriest of Asia (Pergamum)	Ti. Cl. Sokrates, husband of Antonia Caecilia	Thyatira	In.	IGR 4.1239
80-114	highpriest of Asia (Pergamum)	Ti. Cl. Sokrates, husband of Antonia Caecilia	Thayatira	In.	IGR 4.1241
83-96	highpriest of Asia	M. Cl. Valerianus	Eumeneia	Cn.	BM Phrygia 218 #47
83-96	highpriest of Asia	M. Cl. Valerianus	Eumeneia	Cn.	BM Phrygia 218 #48
83-96	highpriest of Asia	M. Cl. Valerianus	Eumeneia	Cn.	CollWadd 6033
83-96	highpriest of Asia	M. Cl. Valerianus	Eumeneia	Cn.	CollWadd 6034
85-130	highpriest of Asia of the temple in Ephesus	T. Fl. Varus Calvesianus Hermokrates, husband of Flavia Ammion Aristio	Phokaia	In.	IGR 4.1323
88/89	highpriest of Asia	Ti. Cl. Aristio	Ephesus	In.	IvE 2.234
88/89	highpriest of Asia	Ti. Cl. Aristio	Ephesus	In.	IvE 2.239

Cont.

Date	Title of office	Name of official	Findspot of data	Medium	Publication
89	highpriest of Asia	Ti. Cl. Aristio	Ephesus	In.	IvE 2.235
89	highpriest of Asia	Ti. Cl. Aristio	Ephesus	In.	IvE 5.1498
89/90	highpriest of Asia	Ti. Cl. Pheseinos, husband of Stratonike	Ephesus	In.	IvE 2.232
89/90	highpriest of Asia	Ti. Cl. Pheseinos, husband of Stratonike	Ephesus	In.	IvE 2.232a
89/90	highpriest of Asia	Ti. Cl. Pheseinos, husband of Stratonike	Ephesus	In.	IvE 2.233
89/90	highpriest of Asia	Ti. Cl. Pheseinos, husband of Stratonike	Ephesus	In.	IvE 2.238
89/90	highpriest of Asia	Ti. Cl. [Aristio? Pheseinos?]	Ephesus	In.	IvE 2.240
90	highpriest of Asia	Ti. Cl. Pheseinos, husband of Stratonike	Ephesus	In.	IvE 2.237
90/91	highpriest of Asia	Ti. Julius Dama Claudianus	Ephesus	In.	IvE 2.241
90-130	highpriest of Asia of the temple in Ephesus common to Asia	T. Fl. Montanus	Ephesus	In.	IvE 6.2063 (verb also attested)
90-130	[highpriest] of Asia of the tem[ple in Ephesus common to] Asia	T. Fl. Montanus	Ephesus	In.	IvE 6. 2062
92-	[th]r[ee times?] high[p]riest [of Asia]	Ti. Cl. Aristio	Ephesus	In.	IvE 2.425 (fragmentary)

Cont.

Date	Title of office	Name of official	Findspot of data	Medium	Publication
96?	highpriest of Asia	[G.] Ju. Lepidus	Sardis	In.	Sardis 7.64
98-	highpriest of Asia	M. Ulpius Trypho Megas Antonianus	Themisonion	In.	IGR 4.882
100-114	highpriest of Asia	Fl. Menophantos	Pergamum	In.	IGR 4.470
100-114	highpriest of Asia	Fl. Menophantos	Pergamum	In.	IGR 4.456
100-150	highpriest of Asia	Ti. Cl. Menogenes Caecilianus, descendant of Ti. Cl. Sokrates and Antonia	Thyatira	In.	IGR 4.1238
102-114	[three times? highpriest of A]sia	Ti. Cl. Aristio	Ephesus	In.	IvE 2.425a
102-114	[. . . highpriest] of Asia	Ti. Cl. Aristio	Ephesus	In.	IvE 2.424a
102-116	highpriest of Asia of the temple in Ephesus common to Asia	T. Fl. Montanus	Akmonia	In.	IGR 4.1696 (corrected version of IGR 4.643)
102-130	highpriest of Asia of the temple in Ephesus common to Asia	T. Fl. Montanus	Ephesus	In.	IvE 6.2061 II ("highpriesthood" also attested)
104	[highpriest of Asia] of the temple [in Ephe]sus common [to Asia]	(generic reference not involving an individual)	Ephesus	In.	IvE 1,1.27 l. 259-60
104	highpriestly year	(does not refer to an individual)	Ephesus	In.	IvE 1,1.27 l. 203-4
114-	highpriest of Asia of the temples in Pergamum	M. Aur. Severus	Aizanoi	In.	IGR 4.577

Cont.

Date	Title of office	Name of official	Findspot of data	Medium	Publication
117-138?	[highpries]t of Asia of the temple in Kyzikos	???	Kyzikos	In.	IGR 4.157
117-138	highpriest of Asia of the temple in Kyzikos	Aebutius Flaccus	Kyzikos	In.	IGR 4.153
117-138	highpriest of Asia	Ti. Cl. Mithridates	Apameia	In.	IGR 4.780
117-138	highpriest of Asia	Ti. Cl. Mithridates	Apameia	In.	IGR 4.787
117-	highpriest of Asia of the temples in Smyrna	Ael. Cl. Lepidus	Aizanoi	In.	IGR 4.586
120-200	highpriest of Asia	Pu. Ael. Zeuxidemos Cassianus	Hierapolis	In.	IGR 4.819
120-215	highpriest of Asia of the temples in Pergamum	Ti. Cl. Pius	Pergamum	In.	AvP 8,3.30
120-	highpriest of Asia of the temple in Kyzikos	G. Orfius Fl. Philographos, husband of Vibia Polla	Kyzikos	In.	IGR 4.155
130-150	[highpriest] of the temples in Ephesus	Ulpius Aristokratos	Ephesus	In.	ÖJh 55 (1984) Haupt. 126-27.
130-150	[highpriest of the temples in Ephesus]	[Ulpius Aristokratos]	Ephesus	In.	ÖJh 55 (1984) Haupt. 126-27
130-211	highprie[st o]f Asia of the temples in Eph[esus]	Ennius Rufus	Ephesus	In.	IvE 3.664b
130-211	highpriest of Asia of the temples in Ephesus	G. Pompeius Hermippos	Ephesus	In.	IvE 6.2069
130-211	highpriest of Asia of the temples in Ephesus	L. Cl. Charidemos Philometor	Ephesus	In.	IvE 3.642

Cont.

Date	Title of office	Name of official	Findspot of data	Medium	Publication
130-211	served well as high-[priest] of Asi[a] of the temple[s] [in E]ph[esus]	M. Ju. Aquila, son of Ju. Damianus	Ephesus	In.	IvE 3.686
130-211	[highpriest] of Asia	T. Oppius Apher Pollius Tertullus	Ephesus	In.	SEG 4.519
130-211	highpriest of Asia	Ti. Cl. Melito, father of Ti. Ju. Reginus	Ephesus	In.	IvE 3.692
130-	served as highpriest of the two temples in Ephesus	Ti. Cl. Piso Diophantos	Ephesus	In.	IvE 2.428 (highly stylized text)
130-	highpriest of Asia of the temples in Ephesus	???	Ephesus	In.	IvE 5.1900(5) (very fragmentary)
130-	highpriest of Asia of the temples in Ephesus	???	Ephesus	In.	IvE 5.1554(1) (very fragmentary)
130-	highpriest(s) of the temple[s in Ephesus]	???, ancestors of Menandra	Ephesus	In.	IvE 3.792
130-	highpries[t of A]sia of the temple[s] in [Ephes]us	[M.] Ulpius Damas [Catullinus]	Ephesus	In.	IvE 6.2067
130-	highpriest of Asia of the temples in Ephesus	Pu. Titius Secundus	Ephesus	In.	IvE 3.722
130-	highpriest of Asia [of the temples in Ephesus]	Ti. Cl. Menandros	Ephesus	In.	IvE 7,2.4354

Cont.

Date	Title of office	Name of official	Findspot of data	Medium	Publication
130-	[...highpriest of Asia] of the temples [in Ephesus...]	Ved[ius...]	Ephesus	In.	IvE 5.1900(3) (very fragmentary)
134/135	highpriest of Asia of the temple in Ephesus	Ti. Cl. Touendianos Magnus Charidemos	Ephesus	In.	IvE 2.279
135-	highpriest of Asia of the temples in Ephesus	Aristokrates of Keramos	Ephesus	In.	IvE 3.618
137	highpriest of Asia of the temples in Pergamum	Temon	Pergamum	In.	APAW 1932:51 #3
138-161	highpriest of Asia	???, ancestor of T. Fl. Julianus	Ephesus	In.	IvE 3.674
138-161	highpriest of Asia	???, father of T. Fl. Julianus	Ephesus	In.	IvE 3.674
138-	highpriest of Asia of the temples of the Sardians in Lydia	L. Ju. Bonnatus	Sardis	In.	IGR 4.1523
150-170	highpriest of Asia	G. Ju. Philippos, father of G. Julius	Tralleis	In.	Sterrett, Journey, 325 #379
150-170	highpriest of Asia	[G. Juli]us Philip[pos]	Tralleis	In.	BCH 29 (1905) 361
150-170	high[priest of Asia]	G. Julius Phili[ppos]	Tralleis	In.	AthMitt 26 (1901) 239 #3
150-180	[...h]ighprie[st...] (provincial?)	[Cn.] Dot[tius Pl]anc[ianus]	Ephesus	In.	IvE 6.2957a

Cont.

Date	Title of office	Name of official	Findspot of data	Medium	Publication
150-200	highpriests of Asia	???, ancestors of Ti. Cl. Campanus Aurelianus	Aizanoi	In.	IGR 4.578
150-200	highpriest of Asia	M. Cl. P. Vedius Antoninus Sabinus	Ephesus	In.	IvE 3.732
150-200	highpriest(s) of Asia	???, ancestors of Julia Marcellina	Synnada	In.	MAMA 6.373
150-	highpriest of Asia of the temples in Sardis	L. Ju. Libonianos	Sardis	In.	Sardis 7.47
160-180	highpriest of the temples in Ephesus	Ti. Ju. Reginus, son of Ti. Cl. Melito	Ephesus	In.	IvE 4.1105
161	designated highpriest of Asia	M. Ulpius Appuleius Eurykles	Aizanoi	In.	IGR 4.564
161-169	highpriest of Asia	Cl. Ant. Lepidus	Sardis	In.	BASOR 158 (1960) 7-10 #4
161-180	served as highpriest of Asia	Ti. Cl. Charidemos Philometor	Magnesia	In.	IvMag 188
165-175	highpriest twice of the temples in Ephesus	Ti. Ju. Reginus	Ephesus	In.	IvE 5.1605
165-175	highpriest twice of the temples in Ephesus	Ti. Ju. Reginus	Ephesus	In.	IvE 5.1611
170-211	highpriest of Asia of the temples in Ephesus	Timaios, highpriest together with wife Amphilla, son of Attalos, father of Aquila	Ephesus	In.	IvE 3.721

Cont.

Date	Title of office	Name of official	Findspot of data	Medium	Publication
180-192	highpriest of Asia of the temples in Ephesus	M. Aur. Mindius Mattidianus Pollio	Ephesus	In.	IvE 3.627 (served 5 days?)
180-192	designated highpriest of Asia of the temples in Smyrna a second time	M. Ulpius Appuleius Eurykles	Aphrodisias	In.	OGIS 509
180-220	highpriest of Asia	Aur. Athenaios	Ephesus	In.	IvE 7,1.3057
180-220	highpriest of Asia	Vedius G. Sabinianus	Ephesus	In.	IvE 7,1.3072
180-220	highpriest of Asia of the temples in Pergamum	Ju. Calpurnius	Philadelphia	In	IGR 4.1639
180-220	twice served as high-priest of Asia	Ti. Cl. Frontonianus	Melos	In.	IG 12,3.209 #1119
188/189	highpriest of the temples in Ephesus	Timaios, son of Attalos	Ephesus	In.	IvE 3.619A
188/189	highpriest of the temples in Ephesus	Timaios, son of Attalos	Ephesus	In.	IvE 3.619B
190-210	highpriest of Asia of the temples in Pergamum	L. Fl. Hermokrates	Pergamum	In.	AvP 8,3.34
190-	highpriest of Asia	L. Aur. Aristomenes, husband of Aur. Tatia	Thyatira	In.	IGR 4.1229
*190-	highpriest of Asia	G. Ju. Hippianos, husband of Corn. Secunda	Thyatira	In.	IGR 4.1244 (210- CE)

Cont.

Date	Title of office	Name of official	Findspot of data	Medium	Publication
193-211	highpriest of Asia	L. Ant. Cl. Dometinus Diogenes I	Aphrodisias	In.	CIG 2777
193-211	highpriest of Asia	L. Ant. Cl. Dometinus Diogenes II	Aphrodisias	In.	MAMA 8.502
193-235?	highpriest of Asia	Pu. Ael. Paullus, husband of Ulpia Marcella	Thyatira	In.	IGR 4.1225
200?	served as highpriest of Asia of the temples in first and twice neokorate Pergamum	Ti. Cl. Celsus Orestianus, husband of Flavia Lycia	Cibyra	kIn.	IGR 4.908
200-250	highpriest of Asia	Demetrios	Synnada	In.	IGR 4.707
200-	[. . . highpriest of Asia of the temp]les in Ephesus	Aurelius [. . .]	Ephesus	In.	IvE 3.626
200-	highpriest of Asia of the temples in Pergamum	(G. Voconius) Ael. Stratonikos	Dorylaion	In.	ÖJh 16 (1913) Beib. 72 #2
210-220	highpriest (of Asia)	Ti. Cl. Lupus	Thyatira	kIn.	IGR 4.1236
211-225	highpriest(s) of Asia	???, parents and grandparents of T. Ant. Cl. Alfenus Arignotus	Thyatira	In.	IGR 4.1213
218-222	highpriest of Asia	M. Aur. Herculanus	Ephesus	In.	IvE 3.625
221-224	highpriest of Asia of the temples in Sardis	Aur. Sept. Apollonios	Olympia	In.	Eckstein 6.221
222-235	highpriest of Asia of the temples in Pergamum	M. Aur. Diadochos	Thyatira	In.	IGR 4.1230

Cont.

Date	Title of office	Name of official	Findspot of data	Medium	Publication
222-235	[highpriest of Asia of the temples i]n Pergamum	M. Aur. Diadochos	Thyatira	In.	IGR 4.1231 (cf. IGR 4.1230)
222-	highpriesthood (provincial?)	M. Aurelius	Ephesus	In.	IvE 7,1.3071
*225?	highpriest of Asia	Proclianus Trypho, husband of Aeliana Regina	Apameia	In.	IGR 4.784 (253-268 CE)
238-244	highpriest(s) of Asia	???, ancestors of T. Aruntius Nikomachos	Temeno-thyrai	In.	IGR 4.617
240?	[...hi]ghpries[t of Asia...]	[Ti. Cl. Dy]nato[s...]	Ephesus	In.	IvE 3.643b
244-249	highpriests of Asia	???, ancestors of Corn. Memmius Charidemos Teuthras	Sebaste	In.	IGR 4.688
???	highpriest of Asia	G. Ju. Julianus	Magnesia	In.	IvMag 151
???	highpriest of Asia	G. Ju. Lepidus, son of Marcus	Thyatira	In.	IGR 4.1246
???	highpriest of Asia	G. Ju. Pytho	Tralleis	In.	BCH 11 (1887) 346 #1
???	highpriest of A[sia]	Ti. Ju. Damianus	Miletus	In.	CIG 2887
???	highprie[st of A]sia	G. Ju. A[...] Saturninus	Dorylaion	In.	Echos d'Orient 10 (1907) 77-78 #2
???	highpriest(s) of Asia	???, ancestors of M. Ant. Popillius Andronikos Flavianus	Aphrodisias	In.	REG 19 (1906) 139-40 #71

Cont.

Date	Title of office	Name of official	Findspot of data	Medium	Publication
???	highpriest(s) o[f Asia. . .]	???, ancestors of Ulpius/Ulpia	Mylasa	In.	IvMyl 1.151
???	[highpr]iest of Asi[a. . .]	???	Ephesus	In.	IvE 5.1549 (very fragmentary)
???	[high]priest of Asia[. . .]	???	Ephesus	In.	IvE 5.1900(6) (very fragmentary)
???	served as highpriest of Augustus (provincial?)	Tiberi[us Cl. . .]	Ephesus	k?In	IvE 4.1404

ATTESTATIONS OF HIGHPRIESTESSES OF ASIA

Date	Title of office	Name of official	Findspot of data	Medium	Publication
*40-59 CE	highpriestess of Asia	Juliane, daughter of Eustratos, wife of Alkiphron	Magnesia	In.	IvMag 158 (54-59 CE)
80-120	highpriestess of Asia	Antonia Caecilia, wife of Ti. Cl. Sokrates	Thyatira	In.	IGR 4.1238
85-130	highpriestess of Asia of the temple in Ephesus	Flavia Ammion Aristio, wife of T. Fl. Hermokrates	Phokaia	In.	IGR 4.1325
89-150	highpriestess of Asia	Stratonike, wife of Ti. Cl. Pheseinos, mother of Claudia Tryphaina	Teos	In.	IGR 4.1571
89-150	h[ighpriestess] of Asia	Claudia Tryphaina, daughter of Stratonike and Ti. Cl. Pheseinos	Teos	In.	IGR 4.1571
97-100	h[ighprieste]ss of Asia	Vedia Marcia, daughter of Publius	Ephesus	In.	IvE 4.1017
130/131	highpriestess of Asia	Skaptia Phirmilla, wife of G. Cl. Verulanus Marcellus	Ephesus	In.	IvE 2.430
130-150	[. . .h]ighpriestess of Asia of the temples in [Ephesus. . .]	???	Ephesus	In.	IvE 3.814
130-211	serving as highpriestess of the great temples in Ephesus	Aelia Ammia, mother of M. Ju. Aquila	Amorium	In.	EpAn 16 (1990) 69-80
130-211	highpriestess of the temples in Ephesus	Aufidia Quintillia, wife of Ti. Cl. Ael. Crispus	Ephesus	In.	IvE 3.637
130-	[high]pri[estess] of Asia of the temples in Ephesus	???, wife of Vetulenius	Ephesus	In.	IvE 5.1553

Cont.

Date	Title of office	Name of official	Findspot of data	Medium	Publication
130-	[h]ighpriestess of [As]ia of the temples in Ephesus	???, wife of an Aelius	Ephesus	In.	IvE 3.994
130-	highpriestess of Asia of the temples in Ephesus	Mindia Stratonike Hegoumene	Ephesus	In.	ÖJh 55 (1984) Haupt. 125
130-	highpriestess(es) of the temple[s in Ephesus]	???, ancestors of Menandra	Ephesus	In.	IvE 3.792
140-160?	highpriestess of Asia	Flavia Papiana, wife of Pu. Vedius Antoninus	Ephesus	In.	IvE 3.729
150-200	highpriestess(es) of Asia	???, ancestors of Julia Marcellina	Synnada	In.	MAMA 6.373
150-200	highpriestess of Asia of the temples in Pergamum	Julia Marcellina	Synnada	In.	MAMA 6.373
150-200	highpriestess(es) of Asia	???, ancestors of Ti. Cl. Campanus Aurelianus	Aizanoi	In.	IGR 4.578
150-214	high[priestess] of Asia of the temples in Smy[rna...]	Aurelia Melite	Smyrna	In.	IvSm 2,1.727
170-211	served as highpriestess (of the temples in Ephesus) with husband	Amphilla, wife of Timaios	Ephesus	In.	IvE 3.721
170-211	highpriestess of Asia	Flavia Appia, wife of Carminius Claudianus II	Aphrodisias	In.	MAMA 8.517b

Cont.

Date	Title of office	Name of official	Findspot of data	Medium	Publication
*180-235	highpriestess twice of Asia	Flavia Priscilla, wife of Aurelius Diadochos, mother of Aurelia Hermonassa	Thyatira	In.	IGR 4.1233 (222-235)
180-	highpriestess of Asia of the temples in Smyrna	Aurelia Melite	Smyrna	In.	IGR 4.1415
180-	highpri[estess of Asia of the temples in Smyrna]	Aurelia Melite	Smyrna	In.	IGR 4.1435 (cf. IGR 4.1415)
190-	highpriestess of Asia	Aurelia Tatia, wife of L. Aur. Aristomenes	Thyatira	In.	IGR 4. 1229
*190?-	highpriestess of Asia	Cornelia Secunda, wife of G. Ju. Hippianos	Thyatira	In.	IGR 4.1244 (210?- CE)
193-235?	highpriestess of Asia of the temples in Smyrna	Ulpia Marcella, wife of Pu. Ael. Paullus	Thyatira	In.	IGR 4.1254
193-235?	highpriestess of Asia	Ulpia Marcella, wife of Pu. Ael. Paullus	Thyatira	In.	IGR 4.1225
200?	served as highpriest(ess) of Asia of the temples in first and twice neokorate Pergamum	Flavia Lycia, wife of Ti. Cl. Orestianos, daughter of Fl. Hiero	Cibyra	In.	IGR 4.908
200-250	highprie[stess of Asia of the temples] in Sardis	???	Didyma	In.	Hellenica 11-12 (1960) 476 l. 5-6
200-	highpriestess of Asia of the temples in Ephesus	Julia Atticilla, wife of Daphnos	Ephesus	In.	IvE 3.617

Cont.

Date	Title of office	Name of official	Findspot of data	Medium	Publication
200-	highpriestess twice of the temples in the most illustrious metropolis, the city of Ephesus	Publia Ael. Tundianus, wife of L. Rupillius Alexandros	Ephesus	In.	IvE 3.714
204/205	highpriestess of Asia	Memmia Ariste Teuthrantis	Sebaste	In.	IGR 4.687
211-225	highpriestess(es) of Asia	???, parents and grandparents of T. Ant. Cl. Alfenus Arignotus	Thyatira	In.	IGR 4.1213
222-235	twice highpriestess of Asia	Aurelia Hermonassa, wife of M. Aur. Diadochos	Thyatira	In.	IGR 4.1233
*225?	highpriestess of Asia	Aeliana Regina, wife of Proclianus Trypho	Apameia	In.	IGR 4.784 (253-268 CE)
238-244	highpriestess(es) of Asia	???, ancestors of T. Aruntius Nikomachos	Temenothyrai	In.	IGR 4.617
???	highpriestess of Asia	Claudia Ammion, wife of P. Gavius Capito	Ephesus	In.	IvE 3.681
???	highpriestess of Asia	Claudia Lorentia	Synnada	In.	IGR 4.706
???	served as highpriestess (provincial?)	Claudia or Claudiane	Dorylaion	In.	Echos d'Orient 10 (1907) 77 #2
???	highpriestess(es) of Asia	???, ancestors of M. Ant. Popillius Andronikos Flavianus	Aphrodisias	In.	REG 19 (1906) 139-40 #71
???	highpriestess(es) o[f Asia...]	???, ancestors of Ulpius/Ulpia	Mylasa	In.	IvMyl 1.151

ATTESTATIONS OF ASIARCHS

Date	Title of office	Name of official	Findspot of data	Medium	Publication
*80-90? CE	twice Asiarch	Fl. Krateros, ancestor of Ti. Cl. Polemon	Cibyra	In.	IGR 4.907 (ca. 200 CE)
*80-90?	twice Asiarch	Fl. Krateros, ancestor of Ti. Cl. Polemon	Cibyra	In.	IGR 4.912 (ca. 200 CE)
89/90	Asiarch	Tatianos	Ephesus	In.	IvE 2.492
90-130	Asiarch	[Ti. Cl]audius [Ari]stio	Ephesus	In.	IvE 3.638
92/93	[Asiarch]	(Ti.) Cl. [Aristio]	Ephesus	In.	IvE 2.461
92/93	Asiarch	Ti. Cl. Aristio	Ephesus	In.	IvE 2.508
100-110?	Asiarch	T. Fl. Peri[gene]s	Ephesus	In.	IvE 4.1270
*100-120	Asiarch	T. [Fl. Py]thio, father of T. Fl. Julianus	Ephesus	In.	IvE 7,2.4342 (130-211 CE)
100-200	[. . .]Asiarch[. . .]	???	Miletus	In.	Milet 1,7.327 #258
100-250	Asiarch	???	Ephesus	In.	IvE 7,1.3055
102-109	Asiarch	T. Fl. Pythio, son of Perigenes; husband of Fl. Myrtos; father of Fl. Aristobulus, and Fl. Julianus	Ephesus	In.	IvE 7,1.3033
102-109	Asiarch	T. Fl. Pythio, son of T. Fl. Perigenes; husband of Fl. Myrtos; father of Fl. Aristobulus and Fl. Julianus	Ephesus	In.	IvE 7,1.3034
102-114	Asiar[ch]	T. Fl. Pythio	Ephesus	In.	IvE 3.858
102-114	three times Asiarch	(Ti.) Cl. Aristio	Ephesus	In.	IvE 2.424

Cont.

Date	Title of office	Name of official	Findspot of data	Medium	Publication
104	those who served as Asiarch	(refers to the office, not to an individual)	Ephesus	In.	IvE 1a.27 l. 240
104-110	Asiarch	Cl. Menandros	Ephesus	In.	IvE 4.1023
115/116	Asia[rch]	T. Fl. Aristobulus	Ephesus	In.	IvE 5.1500
116?	[...A]siarchs	???	Ephesus	In.	IvE 3.670a
117-119	Asiarch	Publius Vedius Antoninus	Ephesus	In.	IvE 2.429
*117-138	Asiarch	Fl. Julianus, father of T. Fl. Julianus, descendent of T. Fl. Pythio	Ephesus	In.	IvE 7,2.4342 (130-211 CE)
117-138	Asiarch	Fl. Julianus, father of T. Fl. Julianus, descendent of T. Fl. Pythio	Ephesus	In.	IvE 3.712b
117-	Asiarch	Ti. Cl. Me[no...]	Pergamum	In.	IGR 4.1688
117-	Asiarch	Aur. Menelaos, father of Aurelia Julia	Kyzikos	In.	IGR 4.154
120-130	three times Asiarch	Ti. Cl. Aristio	Ephesus	In.	IvE 7,2.5101
120-130	three times [Asiar]ch	Ti. Cl. Aristio	Ephesus	In.	IvE 7,2.5113
120-	Asiarch	Pu. Ael. Zeuxidemos Cassianus	Hierapolis	In.	IGR 4.828
120-	Asiar[ch...]	???	Pergamum	In.	AvP 8,3.153
123-	Asiarch	Chersiphron	Smyrna	In.	IGR 4.1431 l. 7

Cont.

Date	Title of office	Name of official	Findspot of data	Medium	Publication
130/131	Asiarch	G. Cl. Verulanus Marcellus, husband of Skaptia Phirmilla	Ephesus	In.	IvE 2.430
130-138	Asiarch	Ti. Cl. Pius Pisoninus	Teos	In.	IGR 4.1567
*130-140	Asiarch of the temples there (i.e., in Ephesus)	Cl. Zeno, ancestor of honorand	Ephesus	In.	IvE 7,1.3072 (ca. 270 CE)
*130-150	Asiarch of the temples there (i.e., in Smyrna)	Cl. Salvius, ancestor of honorand	Ephesus	In.	IvE 7,1.3072 (ca. 270 CE)
*130-150	Asiarch of the temples in Ephesus	Cl. Zeno, ancestor of honorand, relative of Cl. Kallikrates and Cl. Diogenes	Ephesus	In.	IvE 3.810 (ca. 200 CE)
*130-150	A[siar]ch of the tem-ple[s] in Ephesus	Ulpiu[s Ru]fus	Ephesus	In.	IvE 7,1.3017 (200-220 CE)
130-211	Asiarch	Pu. Vedius Antoninus	Ephesus	In.	IvE 6.2039 (extant in two copies)
130-211	Asiarch	G. Pompeius Hermippos	Ephesus	In.	IvE 3.710
130-211	twice Asiarch	???, a[ncestor] of [ ] Aur. Dionysios	Ephesus	In.	Le Bas-Waddington 3.158a
130-211	Asiarch of the tem[ples] in Ephesus	Ti. Cl. Ael. Crispus, husband of Aufidia Quintillia	Ephesus	In.	IvE 3.637
130-211	Asiarch of the first and greatest metropolis of Asia, the city of the Ephesians (who are) twice neokoros of the Sebastoi	T. Fl. Munatios	Ephesus	In.	Le Bas-Waddington 3.158a

Cont.

Date	Title of office	Name of official	Findspot of data	Medium	Publication
130-211	Asiarch	Pu. Vedius Antoninus	Ephesus	In.	IvE 3.697b
130-211	Asiarch [of the temples] of the first and greatest metropolis of Asia and twice neokoros of the Sebastoi city of the Ephesians	T. Fl. Munatios, ancestor of M. Ju. Aur. Dionysios	Ephesus	In.	IvE 3.687
130-220?	Asiarch	Aquila	Amorium	In.	AnSt 18 (1988) 181
130-	Asiarch of the temples in Ephesus	T. Fl. Clitosthenes	Thera	In.	IG 12,3.123 #525
130-	twice Asiarch	(T.) Fl. Clitosthenes	Tralleis	In.	AthMitt 8 (1883) 330-31 #11
*130-	Asiarchs of the temples in Ephesus	???, ancestors of Sem(pronii) Arunc(ii)	Panamara	In.	SIG 2.900 l. 6-7 (310-340 CE)
135	Asiarch	[Ti. Cl]audius Demostratos Caelianus	Ephesus	In.	ÖJh 53 (1981-82) Haupt. 136 #146
135	Asiarch	[Ti. Cl]audius Demostratos [Caelianus]	Ephesus	In.	IvE 7,2.4101b
138-161	Asiarch	???	Ephesus	In.	IvE 4.1162 (fragmentary)
138-161	Asiarch	Pu. Ael. Themistokles	Keramos (Kos)	In.	JHS 11 (1890) 121-22 #5 l. 15
138-161	Asiarch	[Fro]nto?	Sardis	Cn.	CollWadd 5254

Cont.

Date	Title of office	Name of official	Findspot of data	Medium	Publication
138-161	Asi(arch)	(Ju.) Pollio	Pergamum	Cn.	Mionnet Sup 5.440 #1003
138-161	Asi(arch)	(Ju.) Pollio	Pergamum	Cn.	Mionnet Sup 5.440 #1004
138-161	Asi(arch)	(Ju.) Pollio	Pergamum	Cn.	APAW (1910) 93
138-161	Asi(arch)	J(u.) Pollio	Pergamum	Cn.	Mionnet Sup 5.440 #1005
138-161	Asiarch	M. Cl. Fronto	???	Cn.	HuntColl 2.321 #1 (coin of the Ionian League of 13 Cities)
138-161	Asiarch	M. Cl. Fronto	???	Cn.	HuntColl 2.321 #2 (coin of the Ionian League of 13 Cities)
138-161	Asiarch	M. Cl. Fronto	???	Cn.	BM Ionia 16 #1 (coin of the Ionian League of 13 Cities)
138-161	Asiarch	M. Cl. Fronto	???	Cn.	BM Ionia 16 #2 (coin of the Ionian League off 13 Cities)
138-161	Asiarch	(M.) Cl. Fronto	Sardis	Cn.	SNGvA 3154
138-161	Asiarch	M. Cl. Dynatos	???	kCn.	CollWadd 5254
138-180	Asiarch	(Ti. Cl.) Piso Tertullinus	Synnada	In.	MAMA 6.374

Cont.

Date	Title of office	Name of official	Findspot of data	Medium	Publication
*140?	Asiarch twice	Ti. Cl. Hiero, father of Ti. Cl. Polemon	Cibyra	In.	IGR 4.907 (late 2d century)
145-175	Asiarch	Ael. Zoilos	Abydus	Cn.	SNG Cop Troas 60
145-175	Asi(arch)	J(ulius) Pollio	Pergamum	Cn.	Mionnet Sup 5.444 #1021
146/147?	Asiarch	Ti. Cl. Polydeukos Marcellus	Ephesus	In.	IvE 1a.23 l. 35
150-155	twice Asiar[ch of the tem]ples i[n Ephesus]	Ti. Ju. Reginus	Ephesus	In.	IvE 4.1105a
150-200	Asiarch of Asia	M. Cl. Pu. Vedius Antoninus Sabinus	Ephesus	In.	IvE 7,2.4110
150-200	Asiarch	Ti. Cl. Pankratides	Ephesus	In.	IvE 7,2.4346
150-200?	Asiarch	Nemerius Castricius Paconianus	Kos	In.	IGR 4.1075
150-200?	Asiarch	Sellius Sulla	Philadelphia	In.	IGR 4.1643
150-200?	Asiarchs	???, ancestors	Ephesus	In.	ÖJh 55 (1984) Haupt. 134-35
150-211	twice Asiarch	M. Ju. Aur. Dionysios, descendent of T. Fl. Munatios	Ephesus	In.	IvE 3.687
150-	Asiarch	L. Timon	Smyrna	In.	IGR 4.1454
150-	Asiarchs twice	Marcia Cl. Juliane, wife of M. Aur. Zeno	Bournabat	In.	IGR 4.1481
150-	Asiarchs twice	M. Aur. Zeno, husband of M. Cl. Juliane	Bournabat	In.	IGR 4.1481

Cont.

Date	Title of office	Name of official	Findspot of data	Medium	Publication
150-	twice Asiarch	M. Aur. Charidemos Julianus	Smyrna	In.	IvSm 2,1.639
150-	Asiarch	Pu. Vedius Antoninus (Phaedrus Sabinianus?)	Ephesus	In.	IvE 6.2065
150?-	Asiarchs	???, relatives of Aurelia Ju. Papario	Ephesus	In.	IvE 4.1066
*150?-	Asiarch	M. Aur. Manilius Hermippos, father of M. Aur. Manilius Alexandros	Philadelphia	In.	IGR 4.1635 (170- CE)
161-169	Asiarch	Cl. Pollio	Hieropolis	Cn.	Imhoof-Blumer, Kleinas. Münzen, 1.244 #3
161-169	Asiarch	Cl. Pollio	Hieropolis	Cn.	Imhoof-Blumer, Kleinas. Münzen, 1.244 #4
161-169	Asiarch	Cl. Pollio	Hieropolis	Cn.	CollWadd 6189
161-169	Asiarch	G. Ju. Philippos	Olympia	In.	OGIS 498
161-169	Asiar(ch)	(G. Aruntius) Maternus	Temenothyrae	Cn.	SNGvA 4004
161-180	Asiarch	Apollodoros	Miletus	In.	Le Bas-Waddington 3.213
161-180	Asi(arch)	Menandros	Synaos	Cn.	SNGvA 3967
161-180	(A)s(iarch)	Menandros	Synaos	Cn.	SNGvA 3968
161-180	Asiarch	Menandros	Synaos	Cn.	BM Phrygia 390 #18
161-180	Asiarch	G. Asin(ius) Agre(us) Philopappus	Halia	Cn.	BM Phrygia 44 #2

Cont.

Date	Title of office	Name of official	Findspot of data	Medium	Publication
161-180	Asiarch	G. Asinius Agreus Philopappus	Halia	Cn.	BM Phrygia 44 #3
161-180	Asiarch	Pu. Ael. Martialis	Ephesus	In.	IvE 3.621a
161-180	Asiarch	Ti. Cl. Philopappus	Antandros	In.	IGR 4.261
161-180	Asiarch	M. Ulpius Eurykles	Aizanoi	Cn.	CollWadd 5545
161-180	Asiarch	(M. Ulp.) Carminius Claudianus I	Attuda	Cn.	CollWadd 2268
161-180?	Asiarch	(Pu.) Ael. Martialis	Ephesus	In.	IvE 2.214
161-192	Asiarch	G. Aruntius Maternus	Sardis	In.	Sardis 7.77
161-217	Asiarch	M. Aurelius ???	near Smyrna	In.	BCH 1 (1877) 55-56 #4
164-169	Asiarch	(M. Cl.) Pu. Vedius Antoninus (Sabinus), father of Phaedrus Sabinianus	Ephesus	In.	IvE 3.728
164-169	Asiarch	(M. Cl.) Pu. Vedius Antoninus (Phaedrus Sabinianus), son of Sabinus	Ephesus	In.	IvE 3.728
165-175	Asiarch of the temples in Ephesus	T. Fl. Clitosthenes Julianus, father of T. Fl. Clitosthenes	Ephesus	In.	IvE 3.671
165-175	Asiarch twice of the temples in Ephesus	Ti. Ju. Reginus	Ephesus	In.	IvE 5.1604
165-175	Asiarch	Ti. Ju. Reginus	Ephesus	In.	IvE 5.1621
170?	Asiarch	Ti. Cl. Deioterianus, brother of Ti. Cl. Polemon	Cibyra	In.	IGR 4.906

Cont.

Date	Title of office	Name of official	Findspot of data	Medium	Publication
170?	Asiarch	Ti. Cl. Deioterianus	Cibyra	In.	IGR 4.907
170?	Asiarch	Ti. Cl. Polemon	Cibyra	In.	IGR 4.906
170?	Asiarch	Ti. Cl. Polemon	Cibyra	In.	IGR 4.907
170?	Asiarch	Ti. Cl. Polemon	Cibyra	In.	IGR 4.910
170-175	Asiarch	M. Fl. Rufus	Ephesus	In.	IvE 4.1130
170-175	Asiarch twice of the temples in Ephesus	Ti. Ju. Reginus	Ephesus	In.	IvE 4.1130
170-180	twice Asiarch of Asia of the temples in Ephesus	Ti. Ju. Reginus	Ephesus	In.	IvE 3.692
170-	Asiarch	M. Aur. Manilius Alexandros, son of M. Aur. Manilius Hermippos	Philadelphia	In.	IGR 4.1635
175-200	Asiarch	M. Aur. Menemachos	Ephesus	In.	IvE 4.1075
175-200	Asiarch	Ti. Cl. Tatianos Julianus	Ephesus	In.	IvE 4.1182
175-200	Asiarch	Ti. Cl. Tatianos Julianus	Ephesus	In.	IvE 5.1620
175-225	Asiarch	(Ael.) Plotius Leonidas	Thera	In.	IG 12,3.124 #529
175-225	Asiarch	M. Fl. Dometianus	Ephesus	In.	ÖJh 26 (1930) Beib. 57-58
175-225	Asiarch	???, father of M. Fl. Dometianus	Didyma	In.	ÖJh 26 (1930) Beib. 57-58
177-180	Asiarch	M. Ant. Alexandros Appianus	Julia Gordos	In.	IGR 4.1294

Cont.

Date	Title of office	Name of official	Findspot of data	Medium	Publication
180-183	Asiarch	Claudius Kalobrotos	Okokleia	Cn.	Head, Historia Num., 681
180-190	Asiar[ch]	Aur. Meidias	Kyzikos	Cn.	SNGvA 1270
180-192	Asiarch of the temples in Ephesus	(M.) Fl. Dometianus	Didyma	In.	IvDid 168
180-192	Asiarch	G. Aruntius Maternus	Temenothyrae	Cn.	SNG Cop Phrygia 741
180-192	twice Asi(arch)	Ael. Zoilos	Abydos	Cn.	Imhoof-Blumer, Münzen 98 #203
180-192	Asiarch	???, father of (M.) Fl. Dometianus	Didyma	In.	IvDid 168
180-192	Asiar(ch)	G. (Aruntius) Maternus	Temenothyra	Cn.	Imhoof-Blumer, Münzen 202 #640
180-192	Asiarch	Alexandros, son of Deis	Ephesus	In.	IvE 3.613
180-192	[Asiarch]	[Alexandros, son of Deis]	Ephesus	In.	IvE 3.613a (cf. IvE 3.613)
180-192	Asiarch	???, father of M. Fl. Dometianus	Ephesus	In.	IvE 3.951
180-220	Asiarch	M. Ant. Antiochos, son of Apollodoros (II)	Didyma	In.	IvDid 249
180-220	Asiarch	M. Fl. Domitianus	Ephesus	In.	IvE 3.951
180-220	Asiarch	T. Fl. Clitosthenes (Julianus?), father of T. Fl. Clitosthenes, grandfather of T. Fl. Clitosthenes	Ephesus	In.	IvE 6.2070

Cont.

Date	Title of office	Name of official	Findspot of data	Medium	Publication
180-220	Asiarch	[[ ]]	Ephesus	In.	IvE 2.523
180-220	[Asiarch]	???, descendent of Cl. Kallikrates, Cl. Zeno, and Cl. Diogenes	Ephesus	In.	IvE 3.810
180-220	Asiarch of the temples in Ephesus	Cl. Kallikrates, ancestor of honorand, relative of Cl. Zeno and Cl. Diogenes	Ephesus	In.	IvE 3.810
180-220	Asiarch of the temples in Ephesus	Cl. Diogenes, ancestor of honorand, relative of Cl. Kallikrates and Cl. Zeno	Ephesus	In.	IvE 3. 810
*180-220	Asiarch	Aur. Athenaios, father of Aurelia Hermonassa	Thyatira	In.	IGR 4.1233 (222-235 CE)
*180-220	Asiarch	Aur. Athenaios, father of Aurelia Hermonassa	Thyatira	In.	IGR 4.1234 (220-250 CE?)
*180-220	twice Asiarch [of the temples in Ephesus]	Ti. Cl. Zeno	Ephesus	In.	IvE 3.653 (200-250 CE)
180-	Asiarch	Plotius Aur. Gratus	Kyzikos	In.	IGR 4.156
180-	Asiarch	[Fl.] Hermolaos	Hypaipa	In.	IvE 7,2.3802
190-220	Asiarch	T. Fl. Menandros (I), father of T. Fl. L. Hierax	Ephesus	In.	IvE 7,1.3062
190-220	Asiarch	T. Fl. Menandros (II), brother of T. Fl. L. Hierax	Ephesus	In.	IvE 7,1.3062

Cont.

Date	Title of office	Name of official	Findspot of data	Medium	Publication
193-211	Asiar(ch) (a third time?)	(M.) Au[ ]nos (M. Ael. Apion?)	Hypaipa	Cn.	Mionnet Sup 7.358-59 #188
193-211	Asiar(ch) a second time	(M.?) Ael. Apion	Hypaipa	Cn.	Mionnet Sup 7.359 #191
193-211	Asiarch	M. Aurelius	Hypaipa	Cn.	Mionnet Sup 7.359 #192
193-211	Asiarch	Alf(enus) Modestus	Castris Poianis (Thrace)	In.	SEG 1.331
193-211	Asiarch	Fl. Priscus (Negruos)	Akmonia	Cn.	BM Phrygia 13 #62
193-211	Asiar(ch)	Fl. Priscus Negruos	Akmonia	Cn.	Mionnet 4.200-201 #31
193-211	Asiarch	Fl. Priscus (Negruos)	Akmonia	Cn.	Imhoof-Blumer, Monnaies gr., 391 #50
193-211	Asiarch	Glykon	Hypaipa	Cn.	RevNum 1 (1883) 399
193-211	Asiarch	L. Aufidius Euphemos	Ephesus	In.	IvE 4.1171
193-211	Asiarch	M. L. Aurelius	Hypaipa	Cn.	RevNum 1 (1883) 399
193-211	Asiarch	T. Fl. Demetrios	Iasos	In.	BCH 11 (1887) 216 #8
193-	twice Asiarch	M. Aur. Julianus	Smyrna	In.	IGR 4.1433
198-217	Asiarch	M. L. Aurelius	Hypaipa	Cn.	Mionnet 4.55 #285
198-217	Asia(rch)	Fl. Priscus	Akmonia	Cn.	SNG Cop Phrygia 37
193-217	Asiarch	Fl. Priscus	Akmonia	Cn.	SNG Cop Phrygia 34
193-211	Asiarch	(M. Ulpius) Carminius Claudianus (II), husband of Flavia Appia	Attuda	Cn.	SNGvA 2501

Cont.

Date	Title of office	Name of official	Findspot of data	Medium	Publication
198-210	[Asiar]ch of the prytanis	Ti. Cl. Attalos Melior Cle[. . .]	Ephesus	In.	IvE 7,2.4109
198-217	Asiarch	(M. Ulpius Carminius) Claudianus (II), husband of Flavia Appia	Attuda	Cn.	SNGvA 2505
200-212	Asiarch	Alexandros	Otrus	Cn.	CollWadd 6371
200-212	Asiarch	Alexandros	Otrus	Cn.	CollWadd 6368
200-230	Asiarch	[ ]	Ephesus	In.	IvE 3.626
200-250	Asi(arch)	Aur. Hermolaos	Saitta	Cn.	BM Lydia 225 #65
200-250	Asiarch	M. Aur. Artemidoros	Ephesus	In.	IvE 7,1.3058
200-250	Asiarch	L. [Julius?] Apollinarios	Adramytteion	Cn.	CollWadd 614
200-250	Asiarch	Polybius	Attaleia	In.	IGR 4.1168b l. 10-11
200-250	Asiarch	Sulpicius Hermophilos	Sardis	Cn.	Eckhel, Doctrina num. 3 (1894) 115
200-250	Asiarch	G. Aufidius Mindius Polychronios	Ephesus	In.	IvE 3.815
200-250	As(iarch)	???, father of Ju. Charidemos	Synaos	Cn.	SNGvA 3970
200-250	Asiarch	???	Ephesus	In.	IvE 7,2.4345
200-250	Asiarch	Ju. Menekles Diophantos	Smyrna	In.	IvSm 2,1.637
200-	Asiarch	L. Rupillius Alexandros, husband of Pu. Ael. Tundianus	Ephesus	In.	IvE 3.714
200-	Asiarchs	???, ancestors	Didyma	In.	IvDid 239 A II

Cont.

Date	Title of office	Name of official	Findspot of data	Medium	Publication
200-	Asiarch	Cl. Themistokles	Attica	In.	IG 2,2.3704
200-	Asiarch	Pomponius Corn. Lollianus Hedianus	Smyrna	In.	IGR 4.1424
200-	Asiarch	Moschianos	Ephesus	In.	IvE 3.698
202-205	twice Asiarch	Menandros	Hypaipa	Cn.	RevNum 1 (1883) 400
210-220	Asiarch	M. Ful. Publicianus Nikephoros	Ephesus	In.	IvE 2.444
210-220	Asiarch	M. Ful. Publicianus Nikephoros	Ephesus	In.	IvE 2.445
210-230	Asiarch of Asia of the temples in Ephesus	M. Aur. Agathokles	Ephesus	In.	IvE 3.897
210-250	Asiarch	M. (Ful.) Publicianus Nikephoros	Ephesus	In.	IvE 6.2076
210-250	Asiarch	M. (Ful.) Publicianus Nikephoros	Ephesus	In.	IvE 6.2077
210-250	Asiarch	M. Ful. Publicianus Nikephoros	Ephesus	In.	IvE 6.2078
210-250	[Asiarch]	[M. Ful. Publicaianus Nikephoros]	Ephesus	In.	IvE 6.2080 (see IvE 6.2076-78)
210-250	Asiarch	(M.) Ful. Publicianus Nikephoros	Ephesus	In.	IvE 6.2082
210-250	Asiarch	M. Fulvi[us Publicianus N]ikephoros	Ephesus	In.	IvE 7,1.3086
210-250	[Asiarch]	[M. Ful. P]ublici[anus Nikephoros]	Ephesus	In.	IvE 3.679a

Cont.

Date	Title of office	Name of official	Findspot of data	Medium	Publication
210-250	Asiarch	M. Ful. Pu[blicianus] Nikephoros	Ephesus	In.	IvE 4.1087a
210?-	Asiarch	G. Ju. Julianus Tatianos, son of G. Ju. Hippianos and Cornelia Secunda	Thyatira	In.	IGR 4.1244
210?-	Asiarch	G. Ju. Julianus Tatianos, son of G. Ju. Hippianos and Cornelia Secunda	Thyatira	In.	IGR 4.1245
211	Asiarch of the Pergamenes	Ju. Dionysios	Thyatira	In.	IGR 4.1247
211-217	Asiarch	Gaius Antonius Nigrinus	Otrus	Cn.	CollWadd 6369
211-217	Asiar[ch] of the [secreta]riat	[L. Aufidius Euphe]mos	Ephesus	In.	IvE 7,1.3001(2)
211-217	Asiarch three times	Pu. (or ''Lucius'') Ael. Pigres Crispus	Laodikeia	Cn.	SNGvA 3857
211-217	Asi(arch)		Magnesia	In.	IvMag 197
211-217	three times Asiarch	Pu. (or ''Lucius'') Ael. Pigres	Laodikeia	Cn.	CollWadd 7072
212-235	Asiarch of the temples in Pergamum	Aur. Gaius	Pergamum	In.	AvP 8,3.44
212-250	Asiarch of the three temples in Ephesus	M. Aur. Daphnos	Ephesus	In.	IvE 7,1.3070
212-250	Asiarch	M. Aur. Daphnos	Ephesus	In.	IvE 3.616
212-	Asiarch	Attalos, father of Aur. Moschion	Hypaipa	In.	IvE 7,2.3809
212-	served as Asiarch	Lucius? Annianus	Thyatira	In.	IGR 4.1226

Cont.

Date	Title of office	Name of official	Findspot of data	Medium	Publication
212-	Asiarch	M. Aur. Themistokles	Herakleia-Perinthos	In.	IGR 1.798
212-	designated Asiarch	Ulpius Apollonios Plautus	Ephesus	In.	IvE 3.740
212-	Asiarch	Attalos, father of Aur. Moschion	Hypaipa	In.	IvE 7,2.3810
214-	Asiarch	Pomponius Corn. Lollianus Hedianus	Smyrna	In.	IvSm 2,1.638
217-218	Asiarch	Aur. Daphnos	Ephesus	In.	IvE 3.624
217-	Asiarch	Aruntius Marinus	Sardis	In.	IGR 4.1518
218-222	Asiarch	M. Ful. Publicianus Nikephoros	Ephesus	In.	IvE 3.739
218-235	[Asiar]ch	[M. F]ul. Publicianus [Nik]ephoros	Ephesus	In.	IvE 3.679
222-235	Asiarch (lasting four days?)	M. Ful. Publicianus Nikephoros	Ephesus	In.	IvE 7,1.3063
222-235	Asi(arch)	Pu. Ael. Trypho	Apameia	Cn.	BM Phrygia 89 #118
222-235	Asi(arch)	Pu. Ael. Trypho	Apameia	Cn.	BM Phrygia 101 #179
222-235	Asi(arch)	Pu. Ael. Trypho	Apameia	Cn.	BM Phrygia 101 #180
222-235	Asiar(ch)	Pu. Ael. Trypho	Apameia	Cn.	SNGvA 3506
222-235	Asiarch	Pu. Ael. Trypho	Apameia	Cn.	SNGvA 3507
222-235	Asiarch	(M.) Aur. Diadochos, husband of Aur. Hermonassa	Thyatira	In.	IGR 4.1233
222-235	Asiarch	M. Aur. Tychikos, father of M. Aur. Zosimos	Tralleis	In.	AthMitt 21 (1896) 114-15

Cont.

Date	Title of office	Name of official	Findspot of data	Medium	Publication
222-	Asiarch	Ti. Cl. Aristeas	Panamara	In.	BCH 15 (1891) 208 #149
222-	Asiarch	Ti. Cl. Aristeas	Panamara	In.	Benndorf & Niemann, Reisen, 1.156 #134
225-275	Asiarch	M. Aur. Zosimos, son of M. Aur. Tychikos	Tralleis	In.	AthMitt 21 (1896) 114-15
230-250	Asiarch	(Ti. Cl. Dynatos), brother of Ti. Cl. Moschas	Ephesus	In.	IvE 3.892
234-244	Asiarch	Aur. Ael. Attalianus	Sattaai	Cn.	CollWadd 5194
234-244	Asi(arch)	Aur. Ael. Attalianus	Sattaai	Cn.	BM Lydia 216 #22
234-244	Asiarch	Aur. Ael. Attalianus	Sattaai	Cn.	BM Lydia 223 #58
234-244	Asi(arch)	Aur. Ael. Attalianus	Saittaai	Cn.	BM Lydia 224 #62
238-244	Asiarch	L. Ju. Apollinarios	Adramytteion	Cn.	Münzen Mysiens 1.29 #85
238-244	Asiarch	L. Ju. Apollinarios	Adramytteion	Cn.	Münzen Mysiens 1.30 #89
238-244	Asiarch	L. Ju. Apollinarios	Adramytteion	Cn.	Münzen Mysiens 1.30 #90
238-244	Asiarch	???, uncle of (M.) Arunceius (Vedius) Mithridates	Ephesus	In.	IvE 7,2.4336
238-244	Asiarch	Pu. Ael. Artemidoros	Kyzikos	Cn.	Mionnet 2.549 #235
238-244	Asiarch	Pu. Ael. Artemidoros	Kyzikos	Cn.	Mionnet Sup 5.347 #427
238-244	Asi(arch)	(M. Aur.) Tertius	Smyrna	Cn.	Mionnet 3.215 #1198

Cont.

Date	Title of office	Name of official	Findspot of data	Medium	Publication
238-244	Asiarch	(M. Aur.) Tertius	Smyrna	Cn.	Mionnet 3.250 #1410
238-244	Asiarch	(M. Aur.) Tertius	Smyrna	Cn.	Mionnet 3.250 #1411
238-244	Asi(arch)	(M. Aur.) Tertius	Smyrna	Cn.	HuntColl 2.375 #176
238-244	Asi(arch)	(M. Aur.) Tertius	Smyrna	Cn.	HuntColl 2.375 #177
238-244	Asiarch	(M. Aur.) Tertius	Smyrna	Cn.	HuntColl 2.386 #253
238-244	Asi(arch)	(M. Aur.) Tertius	Smyrna	Cn.	SNG Cop Ionia 1318
238-244	Asiarch	M. Aur. Tertius	Smyrna	Cn.	SNG Cop Ionia 1319
240-250	Asiarch	Ti. Cl. Dynatos, brother of Ti. Cl. Moschas	Ephesus	In.	IvE 3.645
240-	Asiarch	L. Pescennius Gessius	Philadelphia	In.	IGR 4.1642
241/242	Asiarch	Apollonios Kouartianos	Diokleia	In.	IGR 4.665
244-249	Asiarch	Aurelius	Synaos	Cn.	BM Phrygia 391 #21
244-249	Asiarch	(Ti. Cl. Dynatos) brother of Ti. Cl. Moschas	Ephesus	In.	IvE 3.737
244-249	Asiarch	Aur. Demetrios	Stektorion	Cn.	Imhoof-Blumer, Monnaies gr., 412 #153
244-249	Asiarch of the native city	Aur. Demetrios	Stektorion	Cn.	CollWadd 6505
244-249	Asiarch	Au(relius) Demetrios	Stektorion	Cn.	SNG Cop Phrygia 692
246-249	Asiarch	Au(relius) Demetrios	Stektorion	Cn.	SNGvA 3961
247/248	Asiarch three times	(Pu.) Ael. Trypho	Apameia	In.	IGR 4.795

Cont.

Date	Title of office	Name of official	Findspot of data	Medium	Publication
250?	Asiarch	Ti. Cl. Dynatos	Samos	In.	Theophanides, AD 9 (1924-25) 103 #2
250-300	[As]iarch of the temples in Eph[esus]	M. Aur. Apoemantus	Didyma	In.	IvDid 315 l. 5
253-260	Asiar(ch)	Aur. Damas	Pergamum	Cn.	SNG Cop Mysia 511
253-260	Asiar(ch)	Aur. Damas	Pergamum	Cn.	SNGvA 1422
253-260	Asiarch	Domitius Rufus	Sardis	Cn.	SNGvA 3164
253-268	Asiarch	Aur. Damas	Pergamum	Cn.	HuntColl 2.285 #68
253-268	Asiarch	Domitius Rufus	Sardis	Cn.	BM Lydia 274 #207
253-268	Asiarch	Domitius Rufus	Sardis	Cn.	BM Lydia 273 #206
253-268	Asiarch	Domitius Rufus	Koula	In.	Keil, "Markttag," 365 l. 3, 26 (= IGR 4.1381)
253-268	Asiarch	???, father of Domitius Rufus	Koula	In.	Keil, "Markttag," 365 l. 2, 25-26 (= IGR 4.1381)
253-268	twice Asiarch	???, father of Domitius Rufus	Sardis	Cn.	BM Lydia 273 #206
253-268	Asiarch	Domitius Rufus	Sardis	Cn.	Imhoof-Blumer, Stadt-münzen, 142
253-268	Asiarch	Domitius Rufus	Sardis	Cn.	CollWadd 7059
253-268	Asi(arch)	(Domitius) Rufus	Sardis	Cn.	SNGvA 3165
253-268	Asiarch	Pu. Cl. Mennipus	Tralleis	In.	AthMitt 22 (1897) 484-85
300?	Asiarch	Macarius	Miletus	In.	Milet 1,9.164-65 #339
301	Asiarchs	???	Hypaipa	In.	IvE 7,2.3803a

Cont.

Date	Title of office	Name of official	Findspot of data	Medium	Publication
372-378	Asiarchate	(refers to office, not to an individual)	Ephesus	In.	IvE 1a.43 (Latin text: l. 7; Greek text, l. 22)
???	Asiar[ch...]	???	Ephesus	In.	IvE 5.1900(8) (very fragmentary)
???	Asia[rch...]	???	Ephesus	In.	IvE 5.1900(10) (very fragmentary)
???	twice Asiarch	???	Ephesus	In.	IvE 5.1900(11) (very fragmentary)
???	[...As]ia[r]ch	[A]ili[anus?]	Hierapolis	In.	IGR 4.817 (fragmentary)
???	Asiarch	Dorotheos	???	In.	Insc. Louvre 84 #72
???	Asiarch	Eunus	Adramytteion	In.	Hellenica 3 (1946) 125 #313
???	Asi[arch?]	[Qui]ntus Lol[lianos]	Pergamum	In.	IGR 4.472
???	Asiarch	L. Ant. Hyakinthos (from Laodikeia)	Rome	In.	IG 14.1402
???	Asiarch	Manilius Alexandros	Philadelphia	In.	IGR 4.1631
???	Asiarch	M. Cl. Nikeratos Cerealis	Eumeneia	In.	IGR 4.740
???	[...]Asiarch[...]	[...M]etrodoro[s...]	Ephesus	In.	IvE 5.1900(2) (very fragmentary)
???	Asia[rch...]	Ofelliu[s]	Ephesus	In.	IvE 3.700

INDEX TO APPENDIX I

Aelius 186
Agathokles
    M. Aur. Agathokles 202
Alexandros 172, 198, 201
    L. Rupillius Alexandros 188, 201
    M. Aur. Manilius Alexandros 195, 197
    Manilius Alexandros 208
Alkiphron 173, 185
Ammia
    Aelia Ammia 185
Ammion
    Claudia Ammion 188
Amphilla 180, 186
Anaxagoras 173
Anninaus
    L.? Anninaus 203
Antiochos
    M. Ant. Antiochos 198
Antonia 176
Antonianus
    M. Ulpius Trypho Megas Anto-
    nianus 176
Antoninus
    Pu. Vedius Antoninus 186, 190, 191, 192
    Pu. Vedius Antoninus (Phaedrus Sabinianus?) 195
Apion
    (M.?) Ael. Apion 200
    M. Ael. Apion? 200
Apoemantus
    M. Aur. Apoemantus 207
Apollinarios
    L. Ju. Apollinarios 205
    L. [Julius?] Apollinarios 201
Apollodoros 172, 195
    Apollodoros (II) 198
Apollonios 172
    Aur. Sept. Apollonios 182
Appia
    Flavia Appia 186, 200, 201
Appianus
    M. Ant. Alexandros Appianus 197
Aquila 180, 192
    M. Ju. Aquila 178, 185

Arignotus
    T. Ant. Cl. Alfenus Arignotus 182, 188
Aristeas
    Ti. Cl. Aristeas 205
Aristio
    (Ti.) Cl. Aristio 189
    (Ti.) Cl. [Aristio] 189
    Flavia Ammion Aristio 174, 185
    Ti. Cl. Aristio 174-176, 189, 190
    Ti. Cl. [Aristio?] 175
    [Ti. Cl]audius [Ari]stio 189
Aristobulus
    T. Fl. Aristobulus 189, 190
Aristokrates
    Aristokrates of Keramos 179
Aristokratos
    Ulpius Aristokratos 177
    [Ulpius Aristokratos] 177
Aristomenes
    L. Aur. Aristomenes 181, 187
Artemidoros
    M. Aur. Artemidoros 201
    Pu. Ael. Artemidoros 205
Aruncii
    Sem(pronii) Arunc(ii) 192
Athenaios
    Aur. Athenaios 181, 199
Attalianus
    Aur. Ael. Attalianus 205
Attalos 180, 181, 203, 204
Atticilla
    Julia Atticilla 187
Aurelianus
    Ti. Cl. Campanus Aurelianus 180, 186
Aurelius 206
    Aurelius [...] 182
    M. Aurelius 183, 200
    M. Aurelius ??? 196
    M. L. Aurelius 200
Au[...]nos
    (M.) Au[...]nos 200

Bonnatus
    L. Ju. Bonnatus 179

Caecilia
　　Antonia Caecilia 174, 185
Caecilianus
　　Ti. Cl. Menogenes Caecilianus
　　176
Caelianus
　　[Ti. Cl]audius Demostratos Cae-
　　lianus 192
　　[Ti. Cl]audius Demostratos
　　[Caelianus] 192
Calpurnius
　　Ju. Calpurnius 181
Capito
　　Corn. Vergilius Capito 173
　　P. Gavius Capito 188
Cassianus
　　Pu. Ael. Zeuxidemos Cassianus
　　177, 190
Catullinus
　　[M.] Ulpius Damas [Catullinus]
　　178
Cerealis
　　M. Cl. Nikeratos Cerealis 208
Charidemos
　　Ju. Charidemos 201
　　Ti. Cl. Touendianos Magnus
　　Charidemos 179
Charinos 172
Chersiphron 190
Claudia 188
Claudiane 188
Claudianus
　　(M. Ulpius) Carminius Claudia-
　　nus I 196
　　(M. Ulpius Carminius) Claudia-
　　nus II 200, 201
　　(M. Ulpius) Carminius Claudia-
　　nus II 186
　　Ti. Ju. Dama Claudianus 175
Cle[...]
　　Ti. Cl. Attalos Melior Cle[...]
　　201
Clitosthenes
　　(T.) Fl. Clitosthenes 192
　　T. Fl. Clitosthenes 192, 196, 198
　　T. Fl. Clitosthenes (Julianus?)
　　198
Crispus 203
　　Ti. Cl. Ael. Crispus 185, 191

Damas
　　Aur. Damas 207

Damianus
　　Ju. Damianus 178
　　Ti. Ju. Damianus 183
Daphnos 187
　　Aur. Daphnos 204
　　M. Aur. Daphnos 203
Deioterianus
　　Ti. Cl. Deioterianus 196, 197
Deis 198
Demetrios 172, 182
　　Au(relius) Demetrios 206
　　T. Fl. Demetrios 200
Demokrates
　　Ti. Cl. Demokrates 173
Diadochos
　　(M.) Aur. Diadochos 204
　　Aur. Diadochos 187
　　M. Aur. Diadochos 182, 183,
　　188
Diogenes
　　Cl. Diogenes 191, 199
　　L. Ant. Cl. Dometinus Diogenes
　　I 182
　　L. Ant. Cl. Dometinus Diogenes
　　II 182
Dionysios
　　Ju. Dionysios 203
　　M. Ju. Aur. Dionysios 192, 194
　　[...] Aur. Dionysios 191
Diophantos
　　Ju. Menekles Diophantos 201
　　Ti. Cl. Piso Diophantos 178
Dometianus
　　(M.) Fl. Dometianus 198
　　M. Fl. Dometianus 197, 198
Dorotheos 208
Dynatos
　　M. Cl. Dynatos 193
　　Ti. Cl. Dynatos 205, 206, 207
　　[Ti. Cl. Dy]nato[s...] 183

Eunus 208
Euphemos
　　L. Aufidius Euphemos 200
　　[L. Aufidius Euphe]mos 203
Eurykles
　　M. Ulpius Appuleius Eurykles
　　180, 181
　　M. Ulpius Eurykles 196
Eustratos 185

Flaccus
　　Aebutius Flaccus 177

Flavianus
    M. Ant. Popillius Andronikos Fla-
        vianus 183, 188
Fronto
    (M.) Cl. Fronto 193
    M. Cl. Fronto 193
    [Fro]nto? 192
Frontonianus
    Ti. Cl. Frontonianus 181

Gaius
    Aur. Gaius 203
Gessius
    L. Pescennius Gessius 206
Glykon 200
Gratus
    Plotius Aur. Gratus 199

Hedianus
    Pomponius Corn. Lollianus Hedi-
        anus 202, 204
Hegoumene
    Mindia Stratonike Hegoumene
        186
Heraklides 172
Herculanus
    M. Aur. Herculanus 182
Hermippos
    G. Pompeius Hermippos 177, 191
    M. Aur. Manilius Hermippos
        195, 197
Hermokrates
    L. Fl. Hermokrates 181
    T. Fl. Hermokrates 185
    T. Fl. Varus Calvesianus Hermo-
        krates 174
Hermolaos
    Aur. Hermolaos 201
    [Fl.] Hermolaos 199
Hermonassa
    Aurelia Hermonassa 187, 188,
        199, 204
Hermophilos
    Sulpicius Hermophilos 201
Hierax
    T. Fl. L. Hierax 199
Hiero
    Fl. Hiero 187
    Ti. Cl. Hiero 194
Hippianos
    G. Ju. Hippianos 181, 187, 203
Hyakinthos
    L. Ant. Hyakinthos 208

Julia
    Aurelia Julia 190
Juliane 173, 185
    Marcia Cl. Juliane 194
Julianus
    G. Ju. Julianus 183
    M. Aur. Charidemos Julianus 195
    M. Aur. Julianus 200
    T. Fl. Clitosthenes Julianus 196
    T. Fl. Julianus 179, 189, 190
    Ti. Cl. Tatianus Julianus 197

Kallikrates
    Cl. Kallikrates 191, 199
Kalobrotos
    Cl. Kalobrotos 198
Kleon 172
    G. Ju. Kleon 174
Kouartianos
    Apollonios Kouartianos 206
Krateros
    Fl. Krateros 189

Leonidas
    (Ael.) Plotius Leonidas 197
Lepidus
    Ael. Cl. Lepidus 177
    Cl. Ant. Lepidus 180
    G. Ju. Lepidus 183
    M. Ant. Lepidus 172
    [G.] Ju. Lepidus 176
Libonianos
    L. Ju. Libonianos 180
Lollianos
    Quintus Lollianos 208
Lorentia
    Claudia Lorentia 188
Lupus
    Ti. Cl. Lupus 182
Lycia
    Flavia Lycia 182, 187

Macarius 207
Marcella
    Ulpia Marcella 182, 187
Marcellina
    Julia Marcellina 180, 186
Marcellus
    G. Cl. Verulanus Marcellus 185,
        191
    Ti. Cl. Polydeukos Marcellus 194
Marcia
    Vedia Marcia 185

Marcus 183
Marinus
     Aruntius Marinus 204
Martialis
     (Pu.) Ael. Martialis 196
     Pu. Ael. Martialis 196
Maternus
     (G. Aruntius) Maternus 195
     G. (Aruntius) Maternus 198
     G. Aruntius Maternus 196, 198
Meidias
     Aur. Meidias 198
     Ti. Cl. Meidias 173
Melior
     Ti. Cl. Attalos Melior Cle[...]
          201
Melite
     Aurelia Melite 186, 187
Melito
     Ti. Cl. Melito 178, 180
Menandra 178, 186
Menandros 195, 202
     Cl. Menandros 190
     T. Fl. Menandros I 199
     T. Fl. Menandros II 199
     Ti. Cl. Menandros 178
Menelaos
     Aur. Menelaos 190
Menemachos
     M. Aur. Menemachos 197
Mennipus
     Pu. Cl. Mennipus 207
Menophantos
     Fl. Menophantos 176
Menophilos 172
Metrodoros
     [...M]etrodoro[s...] 208
Me[no...]
     Ti. Cl. Me[no...] 190
Mithridates
     (M.) Arunceius (Vedius) Mithri-
          dates 205
     Ti. Cl. Mithridates 177
Modestus
     Alf(enus) Modestus 200
Montanus
     T. Fl. Montanus 175-176
Moschas
     Ti. Cl. Moschas 205, 206
Moschianos 202
Moschion
     Aur. Moschion 203, 204

Munatios
     T. Fl. Munatios 191, 192, 194
Myrtos
     Flavia Myrtos 189
M[...]
     Gaius Julius M[...] 172

Negruos
     Fl. Priscus Negruos 200
Nigrinus
     G. Ant. Nigrinus 203
Nikephoros
     (M.) Ful. Publicianus Nikephoros
          202
     M. (Ful.) Publicianus Nikephoros
          202
     M. Ful. Publicianus Nikephoros
          202, 204
     M. Ful. Pu[blicianus] Nikephoros
          203
     M. Fulvi[us Publicianus N]ike-
          phoros 202
     [M. Ful. Publicianus Nikephoros]
          202
     [M. Ful. P]ublici[anus Nikepho-
          ros] 202
     [M. F]ul. Publicianus [Nik]epho-
          ros 204
Nikomachos
     T. Aruntius Nikomachos 183, 188

Ofellius
     Ofelliu[s] 208
Orestianos
     Ti. Cl. Celsus Orestianos 182, 187

Paconianus
     Nemerius Castricius Paconianus
          194
Pankratides
     Ti. Cl. Pankratides 194
Papario
     Aurelia Ju. Papario 195
Papiana
     Flavia Papiana 186
Pardala
     G. Ju. Pardala 172
Paullus
     Pu. Ael. Paullus 182, 187
Perigenes
     T. Fl. Perigenes 189

T. Fl. Peri[gene]s 189
Pheseinos
    Ti. Cl. Pheseinos 175, 185
    Ti. Cl. [Pheseinos?] 175
Philippos
    G. Ju. Philippos 179, 195
    G. Julius Phili[ppos] 179
    [G. Juli]us Philip[pos] 179
Philistes 172
Philographos
    G. Orfius Fl. Philographos 177
Philometor
    L. Cl. Charidemos Philometor 177
    Ti. Cl. Charidemos Philometor
        180
Philopappus
    G. Asin(ius) Agre(us) Philopappus
        195
    G. Asinius Agreus Philopappus
        196
    Ti. Cl. Philopappus 196
Phirmilla
    Skaptia Phirmilla 185, 191
Pigres
    Pu./L.? Ael. Pigres 203
Pisoninus
    Ti. Cl. Pius Pisoninus 191
Pius
    Ti. Cl. Pius 177
Plancianus
    [Cn.] Dot[tius Pl]anc[ianus] 179
Plautus
    Ulpius Apollonios Plautus 204
Polemon
    [Pole]mon 173
    Ti. Cl. Polemon 189, 194, 196,
        197
Polla
    Vibia Polla 177
Pollio
    (Ju.) Pollio 193
    Cl. Pollio 195
    Ju. Pollio 194
    M. Aur. Mindius Mattidianus
        Pollio 181
Polybius 201
Polychronios
    G. Aufidius Mindius Polychronios
        201
Priscilla
    Flavia Priscilla 187
Priscus
    Fl. Priscus 200

Pythio
    T. Fl. Pythio 189, 190
    T. [Fl. Py]thio 189
Pytho
    G. Ju. Pytho 183

Quintillia
    Aufidia Quintillia 185, 191

Regina
    Aeliana Regina 183,188
Reginus
    Ti. Ju. Reginus 178, 180, 194,
        196, 197
Rufus
    (Domitius) Rufus 207
    Domitius Rufus 207
    Ennius Rufus 177
    M. Fl. Rufus 197
    Ulpiu[s Ru]fus 191

Sabinianus
    Pu. Vedius Antoninus (Phaedrus
        Sabinianus?) 195
    Pu. Vedius Antoninus Phaedrus
        Sabinianus 196
    Vedius G. Sabinianus 181
Sabinus
    (M. Cl.) Pu. Vedius Antoninus
        (Sabinus) 196
    M. Cl. Pu. Vedius Antoninus
        Sabinus 180, 194
Salvius
    Cl. Salvius 191
Saturninus
    G. Ju. A[. . .] Saturninus 183
Secunda
    Cornelia Secunda 181, 187, 203
Secundus
    Pu. Titius Secundus 178
Severus
    M. Aur. Severus 176
Sokrates
    Ti. Cl. Sokrates 174, 176, 185
Stratonike 175, 185
Stratonikos
    (G. Voconius) Ael. Stratonikos
        182
Sulla
    Sellius Sulla 194
Tatia
    Aurelia Tatia 181, 187

Tatianos
    G. Ju. Julianus Tatianos 203
Temon 179
Tertius
    M. Aur. Tertius 205, 206
Tertullinus
    (Ti. Cl.) Piso Tertullinus 193
Tertullus
    T. Oppius Apher Pollius Tertullus
      178
Teuthrantis
    Memmia Ariste Teuthrantis 188
Teuthras
    Corn. Memmius Charidemos
      Teuthras 183
Themistokles
    Cl. Themistōkles 202
    M. Aur. Themistokles 204
    Pu. Ael. Themistokles 192
Tiberius
    Tiberi[us Cl. . .] 184
Timaios 180, 181, 186
Timon
    L. Timon 194
    Ti. Cl. Timon 173
Tryphaina
    Claudia Tryphaina 185
Trypho
    (Pu.) Ael. Trypho 206

Pu. Ael. Trypho 204
    Proclianus Trypho 183, 188
Tundianus
    Publia Ael. Tundianus 188, 201
Tychikos
    M. Aur. Tychikos 204, 205

Ulpia
    Ulpius/Ulpia 184, 188
Ulpius
    Ulpius/Ulpia 184, 188

Valerianus
    M. Cl. Valerianus 174
Vedius
    Publius Vedius 185
    Ved[ius. . .] 179
Vetulenius 185

Zeno
    Cl. Zeno 191, 199
    M. Aur. Zeno 194
    Ti. Cl. Zeno 199
    [Lu]cius Anto[nius] Zeno 173
Zoilos
    Ael. Zoilos 194, 198
Zosimos
    M. Aur. Zosimos 204, 205

DATES OF THE ASIARCHS FROM A FAMILY OF CIBYRA

Rosalinde Kearsley presented arguments in "A Leading Family of Cibyra and some Asiarchs of the First Century,"[1] that one family with several generations of Asiarchs could be traced back so that at least one Asiarch could be dated to the late first century BCE. Her conclusion, however, is not correct.

Members of the family from Cibyra are mentioned in several inscriptions from that city (*IGR* 4.883, 906-10, 912) so that the order of the generations can be reconstructed. On the basis of *IGR* 4.908, Kearsley proposed a dating of the family that was earlier than that of Halfmann.[2] *IGR* 4.908 honors Ti. Cl. Celsus Orestianus and his wife Flavia Lycia, who held provincial highpriesthoods in Pergamum. The crucial phrase is in l. 7-9: ἀρχιερατεύσαντας τῆς Ἀσίας τῶν ἐν τῇ πρώτῃ καὶ δὶς νεωκόρῳ Περγάμῳ ναῶν. Kearsley took this phrase to mean "who held highpriesthoods of Asia of the temples in once and twice neokorate Pergamum;" i.e., one held a highpriesthood when Pergamum had one provincial cult and one held a highpriesthood when the city had two such cults. If this were true, it would provide a firm date around 114 CE (when the second provincial cult was established) for the last members of the family; then generations could be calculated back into the first century BCE at approximately 30-year intervals.

This reading of the highpriesthoods phrase is awkward because it requires one plural participle to refer to two highpriesthoods by two different people that are allegedly distinguished by the number of cults in the city at the times of service. More importantly, such a translation of the phrase would be unparalleled in the hundreds of inscriptions naming provincial highpriests and highpriestesses. The normal practice in such an inscription is to use as much praise for

---

[1] *AnSt* 38 (1988) 43-51.

[2] Helmut Halfmann, *Die Senatoren aus dem östlichen Teil des Imperium Romanum bis zum Ende des 2. Jahrhunderts n. Chr.* (Hypomnemata 58; Göttingen: Vandenhoeck & Ruprecht, 1979) 149-51 #61.

the city and the honorand as possible. If a city has two provincial cults, an inscription does not remind the reader that the city once had only one such cult.

The inscription does not refer to Pergamum's first and second neokorate periods. Rather, it uses the city's standard titulature (see above, p. 58) that appears in inscriptions such as *IGR* 4.331 and 4.1688 as a development of Pergamum's claim to be the first city to have a provincial cult of the emperors (see *IGR* 4.456, 470 from the first neokorate period). The phrase does not call Pergamum "once and twice neokorate." It should be translated: "who held high-priesthoods of Asia of the temples in first and twice neokorate Pergamum;" i.e., in twice neokorate Pergamum which was also the first city of Asia to be honored by a provincial cult. This means that the husband and wife can only be dated to some time during Pergamum's second neokorate period (114-215). Since the language used in the group of inscriptions would fit much better in the late second/early third century CE, Halfmann's dating of Orestianus's father, Polemon, to the period of Marcus Aurelius is to be preferred.

Kearsley objected that Halfmann's dating required the identification of M. Deioterianus the Lyciarch (*IGR* 4.907, 912) with the equestrian and tribune Ti. M. Deioterianus (*IGR* 3.472; 500 col. 3, l. 28-30), even though their titles are different (the former is a Lyciarch and not called an equestrian, nor is he named with military offices). She argued that such omissions would be inexplicable.[3] This argument based on the absence of titles is not trustworthy, though. The number and kind of titles listed for an individual could vary according to the nature of the particular inscription, and according to that person's place in that specific inscription. In *IGR* 4.907 (see above, p. 112, n. 177, for the text of the inscription), only Ti. Cl. Polemon, the person honored by the inscription, is described as equestrian; his brother, Ti. Cl. Deioterianus, would have had the same rank but is not listed as equestrian because the dedication was not in his honor. Another example is found in *IGR* 4.912 where their mother is honored as the mother of senators, but the son Polemon is mentioned without any offices or status. This phenomenon is even more clear in two inscriptions from Phokaia: *IGR* 4.1323 honors a certain T. Fl. Hermokrates with a list of offices (imperial, provincial, and municipal) he has held, but he appears as a secondary

---

[3] Kearsley, "Leading Family," 49-50 n. 42

figure without any offices in the parallel inscription· honoring his wife (*IGR* 4.1325).

If we take Halfmann's date and put Polemon at 170 CE (in the middle of M. Aurelius's reign), a rough calculation based on 30-year generations puts the earliest Asiarch, Flavius Krateros, around the year 80 of the first century CE, which fits exactly with the body of data we have examined. This Cibyran family confirms the reemergence of the Asiarchate in the first half of Domitian's reign.

BIBLIOGRAPHY

Akurgal, Ekrem. *Ancient Civilizations and Ruins of Turkey*. 6th ed. Ankara: Türk Tarih Kurumu Basimevi, 1985.

Alderink, L. G. "The Eleusinian Mysteries in Roman Imperial Times." *ANRW* 2.18.2 (1989): 1457-98.

Alzinger, Wilhelm. "Ephesos. B. Archäologischer Teil." PWSup 12 (1970): 1588-1704.

———. "Ephesos vom Beginn der römischen Herrschaft in Kleinasien bis zum Ende der Principatszeit. B. Archäologischer Teil." *ANRW* 2.7.2 (1980): 811-30.

———. "Das Regierungsviertel." *ÖJh* 50 (1972-75): Beib. 249-53.

Asad, Talal. "Anthropological Conceptions of Religion: Reflections on Geertz." *Man* 18 (1983) 237-59.

Balsdon, J. P. V. D. *The Emperor Gaius (Caligula)*. Oxford: Clarendon Press, 1934.

Bammer, Anton. *Architektur und Gesellschaft in der Antike*. 2d ed. Wien: Hermann Böhlaus Verlag, 1985.

———. "Das Denkmal des C. Sextilius Pollio in Ephesos." *ÖJh* 51 (1976-77): Beib. 77 – 92.

———. "Elemente flavisch-trajanischer Architekturfassaden aus Ephesos." *ÖJh* 52 (1978 – 80): Haupt. 67-81.

———. "Römische und byzantinische Architektur." *ÖJh* 50 (1972-75): Beib. 386-92.

———. "Wo einst ein Weltwunder stand. Letzte Ergebnisse österreichischer Forschungen im antiken Ephesos." *Das Altertum* 21 (1975): 27-35.

Bammer, Anton, Robert Fleischer, and Dieter Knibbe. *Führer durch das archäologische Museum in Selcuk–Ephesos*. Vienna: Österreichisches Archäologishes Institut, 1974.

Barnes, T. D. *Tertullian: A Historical and Literary Study*. Oxford: Clarendon Press, 1971.

Bauer, Walter. *Orthodoxy and Heresy in Earliest Christianity*. Philadelphia: Fortress, 1971.

Beasley-Murray, G. R. *The Book of Revelation*. London: Oliphants, 1974.

Benjamin, Anna S. "The Altars of Hadrian in Athens and Hadrian's Panhellenic Program." *Hesperia* 32 (1968): 57-86.

Benndorf, Otto. "Vorläufiger Bericht über die Ausgrabungen in Ephesos I." *ÖJh* 1 (1898): Beib. 53-72.

———. "V. Erzstatue eines griechischen Athleten." In *FiE*, vol. 1, 181-204. Vienna: Alfred Hölder, 1906.

Benndorf, Otto, and George Niemann. *Reisen im Südwestlichen Kleinasien*. Vol. 1 of idem, *Reisen in Lykien und Karien*. Vienna: Carl Gerold's Sohn, 1884.

Beurlier, E. *Essai sur le culte rendu aux empereurs romains*. Paris: Ernest Thorin, 1890.

Bohtz, C. H. *Das Demeter-Heiligtum*. Vol. 13 of *AvP*. Berlin: Deutsches Archäologisches Institut, 1981.

Bookidis, Nancy, and Ronald S. Stroud. *Demeter and Persephone in Ancient Corinth*. Corinth Notes, no. 2. Princeton, N. J.: American School of Classical Studies at Athens, 1987.

Bowersock, Glen. *Augustus and the Greek World*. Oxford: Clarendon Press, 1965.

Brandis. "Ἀρχιερεύς." *PW* 2 (1896a): 471-88.

——. "Asiarches," *PW* 2 (1896b): 1564-78.

Bremen, Riet Van. "Women and Wealth." In *Images of Women in Antiquity*, edited by Averil Cameron and Amelie Kuhrt, 223-42. Detroit: Wayne State University Press, 1983.

Brödner, Erika. *Die römischen Thermen und das antike Badewesen.* Darmstadt: Wissenschaftliche Buchgesellschaft, 1983.

Brooten, Bernadette. *Women Leaders in the Ancient Synagogue. Inscriptional Evidence and Background Issues.* Brown Judaic Studies, no. 36. Chico, California: Scholars Press, 1982.

Broughton, T. R. S. *Roman Asia Minor.* In *An Economic Survey of Ancient Rome*, edited by Tenney Frank, 4:498-918. Baltimore: Johns Hopkins Press, 1938.

Bruneau, Philippe. *Recherches sur les cultes de Délos a l'époque hellénistique et a l'époque impériale.* Paris: E. de Boccard, 1970.

Brunt, P. A. "Charges of Provincial Maladministration under the Early Principate." *Historia* 10 (1961): 189-227.

Buckler, W. G. "Auguste, Zeus Patrôos." *RevPhil* 3d ser., 9 (1935): 177-88.

Burkert, Walter. *Greek Religion.* Cambridge, MA: Harvard University, 1985.

——. *Ancient Mystery Cults.* Cambridge, Mass.: Harvard University Press, 1987.

Burrell, Barbara. *"Neokoroi*: Greek Cities of the Roman East." Ph.D. diss., Harvard University, 1980.

Busolt, Georg. *Griechische Staatskunde.* 2 vol. Munich: Beck, 1926.

Cagnat, R., et al., eds. *Inscriptiones Graecae ad Res Romanas Pertinentes.* 4 vol. Paris: Earnest Leroux, 1906-27.

Campenhausen, Hans Frhr. von. "Bearbeitungen und Interpolationen des Polykarpmartyriums." *Sitzungsberichte der Heidelberger Akademie der Wissenschaften. Philosophisch-Historische Klasse.* 1957, no. 3.

Chapot, V. *La Province romaine proconsulaire d'Asie.* Paris: Emile Bouillon, 1904.

Chapouthier, Fernand. "La Coiffe d'Artémis dans Éphèse trois fois neocore." *REA* 40 (1938): 125-32.

Charles, R. H. *A Critical and Exegetical Commentary on the Revelation of St. John.* 2 vols. International Critical Commentary. Edinburgh: T. & T. Clark, 1920.

Cichorius, Conrad. *Rom und Mytilene.* Leipzig: Teubner, 1888.

Clinton, K. "The Eleusinian Mysteries: Roman Initiates and Benefactors, Second Century B.C. to A.D. 267." *ANRW* 2.18.2 (1989): 1499-1539.

Colin, G., ed. *Épigraphie.* Vol. 3,2 of *Fouilles de Delphes.* Paris: Fontemoing, 1909.

Daltrop, G., U. Hausmann, and M. Wegner. *Die Flavier: Vespasian, Titus, Domitian, Nerva, Julia Titi, Domitilla, Domitia.* Berlin: Gebr. Mann, 1966.

Deininger, Jürgen. *Die Provinziallandtage der römischen Kaiserzeit von Augustus bis zum Ende des dritten Jahrhunderts n. Chr..* Munich: Beck, 1965.

Eck, Werner. "Jahres- und Provinzialfasten der senatorischen Statthalter von 69/70 bis 138/139." *Chiron* 12 (1982a): 315-18.

——. "Prokonsuln von Asia in der Flavisch-Traianischen Zeit." *ZPE* 45 (1982b): 139 – 53.

——. *Die Senatoren von Vespasian bis Hadrian.* Vestigia, no. 13. Munich: Beck, 1970.

Eckhel, J. H. *Doctrina numorum veterum.* 8 vols. Vienna: 1792-98.

Eckstein, F., et al. *Berichte über die Ausgrabungen in Olympia*, vol. 6. Berlin: Deutsches Archäologisches Institut, 1958.

Eichler, Fritz. "Die österreichischen Ausgrabungen in Ephesos im Jahre 1961." *AnzWien* 99 (1962) 37-53.

——. "Die österreichischen Ausgrabungen in Ephesos im Jahre 1964." *AnzWien* 102 (1965): 93-109.

——. "Die österreichischen Ausgrabungen in Ephesos im Jahre 1966." *AnzWien* 104 (1967): 15-28.

Étienne, Robert. *Le culte impérial dans la péninsula ibérique d'Auguste a Dioclétian.* Paris: E. de Boccard, 1958.

Fasolo, Furio. *L'Architettura Romana di Efeso.* Bullettino del Centro di studi per la storia dell'architettura, no. 18. Rome: Casa dei Crescenzi, 1962.

Fleischer, Robert. *Artemis von Ephesos und verwandte Kultstatuen aus Anatolien und Syrien.* EPRO, no. 35. Leiden: Brill, 1973.

Fontrier, A. M. "Β. ΕΠΙΓΡΑΦΑΙ ΕΠΙΣΤΑΛΕΙΣΑΙ ΕΝ ΑΝΤΙΓΡΑΦΟΙΣ." ΜΟΥΣΕΙΟΝ ΚΑΙ ΒΙΒΛΙΟΘΗΚΗ ΤΗΣ ΕΥΑΓΓΕΛΙΚΗΣ ΣΚΟΛΗΣ 3 (1878-80): 147-84.

Fränkel, M. *Die Inschriften von Pergamon.* Vol. 8,1 and 8,2 of *AvP.* Berlin: Deutsches Archäologisches Institut, 1890 and 1895.

Friesen, Steven. "Ephesus A." In *ARNTS,* vol. 2. Philadelphia: Trinity Press International, forthcoming.

——. "Olympia." In *ARNTS,* vol. 1. Philadelphia: Fortress, 1987.

"Funde." *AthMitt* 16 (1891): 140-48.

"Funde." *AthMitt* 26 (1901): 235-40.

Geertz, Clifford. *The Interpretation of Cultures.* New York: Basic Books, 1973.

Gillespie, J. U. "Notes et documents." *RBN* 105 (1959): 211-13.

Grünhage, Wilhelm. "Die Ausgrabungen des Terrassenheiligtums von Munigua." In *Neue deutsche Ausgrabungen im Mittelmeergebiet und im vorderen Orient,* 329-43. Berlin: Gebr. Mann, 1959.

Guiraud, Paul. *Les assemblées provinciales dans l'empire romain.* Paris: Imprimerie Nationale, 1887.

Habicht, Christian. *Gottmenschentum und griechische Städte.* Zetemata, no. 14. Munich: Beck, 1956.

——. *Die Inschriften des Asklepieions.* Vol. 8,3 of *AvP.* Berlin: Deutsches Archäologisches Institut, 1969.

Halfmann, Helmut. *Die Senatoren aus dem östlichen Teil des Imperium Romanum bis zum Ende des 2. Jahrhunderts n. Chr..* Hypomnemata, no. 58. Göttingen: Vandenhoeck & Ruprecht, 1979.

Hammond, Mason. "Composition of the Senate, A.D. 68-235." *JRS* 47 (1957): 74-81.

Hanfmann, George M. A., and Nancy H. Ramage. *Sculpture from Sardis.* The Finds through 1975. Archaeological Exploration of Sardis, no. 2. Cambridge, Mass.: Harvard University Press, 1978.

Hänlein, Heidi. "Zur Datierung des Augustustempels in Ankara." *AA* 3 (1981): 511-13.

Hänlein-Schäfer, Heidi. *VENERATIO AUGUSTI: Eine Studie zu den Tempeln der ersten römischen Kaisers.* Archaeologica, no. 39. Rome: Giorgio Bretschneider, 1985.

Harrison, R. M. "Amorium 1987." *AnSt* 18 (1988) 175-84.

Hasluck, F. W. "Inscriptions from Bizye." *ABSA* 12 (1905-6): 181-83.

Haussoullier, B. *Études sur l'histoire de Milet et du Didymeion.* Paris: Émile Bouillon, 1902.

Head, Barclay V. *Historia Numorum. A Manual of Greek Numismatics.* 2d ed. Oxford: Clarendon, 1911.

Heberdey, Rudolf. "Vorläufiger Bericht über die Ausgrabungen in Ephesos II."
    ÖJh 1 (1898): Beib. 71-82.
——. "Vorläufiger Bericht über die Ausgrabungen in Ephesos V." *ÖJh* 5 (1902):
    Beib. 53-66.
——. "Vorläufiger Bericht über die Grabungen in Ephesos 1902/3." *ÖJh* 7 (1904):
    Beib. 37-56.
Heinz, Werner. *Römische Thermen: Badewesen und Badeluxus im Römischen Reich.*
    Munich: Hirmer Verlag, 1983.
Hepding, H. "Die Arbeiten zu Pergamon 1904-1905. II. Die Inschriften." *AthMitt*
    32 (1907): 241-377.
——. "Die Arbeiten zu Pergamon 1908-1909. II. Die Inschriften." *AthMitt* 35
    (1910): 401-93.
Hölbl, Günter. "Die ägyptische Wasserauslaufuhr aus Ephesos. III. Die ägyp-
    tische Wasseruhr Ptolemaus' II." *ÖJh* 55 (1984): Beib. 21-68.
Hopkins, Keith. "Introduction." In *Trade in the Ancient Economy*, edited by Peter
    Garnsey, Keith Hopkins, and C. R. Whittaker. Berkeley and Los Angeles:
    University of California Press, 1983.

Imhoof-Blumer, Friedrich. *Die antiken Münzen Mysiens.* Berlin: G. Reimer, 1913.
——. *Griechische Münzen: Neue Beiträge und Untersuchungen. ABAW* 18 (1890) 525-798.
    Reprint. Graz, Austria: Akademische Druck- u. Verlagsanstalt, 1972.
——. *Kleinasiatische Münzen.* 2 vols. Vienna: A. Hölder, 1901-02.
——. *Lydische Stadtmünzen.* Geneva: Verlag der Schweizerischen Numismatischen
    Gesellschaft, 1897. Reprint. Bologna: Arnaldo Forni, 1978.
——. *Monnaies grecque.* Amsterdam: J. Müller, 1883.
Inan, Jale, and Elisabeth Rosenbaum. *Roman and Early Byzantine Portrait Sculpture
    in Asia Minor.* London: Oxford University Press, 1966.

Jones, A. H. M. *The Cities of the Eastern Roman Provinces.* Oxford: Clarendon, 1937.
Jones, Brian. *Domitian and the Senatorial Order: A Prosopographical Study of Domitian's
    relationship with the Senate, A.D. 81-96.* Philadelphia: American Philosophical Soci-
    ety, 1979.
Joubin, Andre. "Inscription de Cyzique." *REG* 6 (1893): 8-22.

Karwiese, Stefan. "Der Numismatiker-Archäologe." *ÖJh* 56 (1985): Haupt.
    99-108.
Kaser, Max. *Römische Rechtsgeschichte.* Göttingen: Vandenhoeck & Ruprecht, 1978.
Kearsley, Rosalinde. "Asiarchs, Ἀρχιερεῖς and the Ἀρχιερείαι of Asia." *GRBS* 27
    (1986): 183-92.
——. "Asiarchs, Archiereis and Archiereiai of Asia: New Evidence from Amorium
    in Phrygia." *EpAn* 16 (1990) 69-80.
——. "A Leading Family of Cibyra and some Asiarchs of the First Century." *AnSt*
    38 (1988): 43-51.
——. "M. Ulpius Appuleius Eurykles of Aezani: Panhellene, Asiarch, and Ar-
    chiereus of Asia." *Antichthon* 21 (1987a): 49-56.
——. "14. Some asiarchs from Ephesos," In *New Documents Illustrating Early Chris-
    tianity*, edited by G. H. R. Horsley, 46-55. Macquarie University: Ancient His-
    tory Documentary Research Centre, 1987b.
Keil, Josef. "Die erste Kaiserneokorie von Ephesos." *Numismatische Zeitschrift* N.F.
    12 (1919): 115-20.
——. "Ein Marktag in Maeonien." in *Studies Presented to David Moore Robinson on
    his Seventieth Birthday*, edited by George E. Mylonas and Doris Raymond,
    2:363 - 70. St. Louis, Missouri: Washington University, 1953.

——. "XVI. Vorläufiger Bericht über die Ausgrabungen in Ephesos." *ÖJh* 27 (1932): Beib. 5-72.

——. "XVII. Vorläufiger Bericht über die Ausgrabungen von Ephesos." *ÖJh* 28 (1933): Beib. 5-44.

Keil, Josef, and G. Maresch. "Epigraphische Nachlese zu Miltners Ausgrabungsberichten aus Ephesos." *ÖJh* 45 (1960): Beib. 75-100.

Knibbe, Dieter. "Ephesos vom Beginn der römischen Herrschaft in Kleinasien bis zum Ende der Principatszeit (Historischer Teil)." *ANRW* 2.7.2 (1980): 748-810.

Koester, H. "GNOMAI DIAPHOROI: The Origin and Nature of Diversification in the History of Early Christianity." In *Trajectories through Early Christianity*, idem and James M. Robinson, 114-57. Philadelphia: Fortress, 1971.

——. *Introduction to the New Testament.* 2 vol. Philadelphia: Fortress, 1982.

Kümmel, Werner Georg. *Introduction to the New Testament.* Rev. ed. Nashville: Abingdon, 1975.

Lammer, Manfred. *Olympien und Hadrianeen im antiken Ephesos.* Ph.D. diss., Cologne, 1967.

Larsen, J. A. O. *Representative Government in Greek and Roman History.* Berkeley/Los Angeles: University of California Press, 1955.

Lawrence, A. W. *Greek Architecture.* Revised by R. A. Tomlinson. Pelican History of Art. N. Y.: Penguin, 1983.

Le Bas, Philippe, and W. H. Waddington. *Inscriptions.* Vol. 3 of *Voyage Archéologique en Grèce et en Asie Mineure.* Paris: Firmin Didot, 1870.

Liddell, Henry George, and Robert Scott. *A Greek-English Lexicon.* Revised by Henry Stuart Jones. 9th ed.; Oxford: Clarendon, 1940.

Maccanico, Rosanna. "Ginnasi Romani ad Efeso." *Archeologica Classica* 15 (1963): 32 – 60.

McCrum, M., and A. G. Woodhead, eds. *Select Documents of the Principates of the Flavian Emperors including the Year of Revolution A.D. 68-69.* Cambridge: Cambridge University Press, 1961.

MacMullen, Ramsay. *Paganism in the Roman Empire.* New Haven: Yale University Press, 1981.

——. "Woman in Public in the Roman Empire." *Historia* 29 (1980): 208-18.

Macro, Anthony D. "The Cities of Asia Minor under the Roman Imperium." *ANRW* 2.7.2 (1980) 658-97.

Magie, David. *Roman Rule in Asia Minor to the End of the Third Century After Christ.* 2 vols. Princeton: Princeton University, 1950.

Mallwitz, Alfred. *Olympia und seine Bauten.* Athens: S. Kasas, 1981.

Marquardt, I. "De provinciarum romanarum conciliis et sacerdotibus." *Ephemeris Epigraphica* 1 (1872): 200-214.

Martin, Ronald. *Tacitus.* Berkeley and Los Angeles: University of California Press, 1981.

Merkelbach, R. "Ephesische Parerga 26: Warum Domitians Siegername 'Germanicus' eradiert worden ist." *ZPE* 34 (1979): 62-64.

——. "Der Rangstreit der Städte Asiens und die Rede des Aelius Aristides über die Eintracht." *ZPE* 32 (1978): 287-96.

Meyers, Marvin W. *The Ancient Mysteries. A Sourcebook.* N. Y.: Harper & Row, 1987.

Millar, Fergus. *The Emperor and the Roman World (31 BC – AD 337).* Ithaca, N. Y.: Cornell University Press, 1977.

Miltner, Franz. "XXIV. Vorläufiger Bericht über die Ausgrabungen in Ephesos." *ÖJh* 45 (1960): Beib. 1-76.

Mommsen, Theodor. *Römische Geschichte*. 3d ed. Berlin: Weidmannsche Buchhandlung, 1886.

——. "Volksbeschluss der Ephesier zu Ehren des Kaisers Antoninus Pius." *ÖJh* 3 (1900): Haupt. 1-8.

——, ed. *Digesta Iustiniani Augusti*. Berlin: Weidmann, 1870.

Monceaux, Paulus, *De communi Asiae Provinciae (*ΚΟΙΝΟΝ ΑΣΙΑΣ*)* Paris: Ernestum Thorin, 1885.

Moretti, Luigi. *Iscrizioni Agonistiche Greche*. Rome: Angelo Signorelli, 1953.

——. "ΚΟΙΝΑ ΑΣΙΑΣ." *Rivista di Filologia* NS 32 (1954): 276-89.

Münsterberg, R. *Die Beamtennamen auf den griechischen Münzen*. Subsidia Epigraphica, no. 3. Hildesheim: Georg Olms Verlag, 1973.

Muret, Ernest. "Monnaies de Lydie." *RevNum* 3d ser. 1 (1883) 383-407.

Nilsson, Martin. *A History of Greek Religion*. 2d ed. Oxford: Clarendon, 1949.

Oster, Richard. *A Bibliography of Ancient Ephesus*. American Theological Library Association Bibliography Series, no. 19. Metuchen, N. J.: Scarecrow Press, 1987.

Pappakonstantinou, M. "ΕΠΙΓΡΑΦΗ ΤΡΑΛΛΕΩΝ." *BCH* 29 (1905): 361.

Paris, Petrus. *Quatenus feminae res publicas in Asia Minore, romanis imperantibus, attigerint*. Paris: Ernest Thorin, 1891.

Pekary, Thomas. "Kleinasien unter römischer Herrschaft." *ANRW* 2.7.2 (1980) 595-657.

Pflaum, H. G. *Essai sur les procurateurs équestres sous le Haut-empire romain*. Paris: Adrien Maisonneuve, 1950.

Pick, Behrendt. "Die Neokorie-Tempel von Pergamon und der Asklepios des Phyromachos." In *Festschrift Walther Judeich zum 70. Geburtstage*, 28-44. Weimar: Hermann Boehlaus, 1929.

——. "Die Neokorien von Ephesos." In *Corolla Numismatica. Essays in Honour of Barclay V. Head*, 234-44. London: Oxford University Press, 1906.

——. "Die tempeltragende Gottheiten und die Darstellung der Neokorie auf den Münzen." *ÖJh* 7 (1904): Haupt. 1-41.

Pleket, H. W. "Domitian, the Senate and the Provinces." *Mnemosyne* 4th ser., 14 (1961): 296-315.

Pollitt, J. J. *Art in the Hellenistic Age*. Cambridge: Cambridge University Press, 1986.

Price, Martin Jessop, and Bluma L. Trell. *Coins and their Cities*. Detroit: Wayne State University Press, 1977.

Price, S. R. F. "Gods and Emperors: The Greek Language of the Roman Imperial Cult." *JHS* 104 (1984a): 79-95.

——. *Rituals and Power: The Roman imperial cult in Asia Minor*. Cambridge: Cambridge University Press, 1984b.

Quass, Friedemann. "Zur politischen Tätigkeit der munizipalen Aristokratie des griechischen Ostens." *Historia* 31 (1982): 188-213.

Ramsay, William, "The Province of Asia" *ClRev* 3 (1889): 174-79.

——. *The Social Basis of Roman Power in Asia Minor*. Aberdeen: Aberdeen University Press, 1941.

Reynolds, Joyce. *Aphrodisias and Rome*. Journal of Roman Studies Monographs, no. 1. London: Society for the Promotion of Roman Studies, 1982.

Richter, Giesela M. A. "The Pheidian Zeus at Olympia." *Hesperia* 35 (1966): 166-70, pl. 53-54.

Robert, Jeanne, and Louis Robert. "III. Hierocesaree." *Hellenica* 6 (1948): 27-55.
Robert, Louis. "Le cult de Caligula à Milet et la province d'Asie." *Hellenica* 7 (1949): 206-38.
——. "Études d'épigraphie grecque." *RevPhil* 56 (1930): 25-60.
——. *Les gladiateurs dans l'orient grec.* Paris: Edouard Champion, 1940.
——. "Inscriptions d'Aphrodisias. Premier partie." *AntCl* 35 (1966): 410-11.
——. *Opera minora selecta*, vol. 3. Amsterdam: Adolf M. Hakkert, 1969.
Rogers, Perry M. "Domitian and the Finances of State." *Historia* 33 (1984): 60-78.
Rossner, Margaret. "Asiarchen und Archiereis." *Studii clasice* 16 (1974): 101-42.

Sallet, A. v. "Demeter Horia auf Münzen von Smyrna." *ZfN* 4 (1877): 315-17.
Schowalter, Daniel N., et al. "Athens B." In *ARNTS*, vol. 1. Philadelphia: Fortress, 1987.
Schulthess, Otto, "*Neopoioi*," PW 16 (1935): 2433-39.
Schüssler Fiorenza, Elisabeth. *The Book of Revelation: Justice and Judgment.* Philadelphia: Fortress, 1985.
Scott, Kenneth. *The Imperial Cult under the Flavians.* Stuttgart-Berlin: Kohlhammer, 1936. Reprint. N. Y.: Arno, 1975.
Smith, Jonathan Z. *Drudgery Divine: On the Comparison of Early Christianities and the Religions of Late Antiquity.* Chicago: University of Chicago Press, 1990.
Smith, Wilfred Cantwell. *The Meaning and End of Religion.* N. Y.: Harper & Row, 1962.
Speidel, M. *Roman Army Studies*, vol. 1. Amsterdam: J. C. Gieben, 1984.
Stone III, Shelley C. "The Imperial Sculptural Group in the Metroon at Olympia." *AthMitt* 100 (1985): 377-91.
Stauffer, Ethelbert. *Christ and the Caesars.* Historical Sketches. London: SCM, 1955.
Sterrett, J. R. Sitlington. *An Epigraphical Journey in Asia Minor.* Papers of the American School of Classical Studies at Athens, 1883-84, no. 2; Boston: Damrell and Upham, 1888.
Stillwell, Richard. "The Facade of the Colossal Figures." In *Architecture*, edited by idem, Robert L. Scranton, and Sarah Elizabeth Freeman, 55-88. Vol. 1,2 of *Corinth.* Cambridge, Mass.: Harvard University Press, 1941.
Stoops, Jr., Robert F. "Riot and Assembly: The Social Context of Acts 19:23-41." *JBL* 108 (1989): 73-91.
Sutherland, C. H. V. *The Cistophori of Augustus.* London: Royal Numismatic Society, 1970.

Talbert, Richard J. A. *The Senate of Imperial Rome.* Princeton: Princeton University Press, 1984.
Taşliklioglu, Z., and P. Frisch. "New Inscriptions from the Troad." *ZPE* 17 (1975): 106-9.
Taylor, Lily Ross. "XXII. The Asiarchs." In *The Acts of the Apostles*, 256-62. Part 1 of *The Beginnings of Christianity*, edited by F. J. Foakes Jackson and Kirsopp Lake. London: Macmillan, 1933.
Theophanides, Bas. "Ἐπιγραφη Σαμου." *AD* 9 (1924-25) 95-104.
Thompson, Leonard L. *The Book of Revelation: Apocalypse and Empire.* N. Y.: Oxford University Press, 1990.
Thür, Hilke. "Ephesische Bauhütten in der Zeit der Flavier und der Adoptivkaiser." In *Lebendige Altertumswissenschaft. Festgabe zur Vollendung des 70. Lebensjahres von Hermann Vetters dargebracht von Freunden, Schülern und Kollegen*, 181-87. Vienna: Verlag Adolf Holzhausens, 1985.
Toutain, J. *Les cultes païens dans l'Empire romain.* Vol. 1, *Les cultes officiels; les cultes romains et gréco-romains.* Paris: Ernest Leroux, 1907.

Trell, Bluma. *The Temple of Artemis at Ephesus*. New York: American Numismatic Society, 1945.

Treu, Georg. *Die Bildwerke von Olympia in Stein und Thon*. Vol. 3 of *Olympia*. Berlin: Ascher, 1897.

Vetters, Hermann. "Domitianterrasse und Domitiangasse." *ÖJh* 50 (1972-75): Beib. 311 – 30.

——. "Ephesos: Vorläufiger Grabungsbericht 1983." *AnzWien* 121 (1984): 209-32.

Waddington, W. H. *Fastes des provinces asiatique de l'Empire romain*. Paris: Firmin-Didot Freres, 1872.

Waldstein, Wolfgang. *Römische Rechtsgeschichte*. 7th ed. of the work begun by Gerhard Dulckeit and Fritz Schwarz. Munich: Beck, 1981.

Ward-Perkins, J. B. *Roman Imperial Architecture*. 2d integrated ed. Pelican History of Art. New York: Penguin, 1981.

Wiseman, James. "Corinth and Rome I: 228 B.C. – A.D. 267." *ANRW* 2.7.1 (1979): 438 – 548.

Wood, J. T. *Discoveries at Ephesus, Including the Sites and the Remains of the Great Temple of Diana*. London: Longmans, Green, & Co., 1877.

Yegül, Fikret Kutlu. "The Bath-Gymnasium Complex in Asia Minor during the Imperial Roman Age." Ph.D. diss., Harvard University, 1975.

——. "A Study in Architectural Iconography: *Kaisersaal* and the Imperial Cult." *Art Bulletin* 64 (1982): 7-31.

INSCRIPTION AND COIN INDEX

ABSA
  12 (1905-06) 183: 54
AD
  9 (1924-25) 103 #2: 207
AnSt
  18 (1988) 181: 192
AntCl
  35 (1966) 410-11: 38
APAW
  (1910) 93: 193
  (1932) 51 #3: 179
AthMitt
  7 (1891) 141-44: 54
  8 (1883) 330-31 #11: 192
  21 (1896) 114-15: 204, 205
  22 (1897) 484-85: 207
  26 (1901) 239 #3: 101, 179
  32 (1907) 330 #62: 58
  32 (1907) 331 #63: 58
  35 (1910) 472 #58: 58
  35 (1910) 473 #59: 58
AvP
  8,1.395: 58
  8,1.397: 58
  8,1.431: 58
  8,1.438: 58
  8,1.520: 58
  8,2.255: 51
  8,2.268: 10
  8,2.269: 11
  8,2.374: 15
  8,2.385: 35
  8,2.461: 58
  8,2.489: 39
  8,2.515: 39
  8,3.20: 58
  8,3.23: 39, 58
  8,3.30: 79, 177
  8,3.34: 181
  8,3.37: 58
  8,3.38: 58
  8,3.44: 203
  8,3.153: 190
BASOR
  158 (1960) 7-10 #4: 180
BCH
  1 (1877) 55-56 #4: 196
  11 (1887) 216 #8: 200
  11 (1887) 346 #1: 183
  15 (1891) 208 #149: 205

  29 (1905) 361: 101, 179
Benndorf & Niemann
  1.156 #134: 205
BM Ionia
  16 #1: 193
  16 #2: 193
  75 #215: 119
  83 #261: 65
  91 #305: 63, 66
  92 #306: 65
  198 #143: 25
  268 #263-65: 19
  268 #266: 49
  268 #266-68: 19
  268 #267: 20, 49
  268 #268: 49
  274 #309: 57
  275 #311: 57
  275 #312: 57
  275 #313: 57
  275 #314: 57
  283 #368-71: 115
  294 #440: 115
  295 #443: 115
  299 #473: 115
BM Lydia
  216 #22: 205
  223 #58: 205
  224 #64: 205
  225 #65: 201
  251 #104: 109, 172
  251 #105: 109, 172
  273 #206: 207
  274 #207: 207
BM Mysia
  139 #242: 13
  140 #256: 13
BM Phrygia
  13 #62: 200
  44 #2: 195
  44 #3: 196
  89 #118: 204
  101 #179: 204
  101 #180: 204
  217 #41: 174
  217 #41-42: 109
  217 #42: 174
  218 #47: 174
  218 #47-48: 109
  218 #48: 80, 174

390 #18: 195
391 #21: 206
BM Pontus
105 #10-27: 13
BMCRE
1.114 #705: 12
1.196 #228: 14
2.94 #449: 14
3.12 #79: 14
3.232-33 #1096-1100: 13
Burrell
(1980) 405 #11: 58
CIG
2777: 182
2698b: 10
2782: 103
2887: 183
CollWadd
614: 201
1628: 56
2268: 196
5194: 205
5254: 192, 193
5545: 196
6033: 174
6033-34: 109
6034: 80, 174
6189: 195
6368: 201
6369: 203
6371: 201
6505: 98, 206
7059: 207
7072: 203
Echos d'Orient
10 (1907) 77-78 #2: 183, 188
Eckhel
3.115: 201
Eckstein
6.221: 182
EpAn
16 (1990) 69-80: 185
FiE
2 #48: 29
Fouilles de Delphes
3,2.128: 48, 51
3,2.215: 48, 51
3,2.223: 51
Head
(1911) 681: 198
Hellenica
3 (1946) 125 #313: 208
7 (1949) 206-7: 21-22, 78, 80, 87, 173
11-12 (1960) 476: 187

HuntColl
2.285 #68: 207
2.321 #1: 193
2.321 #2: 193
2.375 #176: 206
2.375 #177: 206
2.386 #253: 206
IBM
3.498: 29
4.894: 90, 172
IG
2,2.3704: 202
12,2.58: 11
12,3.123 #525: 192
12,3.124 #529: 197
12,3.209 #1119: 181
14.1402: 208
IGR
1.798: 204
3.173: 111
3.472: 216
3.500: 216
4.18: 149, 168
4.39: 11
4.146: 54, 55
4.153: 177
4.154: 190
4.155: 177
4.156: 98, 199
4.157: 177
4.261: 196
4.331: 216
4.353: 15
4.433: 9, 153
4.434: 153
4.454: 23, 116
4.456: 95, 176, 216
4.470: 95, 176, 216
4.472: 208
4.498: 15
4.555: 36
4.556: 36
4.564: 180
4.577: 80, 176
4.578: 180, 186
4.582: 36
4.583: 36
4.584: 36
4.586: 177
4.617: 183, 188
4.643: 176
4.652: 86, 87
4.665: 206
4.666: 86, 87

4.687: 188
4.688: 183
4.702: 87
4.706: 188
4.707: 182
4.740: 208
4.780: 177
4.784: 183, 188
4.787: 177
4.795: 206
4.814: 87
4.817: 208
4.819: 177
4.821: 103
4.822: 103
4.824: 115
4.828: 190
4.882: 87, 176
4.883: 215
4.888: 86
4.906: 196, 197, 215
4.907: 100, 112, 189, 194, 197, 215,
  216
4.908: 91, 182, 187, 215
4.910: 197, 215
4.912: 189, 215, 216
4.1064: 15, 115
4.1075: 98, 194
4.1168b: 201
4.1213: 105, 182, 188
4.1225: 182, 187
4.1226: 86, 87, 203
4.1229: 181, 187
4.1230: 103, 182
4.1231: 183
4.1233: 187, 188, 199, 204
4.1234: 199
4.1236: 182
4.1238: 174, 176, 185
4.1239: 80, 174
4.1241: 174
4.1244: 101, 181, 187, 203
4.1245: 203
4.1246: 183
4.1247: 98, 203
4.1254: 187
4.1294: 197
4.1302: 23
4.1323: 80, 84, 174, 216
4.1325: 84, 185, 216
4.1381: 207
4.1388: 58
4.1410: 91
4.1415: 187

4.1424: 202
4.1431: 190
4.1433: 200
4.1435: 187
4.1454: 98, 194
4.1474: 103
4.1481: 110, 194
4.1518: 204
4.1523: 95, 179
4.1524: 21, 80, 173
4.1567: 191
4.1571: 163, 185
4.1631: 208
4.1635: 195, 197
4.1639: 80, 181
4.1642: 206
4.1643: 194
4.1688: 190, 216
4.1696: 176
4.1756: 23, 79
ILS
6964: 83
Imhoof-Blumer
  (1883) 391 #50: 200
  (1883) 412 #153: 206
  (1897) 142: 207
  (1901-02) 1.211 #683: 109
  (1901-02) 1.244 #3: 195
  (1901-02) 1.244 #4: 195
  (1913) 1.29 #85: 205
  (1913) 1.30 #89: 205
  (1913) 1.30 #90: 205
  (1972) 98 #203: 198
  (1972) 202 #640: 198
  (1972) 211 #683: 174
Insc. Louvre
  84 #72: 208
IvDid
  168: 198
  239 A II: 201
  249: 198
  315: 207
IvE
  1a.6: 43
  1a.17: 173
  1a.21: 43
  1a.22: 43
  1a.23: 194
  1a.27: 37, 57, 176, 190
  1a.43: 105, 106, 208
  2.203: 39
  2.213: 149
  2.214: 196
  2.232: 29, 47, 138, 175

2.232a: 29, 47, 175
2.233: 29, 32, 34-40, 47, 153, 156, 175
2.234: 30, 31, 37, 46, 48, 102, 174
2.235: 31, 46, 102, 175
2.236: 57, 157, 158
2.237: 29, 47, 153, 156, 175
2.238: 29, 47, 175
2.239: 31, 46, 102, 174
2.240: 31, 47, 175
2.241: 29, 35, 47, 175
2.242: 29, 47, 137
2.264: 57
2.266: 57
2.267-71: 118
2.270: 118
2.279: 179
2.424: 102, 111, 162, 189
2.424a: 34, 162, 176
2.425: 102, 175
2.425a: 102, 176
2.428: 178
2.429: 34, 190
2.430: 122, 123, 185, 191
2.444: 202
2.445: 202
2.449: 154
2.461: 189
2.492: 189
2.508: 122, 123, 189
2.518: 122, 123
2.523: 199
3.613: 198
3.613a: 198
3.616: 203
3.617: 187
3.618: 179
3.619a: 181
3.619b: 181
3.621a: 196
3.624: 204
3.625: 182
3.626: 182, 201
3.627: 103, 181
3.633: 137
3.634: 42
3.637: 42, 185, 191
3.638: 189
3.642: 42, 79, 177
3.643b: 183
3.644: 42
3.645: 206
3.653: 97, 199
3.661: 137

3.664b: 177
3.670a: 190
3.671: 196
3.674: 179
3.679: 204
3.679a: 202
3.681: 86, 188
3.686: 178
3.687: 97, 192, 194
3.688: 174
3.692: 97, 100, 101, 178, 197
3.697b: 192
3.698: 202
3.700: 208
3.702: 9
3.710: 191
3.710b: 37
3.710c: 37
3.712b: 190
3.714: 188, 201
3.719: 149
3.721: 180, 186
3.722: 178
3.728: 196
3.729: 186
3.732: 180
3.737: 206
3.739: 204
3.740: 204
3.792: 178, 186
3.810: 191, 199
3.814: 185
3.815: 201
3.858: 34, 189
3.892: 205
3.897: 97, 202
3.951: 198
3.994: 186
4.1017: 185
4.1023: 190
4.1066: 195
4.1075: 197
4.1087a: 203
4.1089: 135
4.1104: 135
4.1105: 180
4.1105a: 100, 194
4.1124: 34
4.1125: 135
4.1130: 99, 100, 197
4.1155: 135, 137
4.1162: 192
4.1171: 200
4.1182: 98, 197

4.1270: 189
4.1393: 35, 80, 172, 173
4.1404: 81, 184
4.1451: 39
5.1457: 39
5.1466: 39
5.1498: 29, 46, 175
5.1500: 190
5.1549: 184
5.1553: 185
5.1554 (1): 178
5.1556: 118
5.1604: 196
5.1605: 100, 180
5.1611: 100, 180
5.1620: 98, 197
5.1621: 98, 196
5.1900 (2): 208
5.1900 (3): 179
5.1900 (5): 178
5.1900 (6): 184
5.1900 (8): 208
5.1900 (10): 208
5.1900 (11): 208
6.2039: 191
6.2047: 36
6.2048: 29, 46, 137
6.2053: 43
6.2054: 43
6.2055: 43
6.2056: 43
6.2061 II: 103, 176
6.2062: 175
6.2063: 175
6.2065: 195
6.2067: 178
6.2069: 177
6.2070: 198
6.2076: 202
6.2077: 202
6.2078: 202
6.2080: 202
6.2082: 202
6.2957a: 179
7,1.3001 (2): 98, 203
7,1.3005: 139
7,1.3017: 191
7,1.3033: 189
7,1.3034: 189
7,1.3038: 37
7,1.3040: 103
7,1.3049: 39
7,1.3055: 189
7,1.3056: 103

7,1.3057: 181
7,1.3058: 201
7,1.3062: 199
7,1.3063: 204
7,1.3066: 9
7,1.3070: 99, 203
7,1.3071: 183
7,1.3072: 181, 191
7,1.3080: 103
7,1.3086: 202
7,2.3272: 34
7,2.3801: 80
7,2.3801 II: 80, 91, 139, 173
7,2.3802: 199
7,2.3803a: 207
7,2.3809: 203
7,2.3810: 204
7,2.3825: 89, 115, 172
7,2.4101b: 192
7,2.4109: 98, 201
7,2.4110: 97, 194
7,2.4336: 205
7,2.4337: 35
7,2.4342: 189, 190
7,2.4345: 201
7,2.4346: 98, 194
7,2.4354: 178
7,2.5101: 102, 190
7,2.5102-03: 105
7,2.5113: 102, 190
7,2.5153: 111
IvI
1.41: 39
1.51: 39
1.56: 39
1.59: 39
1.62: 39
1.73: 39
1.74: 39
1.82: 39
1.91: 42
1.107: 87, 117
1.108: 117
1.109: 117
1.110: 115
1.118: 42
1.122: 39
1.153: 39
2.609: 39
IvMag
149b: 87
151: 183
157b: 78, 80, 173
158: 85-88, 173, 185

188: 180
197: 203
IvMyl
1.151: 184, 188
2.866: 39
IvPr
61: 39
105: 43, 44, 89, 139, 172
108: 39
109: 39
117: 39
IvSm
2,1.594: 21, 58
2,1.596: 21
2,1.635: 115
2,1.637: 98, 201
2,1.638: 204
2,1.639: 21, 39, 195
2,1.640: 58
2,1.653: 39
2,1.654: 39
2,1.696: 58
2,1.727: 21, 79, 186
IvStr
2,1.1008: 35
JHS
11 (1890) 121-22 #5: 192
Le Bas-Waddington
3.158a: 191
3.213: 195
MAMA
3.449: 35
3.454: 92
3.514: 92
6.104: 80, 173
6.373: 91, 180, 186
6.374: 193
8.502: 182
8.517b: 186
McCrum and Woodhead
(1961) 52-53 #128: 83
Milet
1,7.327 #258: 189
1,9.164-65 #339: 207
Mionnet
2.549 #235: 205
3.93 #253: 53
3.215 #1198: 205
3.250 #1410: 206
3.250 #1411: 206
4.55 #285: 200
4.200-201 #31: 200

6.319 #1564: 67
Mionnet Sup
5.347 #427: 205
5.440 #1003: 193
5.440 #1004: 193
5.440 #1005: 193
5.444 #1021: 194
7.358-59 #188: 200
7.359 #191: 200
7.359 #192: 200
Moretti
(1953) 156-59 #60: 115
(1953) 174-79 #65: 115
(1953) 181-83 #66: 117
Mouseion Smyrna
3 (1878-80) 180: 29
Numismatische Zeitschrift
12 (1919) 115-20: 56
12 (1919) 118 no. 12: 35
OGIS
222: 9, 153
437: 10
456: 11
472: 39
498: 101, 195
509: 181
ÖJh
7 (1904) H. 2: 67
16 (1913) B. 72 #2: 182
26 (1930) B. 57-58: 197
53 (1981-82) H. 135 #31: 118
53 (1981-82) H. 136 #146: 192
55 (1984) H. 125: 186
55 (1984) H. 126-27: 177
55 (1984) H. 134-35: 194
PASCSA
(1883-84) 100 #6: 101
(1883-84) 325 #375: 101
Pick
(1906) 234-44: 53
(1906) 236: 56
REA
40 (1938) pl. 3 #3-6: 63, 65
REG
6 (1893) 8-22: 54
19 (1906) 139-40 #71: 183, 188
RevNum
1 (1883) 399: 200
1 (1883) 400: 202
Sardis
7.47: 180
7.64: 176

7.77: 196
7.8: 79
7.8 VII: 90, 172
7.8 VIII: 90, 172
7.8 IX: 172
7.8 X: 172
SEG
  1.331: 200
  4.519: 178
  17.315: 53
SIG
  2.799: 54, 55
  2.898: 52
  2.900: 192
  3.981: 52
  3.1065: 15
SNG Cop
  Ionia 391: 121
  Ionia 1318: 206
  Ionia 1319: 206
  Mysia 511: 207
  Phrygia 34: 200
  Phrygia 37: 200
  Phrygia 692: 206
  Phrygia 741: 198
  Troas 60: 194

SNGvA
  1270: 198
  1422: 207
  1879: 119
  2501: 200
  2505: 201
  3154: 193
  3164: 207
  3165: 207
  3506: 204
  3507: 204
  3591: 109, 174
  3857: 203
  3961: 206
  3967: 195
  3968: 195
  3970: 201
  4004: 195
Sterrett
  (1883-84) 325 #379: 179
Trell
  (1945) pl. 6 #3-5: 65
  (1945) pl. 7 #1-3: 65
ZfN
  4 (1877) 315-17: 67
ZPE
  17 (1975) 106-9: 51

GENERAL INDEX

Acts 19
 Asiarchs, 93
 neokoros, 54-56
Aelius Aristides, encomium to Roman
 rule, 151-155
Agrippina, priestess of, 87
Aizanoi, plan of Bath-Gymnasium, 126
aleitourgesia, 95-96
Antiochos I, 8-9, 153
Antonia Tryphaina, 54-55
Antoninus Pius, 63, 95, 135, 151-152
Apollonios of Tyana, 141
Aristonikos, 3
Artemis of Ephesus, 18-19, 48, 52-54,
 56, 75, 119, 167
Asia
 cities of, 37-38, 40, 156-158
 early Christian groups, 145, 165
 proconsular year, 44
 province of, 3
 religious traditions, 62, 67, 68, 70,
 75, 164, 166, 167
Asiarch
 animal battles, 98, 103
 agonothete, 108
 benefactor or official, 110-11
 Cibyra, alleged early dates for a family of, 215-217
 functions of, 97-99, 113
 gender, participation according to,
 110-11
 gladiators, 98, 103, 108
 koinon, relation to, 106, 108-9
 length of term, 99
 literary references, 92-97
 Modestinus, according to, 93-97,
 99
 municipal service, 96-98, 109-113
 numismatic evidence, 98, 109-10
 priest or official, 94-95, 104
 problems in interpretation, 76,
 99-106
 provincial festivals, 105-6, 108
 provincial highpriesthood, relation
 to, 92-110, 113
 Republican period, during, 106-7
 Strabo, according to, 93, 107
 title, diversity in, 97-98
 title, during or after service, 111-12
 title, reemergence in late first cen-

tury CE, 107-8, 113, 155, 217
 title, reference to imperial cults in,
 97, 100, 102
 title, temporal distribution of, 107,
 108
Asklepieion (Kos), 70
Athens
 Erechtheum, 72
 Olympieion, 43, 118
 the lsmophoria, 144
Attalos III, 3
Augustus, 2-3, 9
 battle at Actium, 7
 Kyzikos inscription, 55
 on cistophoroi, 12
 provincial cult at Pergamum, 8,
 10-11, 15, 20
 provincial cults, 167
 reorganization of Asia, 158
 statue of, 63
 temple statue of, 13, 14
 see also Rome and Augustus

Bammer, Anton, 67, 72-73
bath-gymnasium complexes of Asia
 Minor, 123-128, 134
bathing facilities with hot water, 124,
 161
benefaction, 39-40
 see also reverence, grace, goodwill
Bithynia
 provincial cult, 10
 Rome and Augustus temple, 13
 Rome and Augustus temple
 statues, 14
Brooten, Bernadette, 85
Burrell, Barbara, 50

city titles, 56-59
Claros, 63
Claudius, 27, 36, 41, 53
Cleopatra VII, 7
colossal statues, 63
contextual interpretation, 5, 76
Corinth
 Captives Facade, 71, 72
 Demeter, precincts of, 144, 145
Cult of the Sebastoi
 Aphrodisias, inscription of, 32-33,
 35, 37-39, 43

Asians and, 142, 164, 165
cities of Asia and, 37, 38, 40, 41, 49
dedicatory inscriptions, 29, 30, 32, 34-38, 40, 42-48, 137-140, 163
Domitia in, 35-36, 49, 62
Ephesus, effect on city of, 38, 68-70, 154, 161, 163
Flavian dynasty and, 35, 36, 49, 156
free cities, inscriptions of, 32-34
imperial authority, 154, 166
Keretapa, inscription of, 30, 31, 48
neokoros, 56, 75
proconsul of Asia, 41-42, 44
provincial elite, 160, 162-164, 166-168
regionalization, 154, 155
Titus in, 41, 49, 62
Vespasian in, 37, 41, 49, 62
see also Temple of the Sebastoi
cult, definition of, 1-2, 143

Deininger, Jürgen, 79, 83-84, 89, 104, 107
Delos, 52
Demeter, cults of, 144-145
Domitia
    Cult of the Sebastoi, in, 35-36, 49, 62
    Ephesian coin, on, 56-57
Domitian
    Asians and, 159-60
    assassination of, 36, 37, 140-41
    Cult of the Sebastoi, in, 34, 36, 49, 62, 165-167
    Ephesian coin, on, 56
    Ephesian Olympics, 118, 119, 137-140
    Harbor Bath-Gymnasium, 123
    provincial elite of Asia and, 138, 160
    Zeus Olympios and, 119

Eleusis, 144
elite, definition of, 5
emperor
    cities of Asia and, 37, 38, 156
    Cult of the Sebastoi and, 73, 166
    imperial cults and, 22, 34
    imperial cults, in, 81
    provincial cults and, 22, 27, 28, 40, 167

statues in precincts of gods, 73-75, 147, 148
Ephesus
    bath designs in the city, 136
    Celsus Library, 138
    Chalcidicum, 63
    Christian groups in, 145
    cities of Asia and, 38-40, 156-159
    Domitiangasse, 69
    neokoros, 53-54, 56-58
    Olympic games, 117-119, 139-40
    Olympic games, agonothete of, 139-40, 163
    Olympic games, date of, 137, 139
    "Parthian Monument," 59
    provincial cult, 29, 41, 158-59, 161
    Rome and Divus Iulius, cult of, 10, 27
    Rome and Divus Iulius, temple of 11, 12
    Royal Stoa, 63
    slope houses, 69
    Temple of Artemis, 65, 68, 121
    Upper Agora, plan of, 59
    Vedius Baths, 134-35
    Verulanus Halls, 122
    Zeus Olympios, 118, 119
    see also Harbor Bath-Gymnasium, Temple of the Sebastoi, Cult of the Sebastoi, Rome and Divus Iulius

Flavia Lycia, 215-16

Gaius Caesar
    Kyzikos and, 54-55
    provincial cult at Miletus, 21-22, 24-27, 36
Gaius Julius Philippos, 101
Geertz, Clifford, 5
Germanicus, 36
gladiators and Asiarchate, 98, 103, 108
goodwill, 39, 40, 156, 157
    see also reverence, grace
grace, 38, 166, 167 *see also* reverence, goodwill
gymnasium, function of, 161

Hadrian, 15, 43, 57-58, 117-18, 120, 167
Harbor Bath-Gymnasium
    ancient name of, 134-37
    bath building of, 124
    date, 121-123
    discovery, 121

Ephesian Olympics, 128, 137, 139-40
gymnasium of, 126-27, 160-61
Olympia facilities, comparison with, 128-134
palaestra of, 124-126
plan of, 120
honorific inscriptions, 105

imperial cults
diversity and development of, 142-145
divinity of emperor, 146-152
invention of provincial organization, 144
marble halls, 129
municipal autonomy, 152-154
prayers to emperors, 151-52
sacrifice, 146-150

Julia Lydia Laterane, 162
Juliane (first known provincial high-priestess), 85-89
Julius Caesar, 9, 15

Kearsley, Rosalinde, 84, 94-95, 102, 107, 110-112, 215-217
Koester, Helmut, 6, 54, 145
koina Asias, 114-116
koinon
Asiarchate and, 103, 106, 108-9
changes in, 91-92
dedicatory inscriptions for Cult of the Sebastoi, 40
definition of, 2
end of, 78
legal proceedings, 16
participation of women, 91
provincial cult at Pergamum and, 7-8
provincial games, 114-15
provincial highpriesthood and, 89-92
Kyzikos, neokoros, 54-56

Lammer, Manfred, 118, 139
lex Narbonensis, 83
Livia
as New Hera, 35
deification of, 88
provincial cults, 16, 17, 20
Sebaste, 36
statue of, 63
Lucius Luscius Ocrea, 42, 47

Lucius Mestrius Florus, 41-42, 46, 48, 67-68, 149

Magie, David, 77-78, 83, 109-10, 116
Magnesia on the Meander
inscription of first provincial high-priestess, 85-86
temple of Artemis Leukophryene, 68
Malalas, 135
Marcus Fulvius Gillo, 42, 46, 48, 107
Mark Antony, 7, 10, 54
Miletus
Didymeion, 18, 21, 23, 25-26
plan of, 125
provincial cult, 21-27, 78, 80, 155, 167
provincial temple, 23-25
Mitten, David, 6
Modestinus and Asiarchate, 93-97, 99
Moretti, Luigi, 114-15, 117

neokoros, 23, 38, 40, 45, 48, 50, 75
city title, 53-59, 156-58, 167
definition of, 2
free cities, rhetoric of, 40, 153-54
gender, participation by, 50
Kyzikos, 54
Macedonia, 53, 58
priest(esse)s, 51
twice, 56, 57, 119, 167
variety of functions, 52-53
neopoioi, 22-24

Octavian, see Augustus
Olympia
217th Olympiad, 117, 139
Artemis of Ephesus at, 52
bath buildings, 134
gymnasium, 130-132
Metroon, 64
Olympic games, 140
palaestra, 128-130
plan of, 133

Pergamum
Athena and Zeus, altar of, 68
Athena Nikephoros, 51
capital of Asia, 3
city titles, 58
provincial cult, 7-10, 16, 19, 27, 79-81, 158
provincial cults, 215-16
provincial games, 14-15, 114-116

Rome and Augustus temple, 11-14
Rome and Augustus temple
    statue, 13-14
Philadelphia, 157
Price, Simon
    continuity and change in imperial
        cults, 142-145, 154
    neokoros metaphor, 50
    sacrifices to emperors, 146-150
    statues of emperors and gods in
        temple precincts, 73-74
Priene, plan of, 132
provincial cults
    Africa, 26
    Ankyra, 26
        athletic games and, 14-15
    Baetica, 26, 83-84
    Britian, 26
    cities of Asia and, 7, 24, 166
    city, effect on, 18
    city, factors in choice of, 17-19, 24
    emperors and, 81, 167
    Germania, 26
    highpriestly year, 44
    Hispania Citerior, 26-27
    Hispania Ulterior, 16
    imperial authority, 154-156
    invention of, 144
    Lugdunum, 26
    Lusitania, 26
    Lycia, 26
    Macedonia, 26
    Narbonensis, 26, 83
    Noricum, 26
    Olympian religion, 166
    organization of, 23
    provincial elite and, 81, 161-62
    role of Senate, 15-18, 22, 27, 147
provincial games and imperial cults,
    114-15
provincial highpriestess
    first known, 85-89, 113
    history of interpretation, 81-85
    married to highpriest, 82-84, 104
provincial highpriesthood
    Asiarchate and, 85
    changes in, 91, 113
    highpriest of Asia, 79-81, 92, 113
    history of interpretation, 76-78
    koinon and, 89-92, 113
    late imperial period, attestations
        from, 107

number at one time, 77-79
numismatic evidence, 109-10
Pergamum, 215-16
sacerdotal function, 92
temple mentioned in title, 77-79
see also Asiarch
Publius Servilius Isauricus, 9-10, 153

religion, 2
    Olympian, 166
    salvation, 72-73
    society and, 1, 3-4, 152
reverence, 38-39, 55, 147, 150, 156-57,
    166-67
    see also goodwill, grace, benefaction
Rhodes, Temple of Athena Lindia, 70
Rome
    Agrippa, Baths of (plan), 127
    Augustus, Forum of, 71, 72
    Capitoline games, 117
    Nero, Baths of (plan), 128
    Titus, Baths of (plan), 130
    Trajan, Baths of (plan), 131
Rome and Augustus, cult of
    Asia and, 27
    athletic games, 114-15
    Bithynia, 10
    highpriesthood, 80-81, 89-91
    Pergamum, 8-9, 15, 167
    provincial games, 116
    temple statues, 13
Rome and Divus Iulius, cult of
    Asia, 10-11, 21, 27, 167
    Bithynia, 10
    Ephesus, 9, 67
Rossner, Margaret, 79, 102-106
ruler cults
    Hellenistic, 8-9, 152-154
    Roman officials in, 9-10, 23, 153

Sardis, 57, 63
Sayers, Dorothy L., 6
Scott, Kenneth, 146
Sebastos, 2-3, 35-36
Smith, Wilfred Cantwell, 2
Smyrna
    city titles, 57-58
    provincial cult, 15-19, 21, 27, 88,
        91-92, 113, 155, 167
    provincial temple, 19-20
    provincial temple statues, 20
    provincial temple title, 21

society and religion, 1, 3-4, 152
Stabian Baths (Pompeii), plan of, 129
Strabo and Asiarchate, 93, 107

Temple of the Sebastoi
    altar, 67, 68
    architecture, 65-68
    cella, 63-64
    date, 41-49
    excavations, 59-60, 62, 69
    floorplan, 63, 64, 68
    identification of, 59-62
    lower plaza, 70, 75
    name of temple, 35-37
    neokoros of, 45, 48, 138, 140, 163
    north facade, 70-72, 74-75
    precincts, 65-68
    religious symbolism, 74-75, 161
    terrace, 66, 68-70, 75, 119-20
    Titus, statue of, 60-63
temples
    Greek and Italian styles, 11, 67
    pseudodipteral design, 68
    sculptures related to, 74
theos
    use of term in imperial cults,
        22-23, 34, 116, 147
Tiberius Caesar
    Asia and, 15, 16
    highpriest of, 81
    Kyzikos, 55
    provincial cults, 28, 167

provincial cults of Asia, 15-17, 20,
    27
    priest of, 116
    temple statue of, 20
Tib. Cl. Aristio, 45-47, 102, 111-12,
    138, 140, 162
Tib. Cl. Celsus Orestianus, 215-216
Tib. Cl. Pheseinos, 47, 139, 162-63
Tib. Cl. Polemon, 216-17
Tib. Ju. Dama Claudianus, 47, 162
Tib. Ju. Reginus, 100-101
Tib. M. Deioterianus, 216
titles
    absence in inscriptions, 84-85,
        104-5
    first of the city, 86-87
Titus Caesar
    Cult of the Sebastoi, in, 41, 49, 62
    statue of, 60-63
T. Fl. Krateros, 217
T. Fl. Metrobius, 87, 117, 139
Trajan, 58, 162

urban institutions, changes in, 143-44,
    154, 166

xystos, 127, 130, 132, 135, 137, 141

Yegül, Fikret, 123-24, 126

Zeus, 63, 117-119, 151, 166-67

RELIGIONS IN
THE GRAECO-ROMAN WORLD

Recent publications:

114. GREEN, T.M., *The City of the Moon God.* Religious Traditions of Harran. 1992. ISBN 90 04 09513 6

115/1. TROMBLEY, F.R., *Hellenic Religion and Christianization c. 370-529.* 1993. ISBN 90 04 09624 8

115/2. TROMBLEY, F.R., *Hellenic Religion and Christianization c. 370-529.* 1993. ISBN 90 04 09691 4

116. FRIESEN, S.J., *Twice Neokoros.* Ephesus, Asia and the Cult of the Flavian Imperial Family. 1993. ISBN 90 04 09689 2

117. HORNUM, M.B., *Nemesis, the Roman State, and the Games.* 1993. ISBN 90 04 09745 7